THE

HONOR OAK
SCHOOL

Presented to

MAUREEN SMITH

The L.M. Collins Prize
for Mathematics

M.A. Willis
....
HEADMISTRESS

20 October 1972

Theatre 72

FRONTISPIECE (*overleaf*): *John Gielgud as Sir Geoffrey Kendle in* Veterans *by Charles Wood, Royal Court Theatre, London, March 1972*

Theatre 72

**Plays
Players
Playwrights
Theatres
Opera
Ballet**

Edited by **Sheridan Morley**

HUTCHINSON OF LONDON

HUTCHINSON & CO (*Publishers*) LTD
3 Fitzroy Square, London W1

London Melbourne Sydney Auckland
Wellington Johannesburg Cape Town
and agencies throughout the world

First published 1972

This book has been set in Scotch Roman type,
printed in Great Britain by Anchor Press, Tiptree, Essex, and
bound by Robert Hartnoll Ltd, Bodmin

ISBN 0 09 113780 2

Contents

Sheridan Morley

Prologue

As one who has been for nearly ten years now a member of that mildly underprivileged brigade known as the second-night critics, I am well aware of the problems inherent in following a première: if the opening has been successful, there is a danger of smug repetition, if disastrous then of understandable despair. Happily we are here trying to live up to a success rather than down a failure; THEATRE 71, which launched this series of annuals a year ago, seems to have found its market and it would I suppose have been feasible to produce an updated replica involving new contributions from precisely the same team of admirable writers. But it seemed to me that if these annuals were to reflect widely different aspects of our theatres in the seventies, then as many opinions as possible should be involved; for that reason, only four of this year's nineteen contributors will be familiar to readers of THEATRE 71, though I hope that others will be reappearing later in the series.

The aims however remain unchanged: to provide a kind of international theatrical balance sheet, a picture of the theatre past, present and future as it appears to a widely-assorted group of critics, playwrights, actors and directors in each passing year. For this purpose I have taken 'theatre' to include plays, operas and ballets both conventional and experimental, commercial and subsidised, in some of the capital cities and regional centres of Europe, Asia and America.

Inevitably, within the width of this brief, there are going to be some differences of opinion not only between writer and reader but also between writer and writer; this year, for instance, hugely dissimilar views of John Osborne's *West of Suez* are offered by B. A. Young in his London Theatre roundup and by John Lahr in his essay 'Poor Johnny One-Note'. In this last context, and in the light of the fact that Mr Osborne is known to be less than charitably disposed towards many British drama critics, it is only fair to point out that Mr Lahr's transatlantic views of his work are not so far as I know shared by any other contributor to this annual, nor indeed by its editor who remains nonetheless convinced that there is a place for them in an anthology of this nature.

Other contributions need little introduction, though to allay charges of nepotism it should perhaps be noted that despite certain filial connections with 'The One That Got Away' the decision to include it here was not mine alone. Those of last year's readers who remarked on a shameful exclusion of the Irish theatre I would refer to Micheál Mac Liammóir, and to those who felt the same about Scotland I can only promise a section of THEATRE 73.

The year under review was in many ways an uneasy one for the British theatre: bitter struggles over the Industrial Relations Bill and the imposition of Value Added Tax trapped Equity between militant members on one side and a generally unyielding government on the other. Plans to redevelop Piccadilly Circus severely threatened the future of the Criterion Theatre, and gave rise to fears that some of the other twenty-three West End theatres supposedly 'of architectural or historical importance' might also be at risk.

It was a year, too, of resignations: Lord Goodman handed over the 'tattered banner and the dented sword' of the Arts Council chairmanship to Patrick Gibson, and in a considerably less elegantly stage-managed transfer of power it was announced that Peter Hall would take control of the National Theatre following the retirement of Lord Olivier in 1974, by which time the company that Olivier has served with such distinction should theoretically be safely installed in their new South Bank theatres.

In the past twelve months Manchester has gained one theatre and lost another, the Bristol Old Vic and the Royal Shakespeare at Stratford have been given multi-thousand-pound facelifts, and new theatres of varying shapes and sizes have opened at Swindon, Southampton, Colchester and Grays in Essex. Sunday opening for theatres throughout England was approved at long last by Parliament, and in London a multitude of lunchtime and late-night theatre clubs are now offering playwrights, actors and audiences alike the chances denied them by an increasingly con- servative West End. One other hopeful development: the begin- nings of a long-overdue British Theatre Institute which, although only in working-party stages, may hopefully grow into an organisation capable of doing for the theatre what the BFI has throughout a quarter of a century done for the cinema.

So much for the facts: what follows is comment, criticism, idealism, despair, optimism, fear, ambition, admiration, distaste and nostalgia . . . in short a cross-section of the theatrical writing for which no other publication offers any but the most ephemeral of homes. That, more or less, was what I said of THEATRE 71 and I fervently hope it's what I'll be able to say of THEATRE 73. But once again, it depends on you.

For their help in the preparation of this book my thanks must go first as always to the contributors themselves, many of whom gave up valuable time stolen from other projects; I am additionally grateful to John Percival and Tom Sutcliffe for providing the reference and photographic material in their fields of ballet and opera, and to Terry Hands, Naseem Khan, Martin Gottfried and John Simon for help with other pictures. I owe thanks to the editors of the *Observer Magazine* and the *Financial Times*, under whose mastheads 'The One That Got Away' and 'In Triumph Through Persepolis' respectively appeared; Michael Behr's profile of Albert Finney is enlarged and adapted from a *Guardian* article, and John Lahr's 'Poor Johnny One-Note' is expanded and up- dated from an essay originally published by the Grove Press in New York. The fourteen remaining contributions are all here making their first appearance in print.

For the information contained in the reference section I owe thanks to *The Stage* and *Plays and Players* as well as to the press officers at the National, Royal Shakespeare, Royal Court and Chichester Theatres. For photographs, I am grateful to Anne

Tayler at *Plays and Players*; the press offices of innumerable theatres up and down the land; Roger Clifford; the Comédie Française; and of course the following photographers: Alex Agor, Bert Andrews, Claude Angelini, Christina Carr, Michael Childers, Donald Cooper, Anthony Crickmay, Alan Daiches, Dominic, Edward Griffiths, Willoughby Gullachsen, John Haynes, Douglas Jeffery, Terence le Goubin, Angus McBean, S. C. Moreton-Prichard, Anthony Pepitone, Roger Perry, Photocall (Manchester), Juliet Rasmussen, Stuart Robinson, Houston Rogers, Nicholas Simmons, Martha Swope, Nicolas Tikhomiroff, John Timbers, Transworld, Vivienne, Jennie Walton, Cordelia Weedon, Reg Wilson, Zodiac.

Finally, a word of thanks to Wendy Garcin for her help in typing parts of the manuscript; to Harold Harris, Martin Bristow and the production staff at Hutchinson for the infinite care taken in the publication of these annuals; and to Margaret my wife for continuing to live with an increasingly neurotic editor.

B. A. Young

The London Theatre

The drama critic and arts editor of the Financial Times *looks back over a farcical year.*

There's no doubt about it, if you want to succeed in the London theatre today there are only two courses before you. One is to get yourself a whacking handout from the Arts Council (and I don't deal with the Arts Council-supported theatre in this article). The other is to find yourself a good old-fashioned farce of the type that first came into style in the 40s and 50s and deck it out with as many dishy girls as the budget will accommodate.

You can't think about farce without thinking about Brian Rix; and sure enough, Mr Rix bounced back to his old haunts at the Garrick Theatre with a farce by Michael Pertwee called *Don't Just Lie There, Say Something!* I can only say that for my money, or rather for my two comps, it was one of the wettest farces I can remember—an odd thing, since Michael Pertwee's last offering there, *She's Done It Again!* (exclamation marks are de rigueur for farces), was way above average. However, there is no need for me to go into detail about why I disliked *Don't Just Lie There,* for it had hardly lain there a month before it was doing record business for the theatre.

Two other farces in the same mould opened during the year, *Move Over, Mrs Markham* (at the Vaudeville) by the experienced team of Ray Cooney and John Chapman, and *No Sex, Please— We're British* (at the Strand) by a pair new to me, Anthony Marriott and Alistair Foot. The two productions are curiously similar. Both

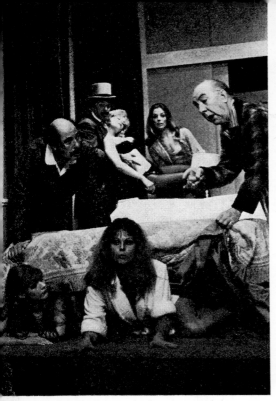

LEFT: '*Wet farce*': Don't Just Lie There, Say Something!
RIGHT: *Prospect's* Hamlet: *Ian McKellen as the Prince*

LEFT: '*A fine comic creation*': *Alan Bates as* Butley, *with Mary Wimbush*
RIGHT: '*A savage indictment of authority*': *Harry Andrews as Bond's* Lear

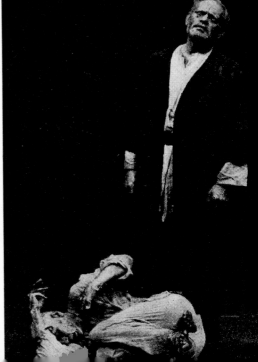

plays are built on a single idea: *Move Over* on the multiple occupation of a single bedroom, which the more generous farce-writers of other days would have tossed in as an extra, *No Sex* on the theory that a bank manager's wife who thought she was applying for the agency to sell Scandinavian glassware could find herself dealing in Scandinavian pornography.

They rely a great deal on the display of pretty young girls, and both employ a clever mature actress (Dame Cicely Courtneidge in *Move Over,* Evelyn Laye in *No Sex*) to demonstrate how farce is played by real experts. *No Sex* adds a male comic as well, Michael Crawford, who displays an aptitude for gymnastics as remarkable as his ability to extract a three-dimensional character from an almost flat part. Both plays lean heavily on the theory that once a character has shut himself, or herself, out of sight behind a door, he or she exists no longer until the need arises for an unexpected encounter.

It may appear that I have no time for farces of this calibre, but this is only partly true. When they are good, like *She's Done It Again!*, I will roll in the aisles with anyone. But it seems to me a pity that managements should take advantage of the theatre-going public's apparently unslakable thirst for this kind of entertainment to offer them anything but the best.

Interestingly enough, a new farce of superior quality made a short appearance in the West End, after an initial appearance at the Dublin Festival in the spring—Hugh Leonard's *The Patrick Pearse Motel*. This extremely ingenious exercise was avowedly modelled on the craft of Georges Feydeau as far as its technique went; but it added an extra quality in its deep and amusing comprehension of Irish middle-class society in our time. And what became of it? It faltered through a little run in the West End, and disappeared while the less sophisticated entertainments at the Strand and the Vaudeville packed the crowds in night after night.

I'd hate it to be thought that I wished ill of any kind of theatrical enterprise. It is not given to every man to relish the subtleties of Strindberg or the *longueurs* of O'Neill; and as long as there is a public to support Brian Rix and Ray Cooney the 'live theatre' remains live, and the actors participating—not to mention the stage-hands, the carpenters, the electricians, and so on—remain available for the next Strindberg when it comes up, if that should be their fate. But farce is potentially an artistic end to be pursued with as much assiduity as any other. I'd be prepared to defend the claim that there is more invention and workmanship in Alan Ayckbourn's *How the Other Half Loves,* which I am glad to say buzzes along as happily as ever after two years at the Lyric, than there is in David Storey's *The Changing Room* (to which I shall come in a moment).

Before leaving the subject of farce—and I make no apology for having given it priority like this, since it's clearly the commercial theatre's trump card—I must record that in 1971 we reached the 50th anniversary of Georges Feydeau's death. This is not a sentimental recollection on my part. It means that Feydeau is out of copyright. The flood of translations that I foresee has not yet made much of an impact; Nottingham has given us a version of *Champignol Malgré Lui,* Greenwich one of *La Main Passe,* the Questors, that admirable amateur company in Ealing, of *Le Dindon.* (Another version of *Le Dindon* went to Broadway by way of Stratford, Ontario.) But it is reported that Ned Sherrin and Caryl Brahms have dealt with virtually the entire works, and it's hardly likely they'll have the field to themselves. We may find ourselves back in the Restoration ambience, when Shadwell was able to say in his preface to *The Miser* (a version of Molière's *L'Avare*), ' 'Tis not barrenness of wit or invention that makes us borrow from the French, but laziness.'

You might think that a public so devoted to farce might have an equal appetite for musicals, but the year's record contradicts this. Naturally, Harold Fielding's re-creation of *Show Boat* (discussed elsewhere in this book by Benny Green) hit the jackpot, but the competition was minimal. At Drury Lane the coaches continued to roll up for *The Great Waltz,* and *Godspell* began to throw its enchantment over the young at the Round House and then at Wyndham's. *Godspell*'s enchantment, I have to say, was not for me, though it encouraged me to see that I'd been right in my estimate of David Essex when I'd seen him in small parts out of London and mentally marked him as a winner. All that simulated childishness, though, is something I find powerfully unattractive.

Then what else was there in the musical line? *Ambassador,* a really disheartening adaptation of Henry James's *The Ambassadors,* full of the kind of clichés about Paris that only Americans can think up, a hotch-potch of midinettes and poules de luxe and clochards and artists in berets and the rest of it, against which the adorable Danielle Darrieux and the imposing Howard Keel struggled in vain.

But at least this was an attempt to put on a big beautiful show. Nothing else came even that far. *Romance!*, which I can only suppose John Spurling wrote either for a bet or through the medium of a broken-down computer, was a shot at the 'little English musical' that flourished in the wake of *Salad Days—Wild Thyme, Chrysanthemum*, that kind of thing. I supposed at the time that it was intended as a satire, but I'm assured this wasn't so. It fell after a five-day innings at the Duke of York's.

Brief, too, was the innings of a musical called *Maybe That's Your Problem* at the Round House. This was a curious show with a story that suggested a film comedy of the 1930s, except that the eponymous problem encountered by the hero was premature ejaculation, not an easy thing to show on the stage (not yet, anyway). True, the same problem appeared in a splendid film called *Closely Observed Trains* and in a gruesome but effective play at the Arts some ten years ago, *Infanticide in the House of Fred Ginger*; but not as the principal theme. I was rather sorry about *Maybe That's Your Problem*; there was some fun in the dialogue, when you could hear it, and some quite tuneful songs, though now I put myself to the test I can't remember one of them.

There was also *His Monkey Wife* at the little Hampstead Theatre Club. John Collier's novel from which it was adapted was an item in the more sophisticated reading of my youth; but the problem of converting it for the stage fell down fairly hopelessly before the matter of having a chimpanzee instead of a girl as the leading lady. Poor Sandy Wilson, he has never had the recognition he deserves, because he goes for subject-matter that is caviare to the general. When I win the Pools I shall put on *Valmouth*, and then *The Buccaneer*; and then I shall have to win the Pools again.

Before washing my hands of the 1971 musicals I suppose I should give a dishonourable mention to *The Dirtiest Show in Town* in which a rather untalented cast project some childishly self-conscious defiance at conventional morality. I said a moment ago that I didn't wish ill of any theatrical enterprise. Shows like *The Dirtiest Show in Town* make this a very hard principle to uphold, for being theatrically worthless themselves, they are occupying a theatre that could be put to better, though doubtless less profitable, use.

Turning at last to the more serious side of the theatre, I am struck, rather pleasurably, by the number of West End productions that have started in the provinces or at one of the outer-circle houses like the Royal Court. This seems to me a desirable kind of progress; it helps the originating theatres, and it keeps the managements' eyes on the increasing displays of talent out of town. The Royal Court provided the West End with two good plays and a *succès d'estime*—John Osborne's *West of Suez*, David Storey's *The Changing Room*, and E. A. Whitehead's *The Foursome*.

West of Suez seemed to me full of unclarity in argument and development; and I thought the influence of Chekhov too obviously paraded. But at any given moment it was always compulsively listenable; and it gave Sir Ralph Richardson a splendid part which he filled to admiration. *The Changing Room* was quite unlike any other play I've seen. The 22 characters who make up a Rugby League side and their attached back-room boys, from the chairman to the cleaner, fulfil no plot, illustrate no theme. They simply go through their routine from arrival on the ground to departure for the continuance of their private lives. For me the effect was quite extraordinary. Without any adventitious empathy, I found my attention riveted on the proceedings, or non-proceedings, from the first moment to the last. This is emphatically not a kind of play I'd like to see proliferating unguardedly; the mind shudders at the prospect of those cricket pavilions, railway signal-boxes, boardrooms, bus-queues and so on from whose daily inactivity ambitious imitators might feel tempted to carve dramas. But *The Changing Room* (like *Home* before it) is an exception to every rule. In his ability to create drama that leaves out so much of what we have always supposed drama must have, David Storey may be called the Mondrian of the theatre.

The Court's other contribution to the West End was a visit to the Fortune from *The Foursome*. This curious little play, which looked in on the not altogether salubrious activities of two young Liverpudlians and their girl pick-ups on a day by the sea, was full of promise, though I did not feel personally that it could be rated more highly than that. It was its author's first-produced play, and

ABOVE: *'Compulsively listenable': Ralph Richardson in Osborne's* West of Suez *with Jill Bennett and Sheila Ballantine*

BELOW: *'Quite unlike any other play I've seen':* The Changing Room *by David Storey at the Royal Court*

won him the enviable position of resident dramatist at the Court; and from this there stemmed *Alpha Beta,* which at the very least can be commended for having tempted Albert Finney back to the stage.

The stripling Greenwich Theatre contributed two plays to the West End, two oddly similar ones. First in was Peter Nichols's *Forget-me-not Lane,* a reconstruction of a boy's youth with his family during and after the war. The way we lived in those days was evoked with a kind of sour nostalgia; but nostalgia was not the theme of the play. We saw this boy growing up into an unwilling simulacrum of the dotty father (we can all make our fathers seem dotty if we try, I suppose) who dominated his home, until he made a final effort to opt out. There must have been many middle-aged people in the audiences for whom the delight in recognising their youth was mitigated by an anxiety in recognising their maturity.

A Voyage Round My Father worked on similar principles, youth being reconstructed with the present kept at hand throughout the evening, so that the growing boy might often be seen in two stages at once. Both plays I take to have been straight biography, and here John Mortimer, who wrote *A Voyage,* had an advantage over Peter Nichols, for his father was a far more flamboyant character, a successful barrister who went blind in the middle of his life and refused to concede the fact. There was some grumbling because Mark Dignam, who played John Mortimer's father at Greenwich, was replaced by Alec Guinness at the Haymarket. Both actors in fact gave superb performances; as I wrote at the time, you would no more say that one was 'better' than the other than that Château Lafite was better than Château Latour.

I suppose the most ambitious import was Prospect's *Hamlet,* with Ian McKellen as the Prince. 'Nor think ambition wise because 'tis brave,' said D'Avenant; I saw this twice, once in rather un-favourable circumstances at a schools matinée in Edinburgh, and what I remember most about Robert Chetwyn's production is Faith Brook's splendid drinking Queen—that and the barbarous way in which the text had been 'simplified' for people unwilling to investigate Elizabethan usage. Mr McKellen's Hamlet was not the

'A year of theatrical autobiographies': Alec Guinness with Leueen MacGrath in John Mortimer's A Voyage Round My Father *at the Theatre Royal, Haymarket*

Hamlet I'd hoped for by extrapolation from his Richard II and Edward II. I am told that my appreciation was affected by the fact that I'd seen about a dozen Hamlets in the previous year, but I deny this. I saw Jean-Louis Trintignant in Paris about the same time and found that, for all its unfamiliarities, a most acceptable piece of work.

Miscellaneous imports were a revival of *The Chalk Garden* from Guildford, in which we saw Gladys Cooper, alas for the last time before her death; *Dear Antoine,* which failed to survive its transplant from Chichester; *After Haggerty,* which Eddie Kulukundis collected from the Royal Shakespeare and displayed at the Criterion with less success than he and everyone else concerned deserved; and a pleasantly nostalgic *Tonight at 8* that migrated from the Hampstead Theatre Club to the Fortune without setting the Thames on fire.

I don't seem to have given the theatre managements much credit for originality so far. Let me now correct the situation, for they haven't done at all badly. It was not an import that won the *Evening Standard*'s award for the best new play of the year, but Simon Gray's *Butley* at the Criterion, sailing under the colours of Michael Codron.

Simon Gray clocked up two productions during the year, *Spoiled* having made a rather unexpected appearance at the Haymarket early in the year. I say 'unexpected' not out of any disrespect for the play (though in retrospect it seems to me that it must have been much better as an hour on television than two hours and a bit on the stage). Unexpected, though, in the rich ambience of the Haymarket (where once I tried to buy an ice-cream for T. C. Worsley in the interval, and was coldly informed by the elegant programme-boy, 'We don't sell ices at the Haymarket'). I was sorry that *Spoiled* didn't do better. It was a modest piece, but there was true sympathy in its story of the schoolmaster who diverted his affection from his pregnant wife to a schoolboy in need of help, and there were three telling performances by Anna Massey, Jeremy Kemp and Simon Ward.

Butley was another matter altogether. It marked a definite step forward by Simon Gray; the characters were depicted in greater depth than he has offered us before, the situations—this time there were more than one—were handled so that they stretched right across the length of the play. Butley, the eponymous hero, was a fine comic creation, and Alan Bates gave a terrific performance in it. (The part was later taken over by Richard Briers, and I found it interesting to see that the play, as a play, remained equally interesting, and was not a piece, like *Inadmissible Evidence*, for example, that depends for its effect on a bravura performance in the lead.)

It's curious to reflect that if the Lord Chamberlain had not been divested of his powers of censorship, *Butley* might easily never have come to the stage, for all the characters but one are either admitted or suspected homosexuals. Yet there isn't an atom of offence in it. In the current climate of opinion, the story of the English lecturer's boy-friend who leaves him to begin an affaire with a publisher is no less of a light romantic comedy than, say, *The Secretary Bird,* which as I write is still bringing them in at the Savoy. On the other hand, the setting in a college of London University is nice and trendy, especially as the staff are all made to look so unadmirable: well, all but one of the staff.

Not only did *Butley* win the *Evening Standard*'s award as the best new play of the year, but Alan Bates won their award for the best performance by an actor.*

Stanley Eveling's *Mister* was a courageous project on the part of Richard Pilbrow, who put it on and directed it (though left the lighting to another hand). Stanley Eveling has for long held a high place among the aficionados of the fringe theatre, and it seemed high time that he should come out with something for the West End, which is still, like it or not, where reputations are won or lost.

Mr Eveling's was neither won nor lost, for *Mister* attracted too little attention. It wasn't at all characteristic of the author; one felt that he had consciously written a conventional piece on the ground that it was going to be seen by conventional audiences. The kooky girl who blunders into an established household and sends the occupants flying in all directions is a favourite character nowadays, and this play added no special quality to her. The three people at the centre—a literary melancholic running an antique-shop, a retired merchant seaman, a 'great galumphing girl' from Bradford—were much nearer stereotypes than you would expect from this writer, who might be encouraged by the reflection that unconventional writers like Simon Gray and Joe Orton have achieved most of their success in the commercial ambience.

* For other awards see p. 277.

The fact is (and we are coming to the point where an argument is likely to crystallise out of my commentary) that apart from the farces there doesn't on the whole seem much future in the West End for the conventional play. A decade ago, who could have failed to foresee a future for *Children of the Wolf*? This is blood-curdling melodrama about a respectable lady who is lured to a deserted house by her two illegitimate children and subjected to mental tortures at the end of which death must have seemed a relief. It was a first play, by John Peacock, who made a very finished job of it. You could say that *mutatis mutandis* it comes into the category of *Night Must Fall*, and it had a performance in it, by Yvonne Mitchell, that was at the top of its class.

But by and large the audiences left it alone. The argument is that this kind of theatre is provided by television, and that the live stage must find something different, and I think this is true. You would never see a play like *Butley* or *The Philanthropist* (which must have had the longest run the Mayfair has ever known) on the television screen—not because of the subject-matter but because of the treatment. Yet both of those have done well, while *Children of the Wolf* (running in the colours, incidentally, of Bernard Delfont, no beginner at the game) faded away.

A similar fate befell another play about sadistic children, *Child's Play* by Robert Marasco. It wasn't such a good play as Mr Peacock's. Fundamentally, as a matter of fact, it was better; there is a good core to it in the tale of jealousy between an old, popular, over-loyal schoolmaster and a younger one who thinks that what matters is to teach the boys to learn and to behave. But this is adulterated with a lot of nonsense about an outbreak of vicious cruelty among the boys that reaches such lengths as crucifixion and the extraction of the eyes. Now I believe that there would have been a public for this kind of thing twenty years ago or more. But you can see horrors far more convincingly enacted in front of the film or television camera. It would be fascinating to see what Simon Gray would have made of the basic plot.

Laurence Harvey played the young schoolmaster, Rupert Davies the veteran. The first of them is a star (if such a beast survives), the second a popular television figure. The tradition remains among managements that stars are vital to a West End success; but it is clear that they will not avert a West End failure.

Kenneth More with Mona Washbourne, Keith Skinner, Brian Cox and Gemma Jones in Alan Bennett's Getting On *at the Globe*

One star at least who had a well-deserved success was Kenneth More, in the part of the Labour MP in *Getting On* that might have been expressly written around his talents and personality. Alan Bennett pronounced himself surprised when he was given an award for having written the best new comedy of the year, but *Getting On* is undoubtedly a comedy, however earnest its intentions. After all, *Man and Superman* and *Getting Married* and *Pygmalion* are comedies and you can't fault *them* for lack of seriousness. *Getting On,* though it has occasional lapses into irrelevant revue material, is not only an excellent comedy but has much to say that is germane to our day. As a bonus, it marked the first, absurdly overdue, appearance of Gemma Jones as a West End leading lady.

Two sports, in the biological sense of the word, deserve mention, for different reasons. At the Cambridge, *Captain Brassbound's Conversion* had a satisfactory run, not, I think, because of any special merit in the production, but because of the presence as Lady Cicely of Ingrid Bergman. Miss Bergman's performance was

variable, but the radiance of her presence is irresistible. To be in
a theatre where she is on the stage is by itself a pleasurable experience, and would I am sure still be so if she did no more than
recite the cardinal numbers from one to a hundred. At any rate she
made *Brassbound* a memorable night for me.

The other sport was Charles Dyer's newest play, *Mother Adam,*
yet another twosome, but dealing this time not with sexual but
maternal affection, if affection is the word I want. After encounter-
ing some lack of sympathy on tour, the play was brought in to the
Arts Theatre with Mr Dyer not only as author but as director and
management as well. On reflection, I admire his determination
more than I admired either his authorship or his direction.

You could also qualify James Bridie's *Meeting at Night* as a
sport, too, in a way. This is a slim little comedy about a con-man
dodging the law in the Highlands of Scotland, and it was presented
to us, no doubt without any intent to deceive, as Bridie's last
play, written shortly before his death in 1951. I am assured on good
authority that it certainly was not; it was an older play that no
one wanted much. No one wanted it much at the Duke of York's,
either, in spite of the serpentine charm of Wilfrid Hyde White,
the blowsy charm of Renée Houston and the dogged detection of
Sydney Tafler.

Lastly, I should mention Joyce Rayburn's comedy at the
Garrick, *Don't Start without Me*. Now I've mentioned it.

A bus-ride from the West End you come across the theatres that
combine the ambitions of the big subsidised companies with the
difficulties of the commercial managements. To the north, the
Open Space in Tottenham Court Road, the Place and the Shaw in,
or almost in, Euston Road, the Hampstead Theatre Club at Swiss
Cottage and the Round House at Chalk Farm; to the east, the
Mermaid in Puddle Dock; to the west, the Royal Court.

Most interesting is, of course, the Royal Court. That theatre's
peaks are currently marked as a rule by John Osborne, David
Storey and Edward Bond, and all three were well represented during
the year. Osborne's *West of Suez*, a strongly Chekhovian study of
British residents in the ghost of a British colony, and Storey's
The Changing Room, an extraordinary group portrait of a Rugby
League side without a plot, I have already mentioned. Bond's

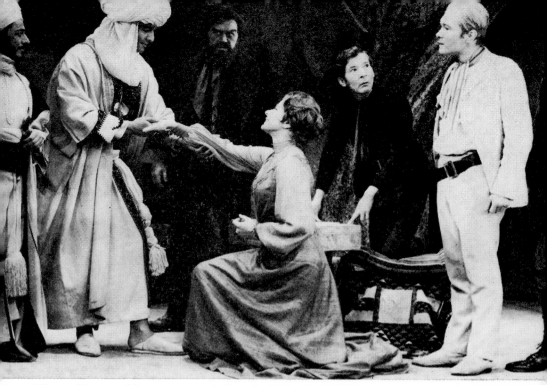

'The radiance of her presence is irresistible': Ingrid Bergman with (centre left and right) *Joss Ackland and Kenneth Williams in* Captain Brassbound's Conversion *at the Cambridge*

Lear is a different cup of tea, for the author appears totally indifferent to public reaction. *Lear* is a savage indictment of authority based vaguely on Shakespeare's initial situation but little on his characters or his plot, and it is disfigured (to my mind) by scenes of nauseating yet rather childlike cruelty. It certainly marks a step forward in Bond's ability to write telling dialogue, though it lacks the humour that has graced some of his earlier work; but an examination of its monumental workings reveals no more than the discovery that all power corrupts. Since Bond is content to present this truth as eternal and immutable, his play reeks of total pessimism. Harry Andrews gave an imposing performance as Lear in William Gaskill's production.

The Court also gave us Dennis Cannan's first new play for a long time, *One at Night*, a somewhat biassed account of the way in which society treats the mentally unsound. It is a moving play, but the author made things too easy for himself by moulding the characters in such a way that those on his side, as it were, were sympathic, and those against him unsympathetic or inefficient.

In *The Lovers of Viorne* (the English title for the multiple puns of *L'Amante Anglaise*) Dame Peggy Ashcroft gave a performance of consummate skill that rates in my mind with Madeleine Renaud's, though it resembled it but little.

The obligatory Brecht was *Man is Man*, very entertainingly directed by William Gaskill. Paving its way a week or so previously was a production in the Theatre Upstairs by Bill Brydon of *The Baby Elephant*, the ten-minute sketch Brecht wrote to be played in the interval. By the time it had been adorned with biographical Brechtiana and sundry extracts from Brecht and Kipling (revealed refreshingly in his democratic colours) it filled the whole of a joyous evening.

One other Court production remains in the memory, and for once it was an undoubted failure. Peter Gill dressed *The Duchess of Malfi* in uniform drab costumes and played it against a featureless set dressed only with kitchen chairs and a cheap table. Consequently the fine shades of class-distinction on which the play so much relies were lost, in spite of some distinguished speaking by the company.

All in all, you may say that it was a very distinguished year for the Court that certainly strengthened the claim that might be made for it as the most influential theatre in the country (though the Traverse provides some powerful opposition over the border).

The Mermaid ought to deserve an article to itself, but its record for the year was hardly outstanding. It is impossible to understand how the same management could have put on a squalid little rustic farce like *The Licentious Fly* in February and then a coruscating production of *John Bull's Other Island* the following May. They had bad luck with *The Old Boys*, a fine adaptation by William Trevor of his Hawthornden Prize-winning novel. I thought this an unusually thoughtful piece, with an array of well-drawn characters and a sequence of dramatic punches; but it opened before the leading player was ready, and his performance, though it contained the core of something really good that I am told flowered effectively on the subsequent tour, hobbled the production in its first days to its inevitable disadvantage. The only other event there that stays in my memory was the visit of the Russian circus from Leningrad, a great feather in the Mermaid's cap.

The Open Space, the Place and the Hampstead Theatre Club don't really come within my purview here (though I recall with pleasure items at all of them). The Shaw does, however. Designed by Elidir Davies, who also designed the Mermaid, it's the best new theatre to have been built in central London for a long time. It was conceived virtually on the back of an envelope; the architect designed a theatre that with a library and attached amenities could form part of a modern office building, and then set about to find someone to order it. It was ordered by Camden Borough, who, having let the office part to an oil firm, were able to pass on the theatre to the National Youth Theatre at a very low rate. There the N.Y.T. indulged its long-held ambition to mount plays with its own professional company. By far the best thing it has shown us thus far was its production of Peter Terson's moving play *The Samaritan,* first seen earlier in the year at the Victoria, Stoke-on-Trent.

The Round House, having failed in its original Weskerian ambition to get itself adopted by the T.U.C., went pretty commercial during the year—to the dismay of some devoted but ill-informed young people who, at the opening night of *Rabelais* in March, made a nude demonstration in the auditorium, complaining that the theatre had been 'stolen' from them, whereas in fact it had simply been enabled to continue as a theatre instead of closing down altogether. *Rabelais,* an English version of Barrault's splendid fantasia, was a fine romp that indicated the unique versatility of the building. In October, another French import, Ariane Mnouchkine's incomparable *1789,* indicated it all over again and even more effectively. The several stages were placed round the circular floor, and the audience stood, as mobile as they pleased, in the middle. *1789* stands out in my mind as the most exciting evening in the theatre I have had for a very long time; I saw it twice (once in Paris, where it was played in a vast disused armoury) and found it just as exciting the second time, even though I was prepared for all the unconventional resources of the production.

The Round House, whose taste is as eclectic as its clientele, also offered Andy Warhol's *Pork,* too much of an in-joke for me, and *Godspell,* a consciously childlike musical version of the Gospel according to St Matthew which may be said to be playing the part of John the Baptist to *Jesus Christ Superstar.*

Naseem Khan

Notes from the Underground

From classical to baroque, from structure to anarchy—the co-editor of Time Out's *theatre section looks at the past twelve months on the* 'fringe':

If you want to look for an incubator of England's underground drama you don't have to go any further than Drury Lane. I remember walking down it in the summer of '68 and noticing a building that had obviously been a warehouse but now was spattered with posters announcing the new 'Arts Laboratory'. It had an open air about it, so I walked in. Inside, in the main area, was a huge pyramid of oranges. They were for anybody who felt like oranges. So I took one.

That haphazard but generous feel was at the heart of Jim Haynes's Arts Lab. It's not surprising then that tracing back the antecedents of the livelier theatre groups working at present one finds some connection with the Drury Lane centre. The first People Shows were staged there. Pip Simmons Theatre Group, Wherehouse La Mama, Portable Theatre, Freehold, all had dealings with the Arts Lab. In terms of hard fact no incipient theatre group could afford to ignore it. For London at that time seemed barren of rehearsal and/or playing space. Charles Marowitz had just acquired the Open Space. Ed Berman was still in the early stages of setting up Inter-Action, initially under the umbrella of Jean-Pierre Voos and of Junior Telfer at Queensway's Ambiance restaurant. A few places offered an occasional roof like the Mercury, LAMDA, the Little Theatre, the Crypt in Lancaster Road where Carlyle Reedy was running her community arts programme. But they were very few.

Invitation to anarchy': Pip Simmons' Do It!
'Crazy and bizarre panache': Alice in Wonderland

'Impressively polished': London Theatre Group's The Trial
'Public art for random audiences': Theatrespiel

Nevertheless it was a case of an ill wind which blew to the advantage of the Arts Lab. Since its closing there is nowhere, at least that I know of, where one can now go in this peculiarly random way to meet people, have a cup of coffee, look at pictures, maybe see a film, a play or a dance performance. It is, without exaggeration, a tremendous loss. As far as the arts themselves were concerned, there was always the possibility of cross-fertilisation at the Arts Lab, both through performances and through actual contact between people. As far as the audience was concerned, it gently pushed people to experiment with things they might have felt were outside their sphere of interest. Today the theatre is in a far stronger position as far as buildings go. But they are tucked away separately, at times pursuing overlapping policies, from Aldgate down to Brixton; and it's hard not to suspect that they serve the *cognoscenti* rather than the casually interested. And as far as overlap between disciplines is concerned, it's a field that is comparatively little explored (other than the absorption of Graham-type movement) except for forays by Geoff Moore's Moving Being. What would be heartening would be to see collaborations of the Cage-Rauschenberg-Cunningham type, for instance, in terms of fringe theatre. But in the past year (March 1971–2) the underground has on the whole remained wedded to the theatre of words. It's a field where, to a certain extent, the ground has been cut away from under its feet by television. It's perhaps time for fringe groups to look more carefully at what it is that theatre can do which the box can't.

The main difference is so obvious that it hardly seems worth mentioning, the fact that theatre has a live audience. On the fringe the audience is a far more positive element than it is in the West End because of scale. For the most part theatres are small, from fifty seats upwards. So this means that even traditional plays like Roy Minton's *Death in Leicester* at the King's Head (a fine play about neurotic obsession) have a far greater impact.

The way in which the fringe is popularly supposed to use its audience is perhaps one reason why straighter audiences steer clear of it. For if the image of the West End is of cucumber sandwiches, the counter-image of the underground curiously enough appears to be of assault, battery, challenge. If you take away the emotion it seems a legitimate enough device. For what happens when you are pinpointed by an actor is that you are forced to respond spontaneously; the situation takes on an immediacy—a decidedly fraught immediacy—which, with our conventions of proscenium-arch divide, we have forgotten. The point is more the way a group uses the divide. Too often it seems the product of vague thinking: it is the easiest thing in the world to make an audience angry by systematic taunts. But then to identify that anger smugly as fury at having been unmasked as middle-class, bourgeois, reactionary or whatever is too glib.

There was an air of manipulation about *Games After Liverpool* at the Almost Free, though one could never accuse The Other Company's director, Naftali Yavin, of glibness. It's a curious play, ostensibly about the My Lai massacre trial, which was acted elliptically and with energy by four members of TOC. In the middle section they broke off and questioned their own reactions to their material and the validity or non-validity of their profession anyhow. It was here that the lights were turned full up on the audience and they were invited—no, dared—to join in. Each night naturally was different, from apathy to walkouts. When I saw it I became quietly angry at a situation that seemed to have an inbuilt bias away from the audience. But this apparently, said some of the cast afterwards, was the point of the exercise. It was meant to bring home the fact that we have virtually no freedom of movement or protest within our society. If that was so, it was a parable which I for one wasn't pushed by the production to extend further.

The laurels for having broken down the actor-audience barrier in the past year have undoubtedly gone to two companies—the People Show at the Royal Court's Come Together (marginally before my brief) and Pip Simmons Theatre Group. The People Show in fact had two shows going, one more selective than the other. The main one ended in a mass exodus from the smoke-filled auditorium to stretchers in Sloane Square. But the smaller one consisted of Mark Long approaching people outside the theatre surreptitiously. Would they like, he'd whisper, a half-minute show including drugs, sex and violence all for one penny? The bold takers were given blank programmes and hastily escorted to a telephone box round the corner where another member of the company was installed. Quickly he told each one a story about de Sade, injected a sugar cube for each of them with red ink and then left them to be embraced by a female member of the People Show.

Pip Simmons on the other hand invited its audience to anarchy. The group's show was *Do It!*, a dramatised version of Jerry Rubin's book, based particularly on the mayhem of the Chicago Convention. Oval House—and later the Theatre Upstairs—resounded with the euphoria of battle and bawdry, which was acted out ironically by the company; for amidst it all they were clearly still making an independent comment on the action. I was away at the time and missed the production, but many people feel it was the most impressive show of the past year.

It has on the whole been an eventful year, and one in which the fringe has slowly spread itself like vegetable marrows. A year ago there were nine fringe theatre bases and three lunchtime theatres (including places like Questors and Studio 68). Today they number sixteen and eight respectively Others are in the planning stage, particularly John McGrath's 7:84 Theatre, which will be a touring group, and the Alternative Theatre which is hoping to set up a circuit of West London pubs. At the same time how you define fringe-work has got harder. There's a strong case for including the Royal Shakespeare Company, for instance, in their season at The Place. And Peter Brook's *A Midsummer Night's Dream*, a caustic and troubling production full of vindictiveness and passion set in a gleaming white ambiguous cube. Nor was Marguerite Duras' spare and abstract *Lovers of Viorne* (at the Royal Court) commercial theatre as we usually think of it. At some point it would be interesting to consider how the techniques of the underground have influenced the overground, for interplay there has certainly been.

As a more underground version of *Lovers of Viorne*, Freehold gave us *Mary Mary*. Both plays are investigations into the mind of a female who commits murder. In Mlle Duras' play it is a middle-aged woman who kills her deaf and dumb cousin. In Roy Kift's it is an eleven-year-old girl who kills two small boys. Marguerite Duras explores Claire's situation by an elaborate and dazzling verbal construct. In this production her characters rarely moved from a static position. Freehold's play on the other hand was a freewheeling but very tightly controlled group exercise (directed as most of their plays are by their founder Nancy Meckler). The group built up a collage-type picture of the repressions and hysteria that was the actual background of Mary Bell (the original 'Mary') via peepshow flashes of her life—at home with an unloving mother, brainwashed by television, with a sadistic priest, at playground games. The group took turns to play Mary so that different aspects of her were fragmented like colours in a kaleidoscope and so that there was never any danger of the audience responding to Mary as a single actress. It was horrifying because it was distanced in this manner, and the production succeeded where Neil Johnston's Oval House group fell short with a similar project.

Neil Johnston's group, a new one and with the same meticulous and expressive style of its parent Freehold, presented an un-scheduled version of the Pauline Jones story during the January Cockpit Festival. But although it's clearly a group to watch, they confused the issue by allowing their own personal indignation to dominate too much.

The Cockpit Festival was one of the highlights of the year's underground drama. Packed into a couple of weeks were Traverse Theatre Workshop's *In the Heart of the British Museum* by John Spurling and directed by Max Stafford-Clark, Pip Simmons' wild *Alice in Wonderland*, Freehold's *Genesis* and Theatre Machine's improvisational show, plus 'surprises' in the foyer by the People Show. All the productions were excellent examples of each com-pany's work; and the whole exercise, arranged by David Aukin, ought to be made an annual event. It served as a splendid antidote to the turgidness of Christmas drama. But if any unsuspecting visitor had wandered into *Alice* expecting a nostalgic and respectful version of Carroll he would have been affronted. Like all Pip Simmons shows it was full of crazy and bizarre panache. The group, arrayed in a strange assortment of undergarments, tuxedos, neatly suspendered socks and sundry hats (plus two rival Alices), leapt vigorously and loudly from scene to scene, waving axes, tossing teacups, singing discordantly. At times it took on the enclosed frightening magic of the original *Alice*, but then lost hold of it again amid the clownery. It was a wild-eyed inventive show that refused to have any truck with convention.

Freehold's show by contrast seemed chastely restrained. For if Pip Simmons was the baroque of the Festival, Freehold was the classical. Their story—scripted as they rehearsed by Roy Kift— was a commentary on the first books of the Old Testament, from Eden to Babel. It was a loose and stylish production that traced the growth of patriarchal authority from democratic innocence to the power struggles embodied in Babel, from harmony to discord.

The Cockpit itself, an ILEA building, was one of the first recruits to the fringe circuit (though at times its productions are more fringe than others). In the past year it's been joined by others. The Almost Free, lurking between the strip shops behind Piccadilly Circus, is another child of Inter-Action. As the name implies, it is almost free—you choose how much to pay for membership and admission. Its plays have been more demanding than its gate policy. Much of the first months were taken up with the playwright Peter Handke, whose *My Foot, My Tutor*, a play entirely without words, was presented at the Open Space by the German Institute earlier in the year. The director for the recent Handke batch— *Offending the Audience, Self-Accusation, Prophecy, Calling For Help* —all by TOC, was Naftali Yavin who pummelled them imaginatively into a dazzling theatrical shape that showed to best advantage in the second play. Handke is an uncompromising and abstract writer, fascinated by semantics, verbal structures and the associations of words; his scripts tend to be blueprints rather than acting versions. *Self-Accusation* was an unbroken first-person monologue on the page which Yavin reallotted to two actors.

Not far to the north of the Almost Free another new theatre opened last spring, the Soho Poly, which is run by Fred Proud and Verity Bargate whose Soho Theatre had previously been based at the King's Head. They started off their new theatre—one of the pleasantest in London—with a delightful and witty spoof of court-room lunacy, *The Trial of St George* by Colin Spencer. Over in the decaying wastes of the old-new East End the enterprising Half-Moon Theatre, based in a magnificent nineteenth-century synagogue, opened its programme with Brecht's *In the Jungle of the City*. Meanwhile up at the King's Head the standard of both plays and productions has been consistently high. The policy of this theatre—housed in what appears to be the old billiards room at the back of this handsome Victorian pub—has always been imaginative and pragmatic. In the past year they've included plays as varied as David Mowat's *Anna-Luse*, Chris Wilkinson's *I Was Hitler's Maid*, John McGrath's *Plugged-in to History* (put on by the Parsnip Theatre Company), Snoo Wilson's *Blow Job*—a violent but stunning work which succeeded in destroying the Edinburgh

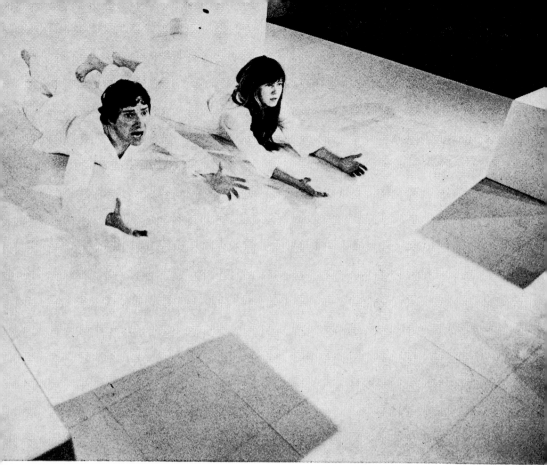

'The growth of guilt between infancy and maturity': Robert Walker and Judy Monahan in Self Accusation, *'a moving ritual of confession'*

theatre it was first staged in—and John Grillo's *Mr Bickerstaff's Establishment*.

For a similarly imaginative policy you have to look south of the river to Oval House, a youth club in Kennington, which has kept open house for a stimulating variety of underground groups. Their own festival in May included Roland Miller and Shirley Cameron's People/Time/Space, the Italian Theatre of the Tiber, Incubus, Cervantes Players and the People Show. Later in the year saw an impressive polished version of *The Trial* by Steven Berkoff's London Theatre Group which was an object lesson in particular of how movement can add a new dimension to a text.

At the Open Space after a burst of public invective at the flabbiness of the Fringe, Charles Marowitz turned up some rewarding parts of it: Portable Theatre writer Howard Brenton's *A Sky Blue Life* which developed into a struggle between Gorki the humanist and Gorki the Marxist, Trevor Griffiths' *Sam, Sam* about two working-class brothers (Sam 1 who stayed in his class, Sam 2 who escaped into the middle-class battlefield—both of them played splendidly by Nikolas Symonds), *Lay By*, a neat and clever play by seven Portable writers, ostensibly about rape, fellatio, etc., but whose Grand Guignol and bursts of porn became funny rather than nasty.

There were also a few companies who weren't concerned with conventional theatre buildings, undoubtedly a good thing. Theatre-spiel took their 'events' on to the underground, into Hornsey Art College, to a recruiting parade. Brighton Combination took their Social Security NAB Show into claimants' unions, youth clubs and the Labour Party Conference. Bruce Birchall's Notting Hill Theatre Workshop dramatised local issues in the streets, church halls and youth clubs, while Hovhaness Pilikian's exuberant black group, the Cervantes Players, followed a similar kind of circuit. The move out of theatres as such and also the move out of London—like Portable's tours and Ken Campbell's Road Show—are the most promising areas of exploration. For there is always the danger with the fringe that it will become too self-contained, that it will be tempted into contemplating its artistic navel until *rigor mortis*, unnoticed, sets in.

As a postscript, I'd like to make clear that, since I work for the London-based *Time Out*, this account is necessarily London-orientated. It includes nothing, for instance, about Albert Hunt in Bradford, about the Welfare State or the Traverse. Nor does it pretend for a moment to be a cool unbiassed report. I have tried on the whole to indicate areas that I find interesting. But the only true guide is to go and see for yourself.

As this book was going to press, news came through of the death of Naftali Yavin, director of Interaction's The Other Company and one of the most imaginative forces at work in the modern theatre. He had, since 1968, been responsible for a wide variety of disciplined, adventurous work from environmental pieces like 'The Pit' and 'Journey' to the formal classicism of Peter Handke's 'Self-Accusation'. And those of us who knew him as a person have lost a man of unusual honesty, warmth and courage.

Micheál Mac Liammóir

Dramatic Accidents

*The Irish Theatre in the twentieth century, viewed by its most
distinguished actor-manager.*

There are creative men who delight in the aftermath of disaster, in
the spectacle of a calamitous beauty shaken into birth by fire or
by lightning or by a falling bomb. Dostoevsky was such a man,
Goya in his warlike phase another, and in our own day among the
painters (forgetting for the moment Picasso who, in the main,
creates his own havoc) one might place Mr John Piper among the
hierarchy.

Yet in the whole fifty-odd years of its existence as a separate
entity the Irish dramatic movement has developed no such conscious
attitude in its creators—even in O'Casey, for while O'Casey at his
best chose war and the rumours of violence for his subject-matter,
his form in those early plays was as conventional as Boucicault's,
and part of its strength lay in its essential theatrical naïveté, as if the
Douanier Rousseau had turned his attention from an amiable wedding to a scene of violence. It was Denis Johnston, who, arriving later
on the scene with James Joyce as father, the German expressionist
movement as mother, with Mangan and other nineteenth-century
Irish romantics as the fairies at the christening, first gave the chaotic
treatment it invited to dramatic expression, and his followers,
though numerous, have not been greatly significant.

Yet the entire Irish theatre movement (conceived in English
by Yeats, himself a formalist, a symbolist, a believer in ceremonial
magic) has contained within itself all the qualities of an accident,

of a toppling over at a certain moment in history of a series of
calamities that proved a suddenly and strangely effective composition, to which the still imperfectly learned English of the country
people made one of the chief contributions. The poet himself, an
educated man with little knowledge of the Irish language and with
no more ear for the English of the peasantry than he had for operatic
music, yet realised as nobody before him had done the dramatic
value of such speech, and if he had never met with Douglas Hyde
who knew the secret fountain of that speech, or with Synge and
Lady Gregory who could use the water of the fountain with such
masterly grace, it would have been necessary to invent them.

For the chief thing that lent to those early Irish plays a quality
that charmed the English and American audiences who witnessed
them—and much of the Abbey's fame was built outside Ireland—
was the twist and turn of the English language, the unfamiliar
music of the voices, the imagery, the phrasing, the construction of
a sentence. Ignorant of Ireland and of her history (and ignorant of
the fact that Ireland, on the threshold of the twentieth century,
was also on the threshold of passing, it may be forever, from one
nationhood to another, from one language to another) the jaded
ears of London and New York heard merely what to them seemed
a delightful quaintness that came they knew not whence but
suggested to them simply that the Irish people had the most
striking way of expressing themselves.

The fact that compulsory English had become fluent but
remained on the lips of the speakers an almost literal though
seldom laboured translation of their own proscribed tongue did not
occur to them and, it may be, would not have greatly interested
them. The fact that if the living Irish language should die at last,
its echo must fade inevitably from the imperfect and accidentally
beautiful dialect of English spoken in Ireland, has occurred only to
a few: the fact that the greatest master of that dialect was but the
chronicler of the briefest of periods—the period of an accident's
aftermath, before the debris has given place to some new and
probably less engaging order—has occurred to still fewer; the fact
that no play of Irish life not using that dialect has had a major
success outside of Ireland has occurred to fewer yet. And indeed
the fact that, as speech is the fundament of dramatic expression,
Ireland without some form of individual speech has no claim to

dramatic individuality beyond that of mere regionalism has occurred, it seems, to nobody at all.

Certainly it had not occurred to Yeats himself, for in 1902, shortly after the birth of what was then called the Irish Literary Theatre, he wrote, of Dr Douglas Hyde: 'Above all I would have him keep to that English idiom of the Irish thinking people of the west which he has begun to use less often. *It is the only good English spoken by any large number of Irish people today and we must found good literature on living speech.*' Today, as one reads these words, so full of that absorption in the moment that is characteristic of a man deeply in love, one cannot but think either that he was unaware of the mortal sickness of his beloved, or that he had refused to reflect on the brevity of her life.

And indeed it is a chilly reflection, for while a dramatist may be unconcerned as to the future of his country and live only to express the life about him in the idiom closest to his hand, thanking heaven for the chance that gave to that life and to that idiom a richness denied to communities less complicated by linguistic upheavals or by national ambitions, the analyst in the theatre must needs speculate on things to come. The Irish dramatic movement grew out of Ireland's insistence on her own individuality, and as it came at a time when the two opposing traditions that have shaped her were in the final throes (the burning bricks and mortar falling about them as they lay half in combat and half in a deathly embrace) it was natural that the playwrights, arriving on the scene like so many journalist-photographers, their cameras in their eager hands, should get to work as nimbly as they might and scoop what they were able to scoop out of calamity.

They themselves, however, hardly saw things in this light. They viewed the clash of events as it were in slow motion and many of them, notably T. C. Murray, Pádraic Colum and Lennox Robinson, recorded their impressions in the gentlest fashion. The twilight described by Yeats as Celtic, though it passed swiftly out of fashion as the setting for the mystical romanticism that he with A.E. and Fiona Macleod had begun to expound in the nineties, still permeated the plays of these new romantic realists, and one is not aware in their work of any violence, any tumbling down of the old order, of any fiery mingling of that old order with the new. Nevertheless the tumbling down, the mingling and the merging were still in

LEFT: *W. G. Fay, the original* Playboy of the Western World
RIGHT: *Frank Grimes,* Playboy *in the centenary production*

LEFT: *J. M. Synge's* Deirdre of the Sorrows (*John Kavanagh and Bill Foley*)
RIGHT: *Brendan Behan's* Borstal Boy (*Frank Grimes*)

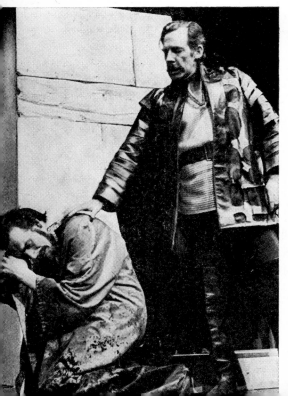

progress, as poets outside the dramatic movement like Pearse and Mac Donagh were fully aware, and they in their own fashion during all those early years of the Abbey's history were preparing for the last stand of the Gaelic world against the overwhelming onrush of the Anglo-Saxon, choosing insurrection instead of the theatre as the medium of their expression. So it was that in 1916 the accident became visible once more, and this, dramatically speaking, was perhaps its chief value, for it fulfilled the prophecy of such plays as *Cathleen ni Houlihán* and *The Rising of the Moon* and paved the way for the discovery of O'Casey.

The accidental quality was not confined to the writers merely: the actors themselves possessed more than a share of it. Most people who care for the theatre and who are old enough will remember the admiration expressed by English and American critics of the stillness and immobility of the players, their marvellous 'economy of movement', as it was termed. Wearied by the expert gyrations and tripping feet, the fluttering hands with their inevitable accompaniment of georgette scarf or telltale document according to sex and situation, the thrown-back chin, the never-failing hesitation on the oak staircase before the epigrammatic exit to the bedroom on an ascending scale of merry laughter beginning on A flat and ending in polite applause, bored to a dull frenzy by these platitudinous accomplishments the critics were revived deliciously by this sombre band of simple people, the women with shawls twisted over their heads, the men in frieze coats, who stood for the most part motionless in their heavy boots uttering such strange music and hardly bothering to raise a hand or a foot to eke out their meaning. 'But the reason of that', said Sara Algood, one of the two great Irish actresses of that time, 'was that when we did more we did it so badly that Willie Fay stopped us doing it. "Stay where you are for God's sake", he'd say to us. "You don't know how to move, by the looks of most of you you'll take a lifetime to learn it, so stay still and let the words tell the story!" '

No crossing and re-crossing the stage could be risked, no declamatory gestures, no sawing of the air with the hands, all were to have the static tranquillity of a Chinese ivory, even though it should lack such delicate precision; passion was to find expression only in the voice and in the eyes, an easy law for Irish people to obey for they are in the main gifted with expressive eyes and voices.

And so it was that another lucky accident came to play its part in the haphazard fabric of the Irish theatre.

It is not my purpose to write of the creation and growth of the theatre in Ireland, for while its birthdays are few its story is already lengthy, complicated and controversial. Besides, it has been told many times, and for my own part in setting down these reflections on its present stage of development I would rather take it for granted that the reader knows enough of its past to speculate a little with me upon its future.

The image of the accident, now that I have evoked it, haunts my imagination and sets me wondering what it is in the rational temperament that has made such a willing and occasionally brilliant contribution to that accident, and how it has been that the Poor Old Woman—no mere poetic conception, as anyone who knows the country at all will I think agree with me, but the most vivid and frequently alarming reality—should have pitched her tent with such enjoyment on the scene of disaster and somehow or other provided a meal, doling out food and drink with a reckless hand and even fishing up a truffle or two out of a surprisingly inadequate-looking bag.

I think in my heart it is the writers who have supplied most of these things: the actors have done little in a practical way beyond lending the charm of their presence to the occasion, and here—I hope I will not be accused of a treacherous heresy in this—they seem to answer to the description which they themselves are most in dread of being: they are, in a literal sense, Stage Irish. Lover and Lever would have bowed before them, and the creator of Con the Shaughraun have crowned their heads with laurel. For, in the main, the Irish actor belongs to that curious type marked down by the authors I have mentioned as being characteristic of the entire nation, that is born with the pleasing conviction that life is a picnic of which he is himself the *pièce de résistance* but to which he has no sort of obligation to contribute.

Or rather, he thinks of his own life in particular—the actor's life—as a picnic, and the theatre as the most diverting of woodland backgrounds with the tents all pitched and ready, the fires alight, and a series of motley disguises magically ready to his hand to while away a possible onslaught of the tedious hours. That the preparation of the festivity is a portion of his own life, his own work, has never occurred to him; the notion that the festivity itself is, like all the arts, a portion of life and that the actor's share in it must be a lifelong dedication to its perfection is one that has rested so lightly upon him that it has led at last to the astonishing conclusion of so many Irish critics and journalists that the amateur movement in the theatre is as significant as the professional if not more so, and that the art of the stage is one that can be practised as a hobby for one's leisure moments.

For this conclusion, as I write these words, has taken so firm a hold on the newspapers, those unsteady guides of popular taste and popular belief, that it cannot be ignored. Ireland, like England, has applauded or derided but rarely understood the actor's art: England, unlike Ireland, has produced from time to time a critic —sometimes a whole coterie of critics—who care in the theatre for little else.

In Dublin, more than any city I know, the play is the thing— not at all in the sense that Hamlet really meant in that most mis-quoted of all his speeches—and the manner and method of presen-ting the play a detail of minor importance. 'They are doing the *Cherry Orchard*', you will hear of this group or that, or 'They are doing *Lear* or *Playboy* or *Charley's Aunt*', in tones of admiration or disdain according to the speaker's feeling for Chekhov, Shakespeare, Synge, or Brandon Thomas; and the speaker, in all probability, will be one who knows the authors he speaks of and has very definite opinions about them and about what he calls 'the drama' in general. Yet, if you ask 'How are they doing it?' you will be gazed upon with that quizzical, vague, abstract, bewildered toler-ance which in Ireland means that you have asked a completely meaningless question.

Acting, direction, casting, décor, lighting, costume, approach, style, pace, handling, all the facets that a production contributes to the diamond of the two hours' traffic, transmuting the author's text to fire or to mud, have been passed over by all but the smallest minority, though this same speaker I have quoted will pierce through a network of fine facets and perceive a poor play under their glamour, just as he will, untroubled by the false facets of an outrageously bad production, perceive through their knotty tangles the elements of a good piece of writing.

This characteristic—I think a true one—leads the man of the

theatre in Ireland to two conclusions. The first is that Irish people have more instinct for literature than for the arts of the stage, that they are more moved by it, more conversant with it, more serious about it: in a word that they understand and sympathise with the professional writer and believe in the existence of his art. The second is that their lack of a profound instinct for visual beauty and their corresponding indifference to visual ugliness, their conviction that acting is a pastime with all the charm and all the absurdity of a pastime practised habitually by themselves without the faintest exertion at all moments of their daily lives, that the native theatre in Ireland is still in its early childhood and the resident Irish professional actor is an eccentric novelty to which they have not yet become accustomed and the reason for whose presence in their midst they cannot grasp—that all these have helped to enable the amateur to command a position of equality with the professional unknown to him in any other community.

It is an evil, not because it praises young men and women who seek a most praiseworthy outlet for energy or refuge from tedium and in whose midst, indeed, the greatest artists of the theatre may well find a first expression, but because in setting side by side the first command of the muses, which is devotion, the existence of the muse of acting becomes at question.

In observing this young theatre in a country whose other arts are older than those of almost any other community of northern Europe, one is tempted to ruminate, to explain, to offer theories, when it would be perhaps of more service to chronicle facts. And yet in speaking of what has been achieved, or of what may be achieved in time to come, it may be necessary to describe the materials that are at hand, and temperament being first among these in any statement on the theatre, and on the men and women who make it, we may do well to examine it. The Irish temperament is, in the main, indolent, gregarious, ruminative, proud, malicious, eloquent, good-humoured, slovenly, and self-absorbed. I do not think Irish people are, as they would have it themselves, outstandingly brave or pure, or, as the English would have it, violently passionate or quarrelsome. Nor is their vanity considerable, though their opinion of themselves is often such that mere vanity, which is but the ambitious dream of the mirror's reflection, is left far behind. What is known to our indulgent neighbours as Irish charm

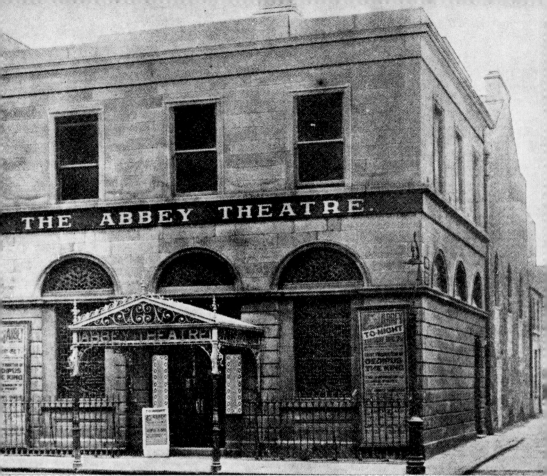

Dublin's original Abbey Theatre

springs in the main from an inner confidence, from an inherent ability (uncommon in most northern countries) to relax, and these in their turn grow from an unshakable conviction that all things in life are unimportant save the moment's savour: that and the certainty of a blissful though vaguely imagined eternity.

These traits, though they have much in them that is common to all people possessing histrionic talent, contain also the elements of destruction. For whereas vanity in the actor will drive him to a cultivation of his best moments, and a comfortable awareness of his effortless power to charm will lend to him a necessary ease, an absence of the former or the smallest excess of the latter will lead to that odd mixture of jaunty condescension and artless make-up that characterises so many Irish performances—as if Hamlet and

Queen Constance had been accepted by Bottom and Doll Tearsheet for the sheer fun of the thing, or in order to lend the poor devil of a producer a helping hand.

Many players spend their hours in long and sometimes futile discussion of their job. Their conversation is limited in scope but illumined by devotion. At its worst it circles round the doings of the great ones of the stage in the way that so much of the talk among the British middle classes circles round the doings of the royal family. At its best it analyses and reveals, it dreams and broods, and sometimes it makes discoveries that lead to a fresh approach to the work of the theatre and the creation of a new style in the art of acting. In Ireland such conversation is rare: the pleasures of living, of drinking, of telling good stories and hearing them are more likely to occupy the actor's mind.

The theatre in Ireland then is confronted, as far as acting is concerned, with a player upon whom the cloak of Thespis sits lightly (if indeed it is not cheerfully fastened with a safety-pin with the philosophical reflection that nobody will know the difference) and with a public which, unused so far to his permanent presence in its midst, is tolerantly disinclined to take him very seriously. It is confronted, as far as the creation of a dramatic literature is concerned, with the dialectic crisis I have indicated and with the question of two languages marked by the accidental and slowly vanishing blend of two idioms.

Ireland, moreover, has been so long a captive that her songs, her stories, her symbols, her mysteries, and at last her plays have all risen out of the conditions in which she perforce has lived.

During her endless years of famine, evictions, and insurrections she had plenty to think about and indeed to talk about, and talk she did: the last thing that came into her head was to follow the example of the Children of Israel and lay up her silent harp on the trees. She played it, indeed, louder than ever, and it was that wild music which gave her most memorable dramatic utterance to the world.

If we take pains to look at life stripped of the excitement of powder and smoke, if we can learn to be as unafraid of the fundaments of life as our soldiers are unafraid of prisons and of sentences of death, if we can free our minds from what we imagine as national principle (which is in reality not a desire to purify our country but a terror of the truth about ourselves) or from what we imagine as religious fervour (which is in reality not a desire for heaven but a terror of hell), if, in short, we can welcome life as we have been ready to bow down to death, our theatre will reflect that welcome and our plays of peace be as powerful and as moving as our plays of violence and of war.

These are some of the thoughts that beset us now, for as is the habit of any living creature who has grown in darkness, in secret, in the perpetual consciousness of being watched lest he escape, the Irish theatre, like all Irish things, like all Irish people, has acquired the habit of a central obsession with a theme grown well-nigh abstract through the passing of the years, together with a method of dealing with its internal problems that is at once shifty and shiftless.

I am discouraged, remembering how we had wished at the Gate Theatre to influence Irish development by showing our people something of the splendour of European masterpieces, when I ponder on the frequent refuge we have taken in reproducing some aesthetically dubious success from Broadway or Shaftesbury Avenue in order to earn a livelihood. I am discouraged, remembering that Yeats had hoped to show some noble image of Ireland in the magical glass of the theatre, when I see that little is reflected in the plays or in the acting of the Abbey today but a complacent photograph of the deathly dull surface of Irish life. Although the Abbey with its origins of poetry and of a poetic nationalism has passed through periods of brilliant productiveness, has produced writers and actors of astonishing talent, yet it has never fulfilled its early promise nor has it made any startling or revolutionary contribution to the art of production—contenting itself where the rarely done plays of Yeats are concerned with an imperfectly mastered style of décor borrowed from Craig and Appia and substituting for the poet's intricate rhythms a facile monotony of speech. Where other writers appear they are interpreted with a photographic treatment already popularised in other countries before the turn of the century.

The Gate Theatre (created in the late twenties by Hilton Edwards, myself and a few friends) has contributed, I think, to the producer's art and to that of décor and of lighting. It has been far more experimental and indeed influential in these spheres than the Abbey and yet, perhaps because it has been so preoccupied with the importing of modern plays from Russia, France, Germany and America and with the classics of Greece and of England, and so busy with the method and manner of presenting them, it has found only two Irish authors of outstanding personality, Denis Johnston and Maura Laverty, and has specialised far less than the Abbey in the perfecting of a unique and individual naturalistic note.

Players like Cyril Cusack, Siobhán McKenna and others make brilliant but occasional appearances at the Gaiety or the Olympia and other places dedicated for the most part to English touring companies. The younger groups are in the main too vague in their aims and too inexperienced in all but the art of flying before they can walk to write about with anything like certainty. They are characteristic of a city where, when all our talk is done, most of our problems revolve about a question of population, for were Dublin's half-million souls to be miraculously increased by, say, two and a half and the rest of the country to undergo a similar multiplication, there would be more work for the Irish artist and less need for him to emigrate to London and Hollywood and New York.

The younger groups, unless I do them an injustice, seem not to understand the necessity for these things, for they in the main belong to that ever-increasing body in Ireland that seems to have no profession but some convenient means of livelihood and a series of hobbies, and their organisations in Dublin appear and disappear in our midst like midnight mushrooms. In this, of course, they are merely doing with the rapidity of youth what all of us who labour in the theatre do in a sort of hypnotic slow motion, for what in the theatre, apart from the writer's work, is not in the nature of a mysterious scrabbling of messages on the sand where at the moon's bidding the tides will rise and wash all away? The important thing is that something of sufficient vitality and truth be written there, some formula so inexorably fixed to the memory that its image will live on in the mind of the future when we and the struggling and self-questioning of our daily preparation, the fretting and fuming of our nightly appearances, are dead and gone.

I wish at times I could believe, as Hilton Edwards believes, that somewhere there lies hidden a formula that would give us a stage for a further freedom, however temporary, as perfect as that which Shakespeare had for his players, as Molière for his, as the

Greeks for those writers and actors who gave the first art of the theatre to Europe. For if I shared this faith completely I could have worked with him at the preparation of the birthplace of a new form, believing that when the house is ready, the fire burning on the hearth, the door left open, the mysterious guest will surely arrive, his pen in his hand. We have indeed, like so many others in Europe and America, experimented with new methods, designed new forms, launched new suggestions, demonstrated new projects, and have hinted to writers, architects and financial men that co-operation would be welcome, but only portions of the dream have found some fragmentary realisation.

We hoped for a development of the evocative form that is hinted at in the later short plays of Yeats, but in too remote and esoteric a fashion to maintain its hold upon the democracy of an essentially popular art, and our hope has so far come to nothing. And how to find a place for blame but in my own lack of faith? I believe with Edwards that a new, imaginative school of the writer's and actor's craft may be discovered some day, and the fanaticism that is part of myself in these matters makes me wish it to be discovered in Ireland. For, remembering the Sheridans and Goldsmiths, the Wildes and the Shaws, and calling to my mind's eye the preoccupation of Yeats with a magic no existing form could satisfy, as well as our own instinctive restlessness, I say to myself that a country which has given so many makers of comedy to her neighbour's powerful tradition in the past may well be called upon to create a model for the imagination to build upon in times to come.

Irving Wardle

Let Them Eat Bread

A year in the life of the National Theatre, reviewed by the drama critic of The Times.

This time last year Ronald Bryden wound up his survey of the National Theatre's shaky 1970 season with two cheers for 1971. The theatre had learned its lesson, he said. With the appointment of Patrick Donnell and Michael Blakemore, and the reinstatement of John Dexter, the perils of one-man rule were over, and the company was all set for a buoyant future.

It was not to be. In terms of publicity, box office receipts, and loss of actors it was a black year. Institutional reputations take time to rise or fall, and possibly it was the mistakes of the year before that made knocking the National such a popular sport in 1971. But, clearly, whatever was wrong with the National Theatre in the past has not been put right yet. And it would be foolish to treat the last twelve months as a self-enclosed episode ending on a note of joyous uplift, even though the record of the period does invite this fairy-tale treatment. It opened promisingly at Waterloo Road, sank to a humiliating nadir with the New Theatre season and the application for an emergency grant, and achieved a sensational recovery at the last gasp of the old year with Olivier's performance in *Long Day's Journey into Night*. Since then the upward curve has been maintained with Tom Stoppard's *Jumpers*.

'A performance of technical and personal fascination': Laurence Olivier with Constance Cummings in Long Day's Journey Into Night

So everything looks rosy just now. Except that there is nothing to stop the whole cycle happening again.

Trusting simply to the evidence that meets the eye, the besetting problem of the National is one of acting priorities. Is it there to show off the best available performers, or to build up its own ensemble strength? The two positions are irreconcilable, but in the past the theatre has balanced them out with tact. The contradiction has emerged more clearly during the past year because the balance has not been kept up. After the failure of company-based productions like *The Idiot* and *Cyrano*, it seems that actor-managerial reflexes have taken over, and what runs through the combined Waterloo Road and New Theatre season is an obsession with stars: star actors and star directors imported to dispense glamour, novelty, and individual flair at the expense of long-term policy. Spokesmen for the National have sometimes argued that the sheer diversity of the repertory and the impact of visiting directors were meant to exercise the company in many different styles. But I doubt whether anyone would still offer this defence for the period under review. Especially as it saw the departure of Robert Stephens, Maggie Smith, Robert Lang, Sheila Reid, Frank Wylie and Jeremy Brett.

For a troupe nominally devoted to the best in world drama and which has yet to pay its respects to German classicism and Golden Age Spain, what scale of priorities can have suggested Arrabal's *The Architect and the Emperor of Assyria* as the opening production of the year? The only plausible answer to that is the availability of Victor Garcia to direct it. Simply as a text, it is hard to believe that this invertebrate allegory would have been accepted for Waterloo Road: and still less as a stylistic trampoline for the company, since it calls for only two actors. But the conjunction of Arrabal and Garcia offered a tempting opportunity of scooping the official British début of the Argentine *Wunderkind* (Garcia's Spanish production of *The Maids* had recently appeared at the Aldwych).

Garcia certainly gave his full money's worth as a visiting maestro. A delicate almond-complexioned dwarf carrying a lady's handbag, he began by inspecting the company and rejecting every one of them apart from Jim Dale. On meeting Olivier he declined to discuss the production and dropped Olivier's annotated copy of the text into a waste-paper basket. 'I hate literature,' he is reported to have said, 'and I hate the theatre. I'm only interested in magic.'

Magic is too absolute a word for the show which reached the public in February, but it did amount to an extraordinary act of transformation, both of the text and of the Old Vic stage. The impression one takes away from reading *The Architect and the Emperor* is of private fantasy masquerading as a universal fable. Two men meet on a desert island (one a native, the other escaping an air crash) and settle down for an extended series of ritual games during which they pass through many identities without acquiring any characters of their own.

As written, the piece is always falling off its stilts: it lacks dignity. And it is precisely this quality which Garcia brought to it, converting its private fetishism and its childish shock tactics into an expression of satanic arrogance. Where Arrabal calls for sex-shop equipment, Garcia restored a classical dimension by restricting costumes to ragged leather cloaks (wound into ropes for flagellation) and turning high-heeled shoes into cothurni. He also introduced his famous fork-lift truck, a patently industrial vehicle like a huge floor-polisher which trundled into service to elevate actors into Genet-like judges, to stage a do-it-yourself crucifixion, and to metamorphose into a spotted pink elephant.

As for the stage, Garcia stripped it to the back wall and packed it with lanterns, including a ground row that opened and shut like a level-crossing and two searchlights facing outwards to sweep over the house. The contrast between this huge battery of equipment and the two nearly naked actors left no doubt of where Garcia's main interest lay.

The actors were Jim Dale and Anthony Hopkins: a skinny Caliban matched against a burly Prospero, and the disconcerting feature of both performances was that in spite of the text's enormous scope for role-playing they hardly changed character; Arrabal's text at least calls for masks. What they offered instead was a high-pressure display of emotion and callisthenics which filled the acting area to its limits and established a general idea of what the fight was all about: a contest between the forces of Dionysus and Apollo for the government of the island. In the circumstances, perhaps it would be unreasonable to ask for more.

A side-benefit of this production was that it brought Mr Hopkins back into the company for two further performances of outstanding quality, as Coriolanus and as the cuckold in Heywood's

LEFT: *Anthony Hopkins and Joan Plowright in* A Woman Killed With Kindness

RIGHT: *Jim Dale and Hazel Hughes in* The Good-Natured Man

LEFT: *Paul Curran and Paul Scofield in* The Rules of the Game

RIGHT: *Anthony Hopkins as* Coriolanus

A Woman Killed with Kindness. The Heywood production also marked John Dexter's return as associate director, and —like his subsequent work—it was in direct contrast to the rest of the season. In a shop-window of gaudy delicacies he offered a basket of home-baked bread: two minor English classics unadorned by any novelty of interpretation or visiting star, and played with vigour and respect by the regular team. As it turned out, both the Heywood revival and Goldsmith's *The Good Natured Man* were lacking in flair, which somewhat offset their evident integrity and solid workmanship: though how much better for the director of a massively subsidised company to put his trust in qualities such as these and proceed with quiet confidence than to compete with the commercial theatre's screams for attention.

Both Dexter's shows were exercises in historical reconstruction, the Heywood being much the more interesting of the two. The piece itself, in which a deceived husband packs his adulterous wife off to another house and leaves her to waste away from guilt, exhibits an aspect of English life rarely celebrated by Jacobean playwrights: a sober provincial society untouched by Renaissance glamour, where offences are punished with Christian judgements instead of daggers. The play is not remarkable for psychological insight or moral curiosity, and Dexter rightly gave his main attention to building up a picture of a vanished way of life: staging it, as Heywood prescribes, on a 'bare scene', and unfurling all the pageantry of feasting and hunting across the platform like splendid carpets unrolled in the desert. Central to the spectacle was the life of the Frankford household, where the master blesses a cottage loaf before dinner and the servants relax with clog dances; and where Puritanism loses none of its austerity, but appears as modest and humane.

Inset within this portrait, Joan Plowright's regally mourning wife and Frank Barrie's foxy lover struck a discordantly theatrical note despite their down-to-earth Yorkshire vowels. But Frankfort himself, as Mr Hopkins played him, took all his strength from the surrounding detail. Swathed in slop breeches and drawing comfortably on a clay pipe, it was a performance at once conveying the unassertive dignity of a man of substance and an extraordinary sense of inner tumult. To see Hopkins rebounding almost in tears from the lovers' bedroom and stopping in the midst of verbally flaying his enemy to wrap a cloak over his naked shoulders, thrillingly enlarged the emotional resources of the part and the play's comment on the nature of charity.

In *The Good-Natured Man* (October) Dexter's attempt to root an old play in its social background was more perfunctory. With a style as enclosed as eighteenth-century comedy it does not help much to open up the genteel hero's living-room to a scene-shifting chorus of brawny tavern roughs, and still less to let them roar out bawdy rat-catching ballads totally at odds with the polite spirit of the piece. If anything, these additions only emphasised the feebleness of a plot in which the hero's friends club together to save him from his improvident impulses. Still, the production's levelling policy was in line with the funniest scene (excluded as too coarse for the original Drury Lane public) in which three blackguardly bailiffs share a tea-party with the wretched Honeywood and his well-bred beloved (an interesting bluestocking performance by Maureen Lipman). And full justice was done to the two meaty comic roles of Lofty the con-man and Croaker the professional pessimist. Goldsmith offered to 'knock out' one of these to give Garrick scope to expand in the other: but as played by Jim Dale, a toothy coffee-house White Rabbit deluging the stage in wig powder, and Bill Fraser, ominously pursing his great lips and speculating with gloomy relish on a mass invasion of Jesuits, there was ample room for them both.

The main comic triumph of the year came in March with Zuckmayer's *The Captain of Köpenick*. Following the Schiller Theater production at the Aldwych, one half suspected that (as before, with *Hedda Gabler*, and afterwards, with *The Rules of the Game*) the World Theatre Season was being raided on behalf of a National star. But within minutes of the opening of Frank Dunlop's production there was no mistaking the descent of the comic spirit. This was a German joke released from the ponderous self-criticism of the Schiller version. The Wilhelmenian background was touched in with military band *entr'actes* and Karl von Appen's delicate settings, suggesting weight with the lightest possible means. John Mortimer's translation worked to the same effect. The hero of the play is not so much Voigt, the old convict turned authoritarian, as the German military uniform which permits this transformation. The uniform confers power and dignity upon its wearer. To this,

Mortimer added the factor of invincible sex appeal—expressed in scenes like the farcical ball and lines like 'I can't stand it, she's sitting on his regimentals'.

Otherwise the production stood out for its rare success in coupling fine company acting with star appeal. Its mainstay was undoubtedly Paul Scofield's Voigt, a shuffling vagrant successively transformed into model prisoner and ramrod Captain, his once bedraggled moustache now bristling with authority and his shifty whine changed to rasping command. But the magnitude of this performance in no way belittled such superb accompanying sketches as John Moffatt's Jewish clothes merchant, Bill Fraser's apopleptically social-climbing Burgomaster, and Kenneth Mackintosh as the gleeful military tailor presiding over the uniform business like a profiteering magician.

It was from this high point that the season began its downward curve. *Coriolanus* arrived at Waterloo Road in July after persistent rumours of internal disagreements. According to Kenneth Tynan, the part was originally intended for Scofield, but went eventually to Christopher Plummer with the invitation to choose his own director. Plummer nominated Manfred Wekwerth and Joachim Tenschert (whose Berliner Ensemble version had visited the Old Vic in 1965), only to find their direction unacceptable and ask for their replacement. However, it was Plummer who was replaced, and the Germans continued work with Anthony Hopkins as the Coriolanus whom the public finally saw.

Hopkins's own contribution was honourable and arresting; an interesting displacement of the character from arrogant pride to narcissistic vanity, too intoxicated with his own sense of superior worth to commit the vulgarity of asserting it. Given Hopkins's own bully-boy physique there was an additional contrast in the modest, almost winsome manner he adopted for Coriolanus. But appearing in the context of a Brechtian production, with its intention of deflating public respect for great men, Hopkins's performance added yet another contradictory strand to an already confused spectacle. The company have indignantly denied striking any compromise with the directors: but, with memories of the Ensemble version, that is what the production suggested.

The Ensemble used the tragedy to expose a parasitic military élite whose hero is finally thrown out by the common people. At the National Theatre, Shakespeare's ending was restored (though Coriolanus was made to wait for the supplicant Volumnia to trail off stage and then to speak the line 'O, mother, what have you done?' in soliloquy). With that concession to the author, the earlier scenes followed the Brechtian line in asserting the civic worth of the people and the tribunes. Impasse. In a letter defending this approach, Kenneth Tynan said: 'The only difference from the conventional version (and it is a big one) is that they are not played as yapping boobies but presented with sympathetic detachment as human beings. In the past they have always been played *as seen through the Patricians' eyes*—as if the only correct viewpoint were the aristocratic one.'

The trouble with that reasonable argument is that Shakespeare himself is among the benighted conformists who view the plebs as a contemptible mob. 'I ever said we were in the wrong when we banished him.' Pity the actor who has to play lines like that as a soberly judicious comment.

Meanwhile the company's second front had opened up at the New Theatre and ensemble policy gave way to actor-managerial tactics. In defence of this sorry episode it may be that the National was determined not to fall into the trap of its previous season at the Cambridge Theatre where successful Waterloo Road productions had fallen upon thin houses. (There was a move to drop Michael Blakemore's brilliant production of *The National Health* from the Old Vic repertory after its failure to pack the Cambridge.) Perhaps there were two publics: one for the Old Vic and one for the West End. In which case something more calculated than 'overspill' programming was necessary.

Whatever the reasoning, the New Theatre formula replenished neither the National's box office nor its reputation. The first show was Pirandello's *The Rules of the Game*, last seen in 1966 in a splendid version brought to the Aldwych by the Compagnia dei Giovani, who revealed the piece as a superb precision instrument. Anthony Page's production paid little attention to the play's intellectual line (such as its virtuoso dramatic imagery), nor to supporting parts, like the party of drunken swells who seemed to have strayed in from a tour of *The Student Prince*. Its interest was reserved for the stars: Joan Plowright as the trouble-making wife and Scofield as the visiting husband. Scofield at least partly redeemed the event with a fascinating lizard-like performance which never let you forget what it had cost the character to edit himself out of life.

Worse was to come in Olivier's production of Giraudoux's *Amphitryon 38* in which Christopher Plummer finally made his National Theatre début. It was a vulgar and empty spectacle, prone on the night I saw it to scenic mishaps, all too compatible with a general air of carelessness variously evident in Malcolm Pride's fretwork clouds, a slap-happy reliance on pre-recorded effects (even for on-stage trumpet calls), and the disappearance of Leda into a supposedly darkened room which a short curtain disclosed as brightly illuminated.

Plummer cut an even cruder mid-Atlantic figure in the name part of Büchner's *Danton's Death* which he carried off with the lumbering gusto of a Civil War general tanked up on Old Grandad. There was no civic or philosophic passion in the performance; only a flashy portrait of a philistine old bull with his back to the wall. Coming upon a line like, 'Everything goes without saying', he would break it in half and speak the two first words as though written by Cole Porter.

Jonathan Miller directed the play not as a political work for today, but as an animated museum-piece. This at least gave Patrick Robertson the pretext for a superbly imaginative set consisting of mobile cages (containing wired Revolutionary costumes), and back-wall projections of classical figures which faded into X-ray skeletons as the guillotine fell. The production did not live up to this frame-work. Not only did it lack the sense of historical occasion, but failed even to identify many of the historical personages. It did contain two fine performances, from Ronald Pickup who built St Just's denunciation into one of the most earth-shaking climaxes I have ever heard, and Charles Kay who played Robespierre with chilling restraint as a glacially smiling and myopic lawyer. Other-wise the piece was disfigured by eccentric banalities, like encasing one of the street commentators in a phrenological head. *Danton's Death* is a play about a whole people, but they looked a few lonely ghosts on that stage.

After *Tyger* (discussed at the end of this chapter by Michael Billington), Olivier returned for his one new performance of the year. In the circumstances, it looked like a superstar speeding to the rescue of a failing enterprise, but in fact Michael Blakemore's

production of *Long Day's Journey into Night* was very much a
company work conceived in devotion to a very great play. Blakemore's main strategy was to approach its black climax from as
distant a point as possible: and the first act, with sunlight streaming
into Michael Annals's seedily spacious replica of O'Neill's Con-
necticut home, presented a family background of peace and goodwill,
with Olivier jovially jingling the change in his pockets and the two
boys romping in like puppies. In this relaxed atmosphere, the
domestic noose began to tighten as involuntary scowls were ex-
changed and poisonous little details started aching under the
surface of the dialogue. But it is a long day's journey, and Blakemore graded it like a long-distance runner.

Of the cast, the big surprise was Constance Cummings who
underwent the transformation from the gentle maternal presence
of the opening to the spectral morphine addict of the last act with
an authority and spiritual intensity that thoroughly earned the
part its central position. Ronald Pickup as Edmund (alias Eugene)
cut through the part's narcissism and coupled passionate contact
with a half-detached viewpoint: while, as the elder brother, Denis
Quilley (a most valuable newcomer to the company) progressed
from Edwardian bounder to a domestic cannibal almost on a level
with the old man.

Olivier's Tyrone was a performance of technical and personal
fascination. Personal because James Tyrone (alias O'Neill's father)
was an actor with the kind of career that Olivier has spent his life
escaping: a strong young talent destroyed by years of profitable
type-casting. We see Tyrone at a stage when he is all too aware of
his self-destruction: and the dejection that settled on Olivier—his
body hunched in its baggy suit, and his mouth cracked into a small
mean line creating a receding chin—expressed a sense of defeat
going much beyond family affairs.

There were touches of the old ham actor: as where Olivier the
showman pulled off a pair of his incomparable tricks in two con-
trasted descents from a table—first swaying vertiginously on his
toes, then leaping off like a gazelle and slapping a hand that offers
him assistance. But what marked out his performance from the
rest was its breadth; all the elements were there simultaneously—
the miser, the old pro, the distracted husband, the ragged Irish
boy. You could argue that the result was too knowing for a charac-

LEFT: *Christopher Plummer as* Danton
RIGHT: *John Moffat & Bill Fraser in* Tyger

ter so much at the mercy of impulse. But the effect was too electrifying to be argued with; and in the desolate last act Olivier abandoned all subterfuge and showed the defenceless face of the man himself.

It was a fitting last production for the year that brought the death of the National Theatre's first Chairman, Lord Chandos. A crack company stretching themselves to the limit in the service of a great work. Not all productions can be on that level; and few of them are likely to list Olivier in the cast. But the integrity of the production is not such a rationed commodity; one can respect shows possessing that and nothing else, while all other qualities are valueless without it. After their switchback year the company have reason to ponder this hoary old commonplace; the reader will know to what effect.

MICHAEL BILLINGTON writes:

Tyger, the National Theatre's first attempt at a musical, was vehemently attacked by the majority of critics. Yet I thought it one of the best things to come out of the National's ill-fated New Theatre season and, in many respects, a highly significant show. It used William Blake as a symbol of the vilified, beleaguered artist forever at war with the philistine English Establishment; it bravely attempted to bring together several different strands in the native theatrical tradition including revue, panto, satire and cod burlesque; and Mike Westbrook's exuberant score showed that the musical form could accommodate the talents of a first-rate jazz musician. Purists hated the show. But who the hell needs purists?

A lot of the argument, of course, centred on Adrian Mitchell's book. People suggested he was using Blake simply as a stalking-horse from which to stage a trendy-lefty attack on contemporary society and showed little feeling either for Blake's poetry or his philosophy. Yet the show was described as 'a celebration of William Blake' and for my money, Mitchell fastened on to the essential quality of the man: that as Northrop Frye once pointed out, he epitomised the English Protestant-Radical tradition which takes the individual as the primary field of operations rather than the interests of society. Mitchell pursued this by showing Blake not only as the devout enemy of the entrenched Establishment but as a genuine visionary who believed that God was the divine essence that existed in every man and woman.

Admittedly the show's structure was somewhat invertebrate and its final image (of the cast dismantling a baroque space capsule and reassembling it in the form of a chimneyfied country house) seemed an inadequate symbol of Blake's vision of a resplendent golden age. Yet the crucial thing is that, for the first time since Arden's *The Workhouse Donkey*, an English writer and composer were attempting to bring a vulgar Dionysiac gaiety on to the stage and showing that the most vital elements of popular theatrical tradition could be reconciled to the exploration of a serious theme. Directors, playwrights and critics are constantly preaching the need for a 'popular' theatre; yet few of them take the trouble to examine the theatrical forms (panto, musicals, variety) that have genuinely widespread appeal. Mitchell, Westbrook and *Tyger*'s directors, Michael Blakemore and John Dexter, had, I felt, done their homework; and the result was an extravaganza that not only celebrated William Blake but also the vitality of the theatre itself. In my memory *Tyger* still burns bright.

Benedict Nightingale

RSC Ascendant

The drama critic of the New Statesman *reviews the year at Stratford and the Aldwych.*

Nineteen seventy-one was the year when the National Theatre could do little right, and the Royal Shakespeare Company little wrong. We critics found ourselves snarling and growling with depressing regularity over what at times looked ominously like the bones of the one, and, like the curs we're commonly held to be, fawning and slavering round the legs of the other. No doubt there was over-reaction, both ways. Nevertheless, I, for one, could not mistake the confident lift of the spirits I invariably felt when I set out for the Aldwych, or Stratford, or even the RSC's short season at The Place. You knew you might find the production wildly presumptuous. At any rate, you could be pretty sure you would disagree with this or that aspect of the director's interpretation, especially when Shakespeare was being performed. But at least there would be something well worth the mental and emotional strain of disagreement. You would never emerge afterwards, as some of us did from the National's *Coriolanus* or *Tyger*, feeling at once exasperated and depressed by the kind of socio-political simplification that seemed to suggest that the audience was only too liable to fall into mass error, and therefore had better not be permitted to think too much; that we were untrustworthy children, whose anxious and earnest questionings were to be fobbed off with dogmatic assertions about the absolute evil of all 'fascists' or the perpetual grossness and grotesquerie of the British 'establishment'.

The RSC always seemed more interested in starting thought than stopping it; and yet, as anyone who saw *Enemies* or *Miss Julie* or *Othello* will confirm, it was very far from being grimly cerebral. There were times when one felt that it, not the other, was the true National Theatre.

Of course, critics are notoriously apt to pontificate about 'trends' on inadequate evidence. The year 1972 could show some switch of fortunes. Indeed, the RSC began it with Peter Hall's reverential production of Albee's sepulchral *All Over*, and the National with Stoppard's *Jumpers*, as exuberantly enjoyable an evening in the theatre as I can remember. Conceivably, some fevered colleague may make the same comparison in next year's edition of this book, with a simple inversion of hero and villain. If I hesitate to believe so, however, it is for three main reasons. First, the RSC would appear to be more adventurously, energetically and youthfully led. Second, it has a history of doing the more interesting new plays, though in this both it and the National must cede to the Royal Court. Third, it has built up a company which may not have any 'house style', whatever that means, but indisputably *is* a genuine company—capable, versatile, and often marvellously responsive, each to each. Although Anthony Hopkins and Ronald Pickup have emerged from the rump in the last year or so, the National is still too disinclined to give its supporting players the chances some of them would seem to deserve. This is especially true of its younger women, none of whom looks like developing into a Judi Dench, Sara Kestelman, Helen Mirren or Janet Suzman, or any RSC equivalent one cares to name, partly because they don't look like being positively encouraged to do so.

What makes a visit to the Royal Shakespeare Company so inspiriting by comparison is the prospect of seeing any of several actors and actresses, all long-standing, experienced members of the company and yet none of them particularly well known to the public-at-large, in parts that may vary from the merest cameo to the most testing Shakespearian lead. Among these, I'd include David Waller, who was seen in 1971 as Bottom in *A Midsummer Night's Dream*; Patrick Stewart, a vindictive, petty-minded factory mogul in *Enemies* and a cool, grim revolutionary in *Occupations*; Emrys James, a good Shylock and a better Iago: Sebastian Shaw, an erratic ex-general in *Enemies*; and, perhaps especially, Elizabeth

LEFT: '*Ensemble acting at its finest*': Helen Mirren, John Wood in Enemies
RIGHT: All Over: *Sebastian Shaw, Angela Lansbury, David Markham, Peggy Ashcroft and Patience Collier*

LEFT: '*Human archetypes*': Colin Blakely and Vivien Merchant in Old Times
RIGHT: '*From ritualistic to casual*': The Balcony—*Estelle Kohler, Brenda Bruce*

Spriggs, an unusually warm, sympathetic Emilia and a notable
Beatrice. These I take to be the RSC's proven backbone, its unsung
troupers; but it also has its share of 'names' and of rising young
players who are in the process of becoming 'names', whatever such
status may be worth. The first category would include Derek
Godfrey, Richard Pasco, Brenda Bruce and Judi Dench, the last
three of whom have been with the company for some time, and
the second, Alan Howard, Sara Kestelman, Helen Mirren, and, on
the evidence of their work in 1971, John Kane and Ben Kingsley.

Not that the year was unrelievedly triumphant. I explained my
unfashionable, unrepresentative, and I daresay by now notorious,
opposition to Peter Brook's *Midsummer Night's Dream* in last
year's edition of this book; and, in 1971, I found myself quite
unable to respond either to its revival or to Etheridge's *Man of
Mode*, an unfunny, mean-spirited piece, nasty even by the standards
of the Restoration—an invitation to laugh along with foppish men
who regard women as mincers might be presumed to regard meat.
Again, there was a somewhat disappointing *Duchess of Malfi* in
Stratford, with oddly muted performances from some of those I've
just named. Jane Austen's Mr Collins seemed on the point of
primly bursting from beneath the purple cassock of Emrys James's
pedantic, moralising Cardinal; Richard Pasco's Antonio was an
apologetic, skulking fellow, lacking magnanimity and warmth; and
Michael Williams's twitching, blinking, erratically beaming Fer-
dinand turned out to be a mildly rabid puppy posing, less than
persuasively, as the mad, bad wolf of Webster's imagination. The
presence of evil was suggested less by the performances than by
one insistent effect: the drag and clank of the spurs Mr Williams
wore throughout, a chilling noise to hear in the corridors of an old
and doubtless haunted palace late at night, but still only a noise. It
was left to Judi Dench to make a stronger case for the forces of
light, and without help from her shoes, clothes, or any other ulterior
agency. Indeed, a strong white light is exactly what she seemed to
radiate at times, so much so that she had no need to emphasise
that traditional assertion of the character's emotional integrity,
'I am Duchess of Malfi still', and could simply drop it into the
conversation as an obvious fact, of which others should scarcely
need reminding. But, by comparison, the rest of the play seemed
not to exist.

And then there was the strange case of Joyce's *Exiles*. I was part of the critical consensus that almost unreservedly welcomed this when it was first revived at the Mermaid in 1970; and yet, a year later, faced with an almost identical cast at the Aldwych, I found myself wondering how I could have been so entranced. The introverted, meditative tone of Harold Pinter's production appeared to have become mechanical, the silences self-conscious and studied. It no longer gave that impression of dark, unpleasant truths lurking beneath plain surfaces so characteristic of Pinter's own work. Where it had seemed profound, it was now often merely downbeat; and Vivien Merchant's Bertha Rowan was more mannered than ever—all raucous pant and tremulous gasp—and altogether too gracious and sure for what's supposed to be a gauche, frightened, shrunken character. The scene in which she described to her husband the details of the advances his best friend had just made to her, which chilled audiences at the Mermaid, simply left those at the Aldwych cheerfully cackling. This was a pity, since the piece was topical and worth revival, showing, as it does, the unease and unhappiness too much marital freedom brings all three sides of its triangle. There was also a superb, and quite unspoiled, performance by John Wood as Richard Rowan himself—now lugubrious and brooding, now sudden and snappish, a reptile with a quick, dangerous tongue. He injected breath into a deflated evening, but not enough, alas, to restore it to its former health.

But the other three offerings at the Aldwych, not to mention those at Stratford and The Place, more than compensated. Indeed, one was the first performance of a play one can readily imagine being revived in 100 or 200 years' time by a National Theatre, Royal Shakespeare Company, or (who knows) Royal Pinter Theatre, centred in Sidcup, Holloway, or beneath the pier of some obscure south-coast resort. This was Pinter's own *Old Times*. Let me admit that some perfectly sensible, indeed intelligent, people managed to sit through it and see little but desultory nostalgia in the conversation of Colin Blakely, Dorothy Tutin and Vivien Merchant, playing, respectively, husband, wife and wife's old friend. It left them as cold and uninterested as Pinter's double bill, *Landscape* and *Silence*, had left me a couple of years earlier. There, I had found only a self-consciously 'lyrical', slightly maudlin tone-poem, a sort of *Finlandia* in words, and I feared for Pinter's future; but

now, surely, he had moved onwards, and decisively, and in a much
more rewarding direction, towards a compromise between the best
of *Landscape* and *Silence* and the more concrete style of *The Caretaker* and *The Homecoming*.

Like *Landscape, Old Times* involved human archetypes, but,
this time, ones that were also sharply individualised. Like *The
Caretaker*, it had a carefully constructed plot, but, this time, one
that occurred almost entirely at an unspoken, subliminal level. In
the most economical way it showed an increasingly bitter and
unpleasant battle between a bluff Mr Blakely and an arty, bubbling
Miss Merchant in which the winner could apparently expect Miss
Tutin's allegiance, and maybe something more, as a sort of trophy;
and it also showed how, in such situations, the real power belongs to
the trophy—to Miss Tutin, sitting back and luxuriously watching,
an amused cat withholding her favours and biding her time. In
short, it was about a very English phenomenon: politeness without,
all social forms duly observed, and violence within. But one had
to keep one's eyes and ears skinned. It was easy to miss a violence
so subtly and obliquely expressed.

Of course, this was uncharacteristic of the season, involving,
as it did, a small cast mainly imported for the occasion. Neither
Miss Tutin nor Mr Blakely appeared in any other production. If
one wanted to see the more permanent members of the company at
their composite best, there was Stratford, or, at the Aldwych,
notable productions of *The Balcony* and *Enemies*. Genet was performed to the intermittent accompaniment of mocking music from
a band tucked away behind what looked like the reticulated gold
frame of a Victorian Christmas card, dominating the stage. Beneath,
there cavorted androgynous dream creatures called Blood, Sperm
and Sweat, imported for the occasion from a previously unperformed
version of the play; the most unpretentious and businesslike of
revolutionaries plotted the destruction of the brothel of the title,
while Brenda Bruce's madame manipulated its clients with concern,
even tenderness; Philip Locke's drably skeletal little clerk clam-
bered, with the help of the tart playing his horse, into enormous
cothurni and a bizarrely padded, bemedalled uniform, Larry the
Lamb gradually transformed into General Patton. The difficulty of
the play, as this suggests, is that it is stylistically very varied, very
confusing: the achievement of the director at the Aldwych, Terry

Hands, was somehow to assimilate all its elements, from the most grotesque to the most mundane, from the ritualistic to the casual, into a whole which had dramatic coherence. In defiance of all pusillanimous rules against 'mixing styles', it worked. I can't recall a production of Genet that more successfully expressed his cheerful, bitter, nihilistic, pious, priapic, cerebral, farcical, histrionic and altogether contradictory spirit.

Enemies was, simply, one of the most enthralling evenings I have spent in a theatre, and a revelation to those of us who had accepted the common wisdom that Gorki wrote nothing worth reviving but *The Lower Depths*. David Jones's production showed us a sunny world where beautiful people sauntered across lawns to what appeared to be a 24-hour running picnic, far from the satanic mills that had actually paid for the silver so casually strewn across the trestle table to the right of the stage. Indeed, it deliberately drew us into it, seducing us into identifying with the characters and enjoying their leisure, almost into tasting the tea in the samovar and the cakes piled next to it, and then it betrayed us, by making it clear that the characters (and we?) were morally misguided and historically doomed. They were well-enough intentioned, most of them, but this was a situation where kindly feelings would be of little further use. The factory boss was shot, the gentry felt it had no choice but to close ranks beside his body. There would now only be greater bitterness, more polarisation: 'enemies'. As a capriciously garnered selection of workers were taken away, hoods over their heads, we understood, and at a level no history book could reach, just why 1917 was unavoidable.

The tone of the piece is tragi-comic, after Chekhov, with grand cosmic generalisations co-existing with nicely observed human foible; and the company proved remarkably sensitive, not only to one another, but to the most subtle ups and downs of atmosphere. One remembers Sebastian Shaw, whimsically cantering across the stage on foot, his batman posing as his horse, while Patrick Stewart's industrial tyrant lay sprawled among the sandwiches, dying. Then there was Alan Howard's grimly fanatical prosecutor, a man who evidently thought that the smallest concession to human weakness (a smile, even) might release the torrents of socialism; Mary Rutherford's bouncing, girlish, ineffective young liberal; John Wood's Yakov, an apolitical, private man born hopelessly out of his time, and far gone in booze, self-loathing and despair. One could go on naming names—but what, finally, is the point? This was ensemble acting at its finest.

In 1969 the RSC presented a season with a distinct theme at Stratford, and in 1972 is presenting another. The one concentrated on the last plays, the other on the Roman plays, though each time with the odd omission of *Cymbeline*, which fits into both categories. In 1971 all that linked the Stratford season was a high standard of production and performance, down to and including the more 'Theatregoround' productions, specially mounted to go out from Stratford to halls and schools elsewhere, with the minimum of stage furniture and so much doubling of parts that the female lead may sometimes be spotted lurking beneath a helmet, playing a soldier.

In John Barton's *Richard II*, a confident, upright young king, attractively played by Richard Pasco, was seen being outmanoeuvred by as cynical and gloating a Bolingbroke faction as I can recall having seen; and yet in his second 'Theatregoround' production, *Henry V*, Barton managed to suggest that it was Hal, the highly principled hero, who had the more capacity for inflicting damage. Michael Williams played him as a pleasant, modest, conscientious boy, the kind every father would like to see dating his daughter, and every son would forgive for beating him at tennis. The trouble, of course, is that he and his age did indeed see war as a somewhat ferocious Wimbledon final, more so (I think) than Shakespeare did, and certainly more so than we do, from our knowing stance in 1972. Barton gave us both the decency and the destruction, letting the contrast speak for itself and in no way distorting Shakespeare in order to make it stronger. Indeed, his inference (no more) was that it was Hal's very decency that made him seductive, and therefore dangerous; or, to translate the point into twentieth-century politics, a John Kennedy is in a way more to be feared than a Johnson, or perhaps a Teddy Kennedy more than a Nixon, since they have charisma, seem purer and tend to receive a more uncritical trust, although in fact they may be no less prone to self-deception and error. The obvious wheeler-dealers—a Johnson, a Bolingbroke— invite scepticism at once, and may hence be less likely to lead us unprotesting to disaster.

LEFT: '*A confident, upright young king*': *Richard Pasco as* Richard II
RIGHT: '*Refreshingly sensible*': *Elizabeth Spriggs and Derek Godfrey in* Much Ado About Nothing

LEFT: '*Grandiloquence and thunder*': *Brewster Mason* (Othello), *with Lisa Harrow* (Desdemona)
RIGHT: '*A strong white light*': *Judi Dench as* The Duchess of Malfi

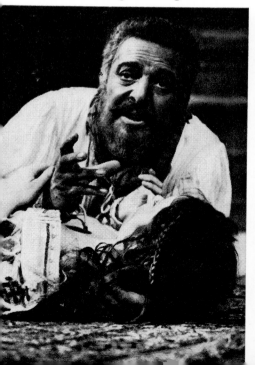

At Stratford proper the season began with an underrated _Merchant of Venice_, set more unambiguously than any production I can recall, in a great imperial capital, very conscious of its wealth and power, but hedonistic and more than somewhat spoiled. Gold dominated the set—one of Portia's caskets, in the form of a human figure, seemed to have been borrowed from the film of _Goldfinger_—and laughter characterised the Christian characters. There can have been few warmer Portias than Judi Dench, with her proneness to explosions of giggles, her burning faith in liberal values, like 'mercy', and, with it, such capacity for disillusion that she actually wept when Bassanio gave away her ring. The trouble with Jonathan Miller's production of the same play at the National was that he accentuated the shallowness of the Christians, and also made them a good deal more obviously malicious than they are, instead of allowing their limitations to emerge of themselves. Terry Hands, who directed at Stratford, resisted both this and the temptation of turning Shylock into a melodramatic Jew of Malta on the one hand, or, on the other, into the kind of dignified, oppressed Rothschild Laurence Olivier gave us at the National. Emrys James was a shaggy, flamboyantly Oriental, dangerous Shylock, baleful when crossed, but by no means unsympathetic. He barked comically and satirically at the Christians, showing them the absurdity of calling him 'dog', and he put across the great speech about eyes and ears notably well, with the bewildered, slightly hopeless air of a teacher explaining an obvious fact for the fortieth time to an inexplicably impervious class—will they never see what is, after all, mere reason? He left us, not with a roar, like Olivier, but with a terrible whisper, his strength quite exhausted. It was a finely balanced performance in a finely balanced production; and there were others to come.

There was, for instance, Ronald Eyre's refreshingly sensible _Much Ado_: a complete answer, as I saw it, to Shaw's attack on Shakespeare for allegedly asking us to believe Beatrice and Benedick 'exquisitely witty persons'. Eyre's point was, simply, that Shakespeare never asked anything of the sort. His Benedick was Derek Godfrey, looking and sounding a bit like Jimmy Edwards, a hearty, genial fellow, everyone's chum in the mess, and capable of announcing his intention to be 'horribly in love' with the kind of salacious growl men sometimes produce when discussing women over drinks; and his Beatrice was Elizabeth Spriggs, a sunny, complacent, busy lady, the sort anyone would approach if a concert party had to be arranged or an invalid visited. In a characteristically intelligent, developing performance, and a characteristically sympathetic one, she slowly and movingly rediscovered a capacity for love she had long since laid aside. Neither of them were 'exquisitely witty', or even particularly sophisticated, but, rather, brought some fairly ordinary banter to the bluff military milieu to which they both belonged. In short, they were very much creatures of their time and place—which meant that, for once, it was quite credible that Benedick should be so accepted and liked by his fellow-soldiers, and, indeed, should *be* a soldier at all, rather than a courtier, poet, comedian or dancing master.

The action occurred in the Regency period, which accentuated the play's comfortable, mellow tone, but did admittedly make 'kill Claudio' an even more improbable injunction than it is already; and the action of John Barton's *Othello* occurred a little later still, in some obscure Victorian colonial outpost, where there was little to do but sprawl, drink, gossip and wait for something to happen. This party obviously needed a life and soul—and found it, logically enough, in Emrys James's excellent and unusual Iago. With his jaunty manner and tiny, round, red, scrubbed, shiny trooper's face, he reminded you of the kind of Cockney sparrow that used to appear in every British war film, always ready with a quip, a song, an attentive ear, a piece of helpful advice, or a quick, ingratiating smile. We had, of course, seen him earlier with Roger Rees's artless, lovelorn Roderigo, so we knew the bitterness of which this Iago was also capable: but to his superiors he was, credibly enough, a simple, 'honest' man, almost embarrassingly grateful for the opportunity to be of service. Lisa Harrow's Desdemona was too innocent, and Brewster Mason's Othello too enamoured of his own lordly splendour, to see him with anything but that mindless complacency with which, even now, the squirearchy is apt to regard its old and supposedly faithful retainers. It was an interesting performance, with obvious topical implications; and I still don't think the approach distorted the play, which is, after all, as much about a morally obtuse society, in which people value the *appearance* of good above all, as about the jealousy of its principal character. At any rate, Barton concentrated on the former and neglected the latter, with the connivance of Mr Mason, whose Othello was full

LEFT: *Julian Glover, Sara Kestelman:* Subject to Fits
RIGHT: *Helen Mirren:* Miss Julie

of grandiloquence and thunder, but surprisingly lacking in passion.

With so much going on in London and Stratford, it seemed odd of the RSC to proclaim, as it virtually did towards the end of the year, that it didn't feel fully stretched. But it is a large company, two of the plays at the Aldwych had small casts, and, more to the point, its two theatres are too large for intimate productions and too costly for experimental ones dubious of success. Hence the short season it offered at The Place, in a tiny rectangle flanked on three sides by steep rakes of the most uncomfortable seats in London. There was Robert Montgomery's *Subject to Fits*, which consisted of somewhat erratic doodles on a general theme of Dostoevsky's *Idiot*, and notable mainly for John Kane's dignified, earnest, bewildered Myshkin; there was Trevor Griffiths's *Occupations*, about industrial unrest in Turin in 1920, notable for Ben Kingsley's Gramsci, with his hunched back and crooked walk, his tentative, questioning smile and solid inner passion; and, above all, Robin Phillips's production of Strindberg's *Miss Julie*.

This was much praised for the precision of Daphne Dare's set, though its admirers seemed unaware that Strindberg himself, who demanded so much attention to detail when he wrote the preface to the play, later changed his mind, pronouncing 'all this pottering about with stage properties' to be 'useless'. And, to be sure, so literally conceived a kitchen did prove somewhat distracting, though not so much as to vitiate the effect of two fine performances. Donal McCann's Jean wasn't very interesting, perhaps, but Heather Canning made a splendidly downright, mulishly decent Christine, and Helen Mirren had never been better than as Julie herself. Miss Mirren's problem has always been an excess of head; and this time, too, you sometimes had the feeling that her body was struggling to keep pace with the demands of an intelligent interpretation. The rivets of the performance occasionally showed: the *idea* predominated. Yet there was fluency, too, and considerable force—'Lackey', she roared at McCann, her whole being quivering with indignant contempt, and the rafters shook. It was as if she was shaken by civil war within, with fear and hatred pulling her one way, and a sort of awful, morbid, fascination with sexuality the other. There was pre-coital torment, her hands flailing angrily at McCann's chest, and post-coital disgust, her nose wrinkling at the smell of stale sperm, and yet also an odd pathos. 'What is love, do you know what love is?' she asked with a sudden, vulnerable simplicity, badly needing to understand—and knowing quite well she never *could* understand.

It would be good to see more such performances at close quarters. Indeed, it's possible that the short season at The Place was the most important event during the year, as far as the now and future health of the company is concerned. Not that there are yet any signs of self-satisfaction, or stasis, or resting on laurels: nevertheless, given its achievements, those are always dangers. The more self-imposed challenge, the better. If a season such as this can be mounted again, perhaps annually, perhaps for longer than the nine weeks it lasted this time, and perhaps with a rather more unorthodox and taxing programme. Well, why not? The Royal Shakespeare Company is so good at the moment that it is worth taking some pains to keep it that way.

John Simon

Broadway

The drama critic of New York *and* The Hudson Review *looks back over another 'lamentable' year.*

I cannot recall reading a piece on any Broadway season that did not begin with a lament about its having been one of the worst ever. Of course, it is possible that critics are insatiable creatures who might have described the London season of 1605–6 as one in which nothing more distinguished happened than *King Lear, Macbeth* and *Volpone*. Or the critic may be an inveterate *laudator temporis acti*, and may wax enthusiastic only about the year in which Plautus wrote the *Mostellaria*. However that may be, I would give anything to be able to start this account with something other than 'The period between 1 January 1971 and 1 February 1972 was one of the worst in recent Broadway memory'.

But, alas, the period between 1 January 1971 and 1 February 1972 was one of the worst in recent Broadway memory. Of the eight musicals worth listing, for example, only one was a new American work; of the seven mentionable comedies, only one was a new full-length American play (not an adaptation, revival, import or group of vaguely related one-acters). Under such circumstances, certain desperate stratagems became veritable trends, but despair is no better as a dramatist than as a counsellor.

'A riotous, madcap mixture of sporadically clever invention and a lot of slapdash horseplay': Two Gentlemen of Verona *with Raul Julia, Jonelle Allen, Clifton Davis and Diana Davila*

Probably the most prominent phenomenon was the non-play or non-musical, a way of getting something on stage without having to write practically anything. Thus in *The Incomparable Max*, those two old slouch-bys, Lawrence and Lee, glued together two unrelated Beerbohm stories, a few anecdotes about Max, and some pallid Lawrence-and-Lee twaddle, and tried to call it a play. Another such attempt, this one more successful, is Julian Barry's *Lenny*. Here the core of the drama is a handful of Lenny Bruce monologues literally transported to the stage, garnished with a few songs and some biographical data, and spiced up with weirdly grandiose production numbers by Tom O'Horgan, America's answer to Peter Brook. O'Horgan's technique is to ransack every old and new, Eastern and Western theatrical style, add to it a few in-jokes or outlandish japes, and then plunk it all down pell-mell on whatever play he happens to be doing. Here he has introduced everything from a creepy tribe of nattering cavemen to naked hippies representing Moses and Jesus, from giant puppets to an enormous, Mount Rushmore-style head of Nixon that opens up to reveal the overdosed, naked and dead Lenny Bruce slumped over his toilet bowl. That Nixon, for all his sins, had nothing to do with Bruce, or that none of O'Horgan's neo-baroque excesses has anything to do with the play, does not seem to deter critics or audiences in the least. Similarly, because Mrs Bruce was a stripper, the actress who portrays her is kept near-naked throughout: questionable logic but an unquestionable box-office coup.

Yet underneath all this nudity and crudity, Barry's play is hardly written and depends chiefly on Cliff Gorman's energetic and dedicated work as Lenny, a character who almost never leaves the stage and hurtles from frantic night-club routines into plaintive, semi-crazed self-justifications before his judges. It is the equivalent of simultaneously performing *Hamlet* and running a marathon race, and Gorman's bravura and stamina are impressive, even if he does not ultimately possess the rich variety of accents and inflections that made Bruce spellbinding.

Even more prevalent than the non-play was the non-musical. Since it is always the book that is the hardest, and usually the weakest, part of the musical, the new solution is simply to leave it out. That this subtraction turns the event into more of a revue or pop concert, a step back or sideways rather than forward, does not

seem to bother anyone much. Here we have two more ventures of
Mr O'Horgan's. The first is *Jesus Christ, Superstar*, the flimsy
British rock oratorio, retelling the last days of Christ in terms of
Tom Rice's contemporary doggerel lyrics and Andrew Lloyd
Webber's eclectic and uninspired rock score. O'Horgan's set,
costume and dance designs are even more unleashed, irrelevant
and irredeemably vulgar in this show, with silks and gauzes often
swathing the entire stage, performers flying in and out on ropes,
large surreal objects being carried on and off constantly and sometimes disgorging or swallowing one or the other cast member. It is
all like a cross between a Ken Russell version of *Peter Pan* and a
Folies Bergère show designed by Aubrey Beardsley and staged by
Baron Corvo.

The sister show is *Inner City*, a street cantata for barrel O'Horgan. It consists of mildly unfunny Mother Goose parodies by Eve
Merriam that catalogue the miseries of megalopolitan existence and
have been around in book form for some years; they have been
provided with a wholly undistinguished musical score and a little
surplus verbiage, and finally decked out with the usual O'Horgan
superbric-à-brac, including an enormous junk pile in the shape of
the Tower of Babel, which appears for a few minutes in the show's
finale, unintegrated into the proceedings and prodigiously wasteful.
But one black performer, Linda Hopkins, belts out some songs with
imposing, controlled power, and would need no trumpet accompaniment to bring down the walls of Jericho.

The blacks, too, have their non-musical in *Ain't Supposed to
Die a Natural Death* by Melvin Van Peebles. Van Peebles, an actor,
writer, film-maker and composer of sorts, had brought out a couple
of record albums in which he performs his monotonous quasi-songs.
The melody is subliminal but shrill, and the lyrics recount the ills
of the black urban proletariat in garish colours and with a reliance
on refrain so maniacal as to be more a jag than an artistic device.
Against a setting of tenements, fire escapes and rabble heaps,
Gilbert Moses, the director, puts a generally proficient black cast
through a speciously melodramatic scenario of violent or grotesque
movements, while a small onstage band seems to improvise proto-
music around these non-songs in pop-*sprechstimme*. Not only is it
all excruciating in its stridency, it is also fanatically anti-white,
which is what must have persuaded a number of swingingly liberal

white reviewers to shower it with praise. Even worse, however, is *To Live Another Summer, To Pass Another Winter*, a coarse, antiquated, inept and totally unmusical Israeli musical. There has been a steady influx of these export items from Israel, especially designed to make New York's overwhelmingly Jewish theatre-goers feel dewy-eyed and exuberant enough to rush out and buy Israel Defence Bonds. More remarkable yet than the execrable lyrics, tunes, dances, performances, sets and costumes was the notion of how to deal with the book: the four principals would line up facing the audience from time to time and tell Jewish jokes —some old, some prehistoric—or bask in fake modesty about Israel's military prowess. Dutifully, several reviewers, led by Barnes of the *Times*, came out with the kind of notices especially reserved for minority groups whose efforts it would be considered racist— and possibly dangerous—to disparage.

The non-play even went so far as to try to elevate itself into a new genre with Paul Sills's invention of something he called Story Theatre. This consists of taking narrative material and trans-planting it to the stage by having the characters narrate events in the first or third person, switch to dialogue where conversations occur, and bring in all kinds of pantomime, musical numbers and fancy scenic effects to try to disguise the fact that this is not really stage material. In 1970 Sills had a modest success with a story-theatricalisation of fairy tales mostly by the Brothers Grimm: these fantastic, naive, childlike stories lent themselves to the primitive spectacle and childish clowning of Story Theatre; as with all transplants, the plant has to be rather young to take root in new terrain. When Sills tried it again in 1971 with Ovid's *Meta-morphoses*, it did not work: Ovid's poems are too elegant, sophisti-cated and, finally, verbal to permit this kind of rumpus-room acting out. Another director, Larry Arrick, tried his hand at Story Theatre with *Unlikely Heroes: Three Stories by Philip Roth*. Despite some sardonic insights and intermittent poignancy, as well as good per-forming and set design, these fictions looked intensely uncomfortable on the stage—three character sketches in search of a dramatic author.

The next best thing to not having to write any kind of play or book for a musical is to adapt a work of fiction in the old (or non-Story Theatre) manner, which is what Archibald MacLeish elected to do with *Scratch*, his dramatisation of Steven Vincent Benét's story, *The Devil and Daniel Webster*. This proved to be a short-lived disaster, what with MacLeish's pathetic attempts to infuse contemporary relevance into Webster's murky pre-Civil War politics —MacLeish's vague, unfocussed liberalism and hazy belief in 'America' clashing unhappily with the simple, unpretentious elements of a good, supernatural thriller. Especially unfortunate was the choice of Patrick Magee for Daniel Webster, who emerged as an Anglo-Irish sniveller. A musical adaptation of Truman Capote's *The Grass Harp*, though slightly more deserving, fared no better. But another musicalisation proved highly successful: *Two Gentlemen of Verona*, which Joseph Papp, artistic director of The Public Theatre and The New York Shakespeare Festival, first presented in Central Park last summer. Rather than trying to do Shakespeare's wobbly juvenilia straight, Papp and Mel Shapiro, his director, called in the young playwright John Guare, whose *House of Blue Leaves* Shapiro had successfully directed, and, together, they updated the story. They placed it, at least partly, in today's New York, and turned most of the characters into Negroes, Puerto Ricans, Jews, Chinese, so as to give a sense of the metropolitan melting pot. Then Guare wrote a considerable number of lyrics for it (on top of that *objet trouvé*, 'Who Is Silvia?') and Galt MacDermot, the composer of *Hair*, provided a score.

The final version, as presented on Broadway, was a riotous, madcap mixture of sporadically clever invention and a lot of 'Varsity-show, slap-dash horseplay—Guare and Shapiro's juvenilia instead of Shakespeare's. The book still follows Shakespeare at a disrespectful distance, but anachronisms and local references (e.g., the Duke of Milan as a Black Panther leader) are everywhere, and not always very funny. The lyrics are wildly uneven and the score, though copious, well below the *Hair*line. The choreography by Jean Erdman, supplemented by Dennis Nahat, is infectious without being truly inventive, and the scenery and costumes have a jovially eclectic, timelessly mixed-up look about them. The performances are inconsistent, but Raul Julia is a captivatingly roguish Puerto Rican Proteus, the sort of villain who charms you even while he is plainly robbing you; and Jonelle Allen, as a black Silvia, proves a bottomless bundle of singing and dancing energy —if a bundle can ever be said to have a bottom. Miss Allen

T.72—F

certainly has one, and, like the rest of her, it is undeniably alluring.

Suppose, however, you have to write your own play, but find the sustained effort of a full-length drama too demanding; you can always eke out an evening with two or more one-acters. Thus Robert Anderson gave us the double bill *Solitaire/Double Solitaire*. The first play, *Solitaire*, about a man's vain rebellion against a mechanised, dehumanised totalitarian society of the future, might just as well be considered an adaptation, so heavily does it borrow from works like *Brave New World, 1984, Fahrenheit 451* and E. M. Forster's story, *The Machine Stops*. The other play, *Double Solitaire*, was a dreamy conversation piece in which various generations voiced their views on love, sex, marriage and divorce in a series of colloquies and monologues, as hackneyed as they were static. More successful was George Furth; in 1970, the musical *Company* was based on a dozen or so playlets of his. Last year, he came up with *Twigs*, four tenuously related one-acters. In these he gives us successive glimpses into the lives of three sisters and their moribund but still tough mother. Neither the family resemblances nor the divergences among these women are of particular interest, but there is a superficial piquancy in the fact that the same actress plays all four women. Sada Thompson switches characters from one playlet to the next without special distinction or distinctiveness even, but the bravos and raves were like those for a one-man orchestra: the fellow may play all four instruments poorly, but let him play them all together and he is considered a sensation.

There is yet another, time-honoured though not necessarily honourable, method of shirking playwriting responsibilities—with a minimal risk, too—and that is to import a full-fledged London hit. If it has British stars, a long London run, and a lot of advance hullaballoo to its credit, such an import is considered a sure bet, particularly in view of the fact that the almighty *New York Times* critic, himself a British import, is presumed to smile benevolently on such an enterprise. And so the year had its share of wholly or partly British productions. The only truly successful one, so far, was Peter Brook's *A Midsummer Night's Dream*, a perversion of Shakespeare's play which, though occasionally clever, serves mostly to exalt the director's gimmickry at the expense of the playwright's intentions. Nevertheless, for a limited run, and with limitless

LEFT: *'Neo-baroque excesses': Cliff Gorman* (top centre) *as* Lenny
RIGHT: *'Irrelevant and irreedemably vulgar:* Jesus Christ, Superstar

LEFT: *'Excruciating in its stridency':* To Die A Natural Death
RIGHT: *'Neil Simon's annual donation':* The Prisoner of Second Avenue

built-in snob appeal, this switched-on Bard run through a Brook synthesiser was loudly acclaimed.

Pinter's *Old Times* fared rather less well here. The cast, though perhaps not so ideally suited to their roles as the London one, was respectable enough (Mary Ure, Robert Shaw and, as the interloper, Rosemary Harris); Peter Hall's direction and John Bury's designs were reproduced in all their diabolical expertise. Clive Barnes came through with a panegyric proclaiming the work a timeless masterpiece, and most of the other reviewers raised a Hallelujah chorus. But the public refused to be taken in for the umpteenth time. They divined the arrogance behind this sixty-minute play, air-cushioned on pauses and bloated with a twenty-minute interval, posing as a full-length drama; they did not quite believe that all those weighty implications necessarily implied much of anything, or anything of much importance; they were not convinced that those interminable pregnant pauses (false pregnancies, for the most part) made Pinter more than a Grand Pauseur.

A play that I found extremely deserving—though, granted, not a masterpiece—fared shockingly badly. This was Christopher Hampton's *The Philanthropist*, with Alec McCowen and Jane Asher re-creating their roles here, Victor Spinetti much less right than Charles Gray for the caddish novelist, and the remaining American actors suitable to varying degrees. Still, it was all quite good enough to deserve a respectable run, despite mixed reviews, if only Broadway audiences had a fine enough palate for polished badinage, superficial-sounding exchanges that carry under the silken word-play the sting of truth. But the combination of absurdity and pathos, fine-spun verbiage and grotesque vehemence, was too changeable, elusive, demanding for this public that will almost always fall for the alleged New, but strongly resists being taken in by the genuinely Subtle. A much less interesting play, Robert Bolt's diffuse and rather pointless exercise in rapid-fire historical reconstruction, *Vivat! Vivat Regina!*, with an uneven Anglo-American cast (whose highlight is, once again, Eileen Atkins as Elizabeth I), may chalk up a fair run, given our democratic public's inexhaustible fascination with absolute monarchs.

Ronald Millar's *Abelard and Héloïse*, however, deserved the short shrift it got, lacking as this version of the oft-told tale was in electricity, intensity, panache. With its general posturing, its ubiquitous chorus of swaying monks and nuns, and its language more castrated than its unhappy hero, the thing looked and sounded like a Menotti libretto without even the puny benefit of a Menotti score. The acting of Diana Rigg and Keith Michell seemed no less tepid and perfunctory than the gingerly and half-hearted nude scene hustled past us with lights studiously dimmed. *Wise Child*, by Simon Gray, came here after too long a time lag to benefit from whatever London success it had. Though not an outstanding play, with Donald Pleasence performing manfully *en travesti*, it could have run for a little while despite an inadequate juvenile and edulcorating staging. But studies in the nature of perversion and varieties of evil, particularly when treated as farce, are not to the taste of a Broadway audience. In fact, very little is to the taste of a Broadway audience, and that little as predictable as it is skimpy.

Another London hit, Alan Ayckbourn's farce, *How the Other Half Loves*, was, by way of double precaution, adapted to an American setting. It still failed, proving that even if you wear both belt and suspenders, you can still lose your shirt. Over here, the joke wore thin very quickly.

But there is yet another way of evading the rigours of producing a new play, and that is reviving an old one. Revivals have become more popular than ever on Broadway because they automatically cater to the nostalgia of the middle-aged and old, who, at the present price of Broadway tickets, are virtually the only ones who can afford to go. Moreover, the social and political evils of our society have now caught up with even the most ostrich-like bourgeois, and the craving for total escape is the natural struthious answer: escape into the sweet never-neverland of one's youth. Hence all these revivals of plays with, not artistic, but nostalgia value, mindless moneymakers from the rosy past. Foremost among them is the still running, vastly successful revival of the 1925 musical *No, No, Nanette*, trash even in its own day. The silly little Otto Harbach book comes equipped with one of Vincent Youmans's lesser scores and some piddling lyrics by Irving Caesar, including the profoundly silly 'Tea for Two', significantly the biggest bonanza of Caesar's career. Busby Berkeley was called in to oversee the production, but the work was done by the clever director, Burt Shevelove, and the conscientious choreographer, Donald Saddler. Raoul Pène du Bois's Art Deco sets and costumes were less spectacular than one expected from him, but there were rumours of the producers severely curtailing his original designs. The chorus boys and girls, very important in a show of this nature, were less than appealing, and, among the principals, Ruby Keeler and Patsy Kelly contributed little beyond nostalgia value. Jack Gilford, was ill at ease as a Protestant Bible publisher suspected of womanising. Helen Gallagher and Bobby Van were fine, but one could not escape the sense of being in a geriatric ward, with everything from jokes to leading actresses exuding a stale aroma of senescence verging on rigor mortis. But while the memory-laden foolishness of it pleased the old-timers in the audience, the campiness (there was considerable rewriting on the book) delighted the camp-followers, who stamped their feet, shrilled their bliss, and dithered throughout. People sang along with the performers, jumped up from their seats in sheer ravishment, rapturously applauded the first bars of every song they recognised, and uttered astonished little 'oh's' when a song happened to be a towering classic like 'Tea for Two', the like of which they had not expected to encounter here. Critics like Walter Kerr and Brendan Gill overflowed with avuncular ecstasy as Broadway took another giant step backwards.

A further musical revival was *On the Town*, by the popular team of Comden and Green, and with music by Leonard Bernstein. Though a better show than *Nanette*, it was given a mediocre production, and it was now hard to see New York in wartime with the sentimental innocence with which one could still make oneself see it in 1944. The gags and lyrics had dated badly, but were not quite hoary enough for camp; the new choreography by Ronald Field, who also directed, was drably routine. The new sets were less interesting than Oliver Smith's for the original production, and there were no such outstanding performers as, for instance, the exquisite Sono Osato. Even Bernstein's score, except for two or three numbers, now seemed tepid compared to such later work of his as *Candide*.

Even more misguided was the revival, after less than eight years, of Lorraine Hansberry's *The Sign in Sidney Brustein's Window*. This comedy-drama was first presented while its author lay dying of cancer, and the entire theatrical establishment united in propagandising for it. Even so, it closed after her death and a hundred

ABOVE: *Broadway's giant step backwards:* No, No, Nanette—
'Trash even in its own day'

BELOW: *'The ghosts of showgirls past': Alexis Smith, Yvonne de
Carlo and the cast of* Follies

performances. This time, made even less palatable through the addition of an oafish singing and dancing chorus—strictly 1972, while the central action, despite tinkering, remained 1964—it could not last out a week. The adapter was Robert Nemiroff, the playwright's husband and literary executor, who has become an industry for digging up unsuccessful or unproduced Hansberriana, usually unfinished work, and finishing it off in more ways than one. In the rather poorly acted and misadapted revival, the basic exiguities of plotting, characterisation and dialogue became depressingly apparent, and there was one performance—by Zohra Lampert—that for sheer tics and hysteria underpassed even Sandy Dennis.

Characteristically, the year's one original musical, *Follies*, also depended largely on nostalgia. It takes place in a half-torn-down theatre whose manager, modelled on the late Flo Ziegfeld, gives a farewell party to bygone glory on this bizarre site. The guests are former stars and showgirls, along with their sundry friends and consorts, which permits the dragging out of any number of nostalgically doddering performers, some of them actually ex-Ziegfeld girls. The ghastly are haunted by the ghostly: ghosts of showgirls past are drifting by, high-kicking or lolling about in eerie black-and-white costumes and make-up. And the principals, two quondam showgirls now in early middle age and their husbands—all four of them once friends and complicatedly criss-crossed in love—are shadowed by their youthful selves, reenacting the past. The idea of love among the ruins, with the lovers themselves ruinous, is not uninteresting, and Florence Klotz's costumes and Boris Aronson's sets have both extravagance and real style, and work effectively as both spectacle and mild satire. But the book, by James Goldman, is banal and flat; its cataloguing of past and present, always unsatisfactory, relationships as trivial as it is clichéd. Stephen Sondheim's lyrics are clever as always, but his tunes are pastiches of old melodies, equally disturbing whether they come too close to the originals for comfort, or wrenchingly try to change courses in midstream. Harold Prince and Michael Bennett have staged *Follies* neatly, and the latter's choreography has his customary blend of resourcefulness and essential simplicity. Nevertheless, the whole enterprise remained, for the most part, cumbersome, bloated and insignificant, and ended on a blatantly false note of spurious reaffirmation of things as they are. Since it cost a great deal to put on and keep on the boards, its soon-to-be-ended run represents less than a real success. But one of the performers, Alexis Smith, a retired B-movie actress, made a triumphant come-back, demonstrating hitherto hidden histrionic depths as well as a cool loveliness the advancing years seem merely to have stressed.

What, then, were the original, full-length, domestic contributions to our non-musical theatre? There is the annual donation from Neil Simon, called this year *The Prisoner of Second Avenue*. Its theme is currently very popular on stage and screen: the small and huge distresses of life in New York, where those rival furies, anomie and entropy, compete in destructiveness. Simon treats the matter comically, although the various ills he heaps on his characters— everything from a malfunctioning luxury apartment, through burglary and unlivable-with neighbours, to loss of livelihood owing to layoffs caused by the recession—are painful enough. But Simon's farce, even when laced with bitter realities, never pricks deep, and lacks even a sharp eye for existential details. Its ear is better, and its ability to toss out a plethora of gags better yet. But one never has the feeling of the characters having a life of their own, shooting up beyond the author's calculations, as they do in the superbly humane farces of a Feydeau or Courteline. Here the adroit staging of Mike Nichols is matched by the expert set design of Richard Sylbert and coruscating performances from Peter Falk, Lee Grant and a quartet of supporting pranksters, but the final effect is deadening rather than exhilarating: a firm foundation in humanity is lacking.

The one dramatic contribution was Edward Albee's *All Over*, a play as pretentious and dreary as only Albee can get produced on Broadway nowadays. While some unspecified great man, attended by a physician and nurse, is dying behind a screen in his living room (why there?), his wife, mistress, best friend, son and daughter reminisce, philosophise, wax wroth or bitchy, moan or rage about one another, themselves, the world. Not only the dying man, all of them are behind a screen: the screen of Albee's grandiloquent but juiceless and unwieldy diction, his remoteness from flesh-and-blood creatures, and his flagging, fuzzy wit—once his brightest, most penetrating instrument. Under John Gielgud's direction—blindly groping its way ahead amid the walking cenotaphs and verbal simulacra—Colleen Dewhurst and Jessica Tandy did well enough as Mistress and Wife (the characters are all labelled with such capitalised abstractions), but the others seemed lost, or both lost and inept. *All Over* closed quickly; if the play struggled vainly to be poetic, at least the title succeeded in being prophetic.

Finally, there was one comedy-drama, *And Miss Reardon Drinks a Little*, by Paul Zindel, whose *The Effect of Gamma Rays on Man-in-the-Moon Marigolds* seemed to me one of the more likeable plays of the previous year. In this, apparently earlier, work, Zindel examines the lives of three sisters, two schoolteachers and one school supervisor. The last-named is ambitious and greedy, the other two are victims, one of her tormented psyche, the other of having had to care for a psychotic mother. All have been marked by their dead mother, almost as much as Zindel's dramaturgy by Tennessee Williams, and I could not help feeling that both the drama and the humour were forced, exacerbated, straining for effects that, even had they come off completely, would still have seemed rather trumped-up. As the most chaotic sister, Julie Harris once again give us her customary mixture—half Sarah Bernhardt, half Shirley Temple—that has lost what fey charm it may ever have had.

Two classics were mounted: Molière's *The School for Wives* in Richard Wilbur's dazzling new translation; and, imported from Stratford, Canada, Feydeau's *Le Dindon*, adequately adapted by Suzanne Gorossmann and Paxton Whitehead as *There's One in Every Marriage*. The former had a modest run, but might have lasted longer if Brian Bedford had been a less schematic and repetitious Arnolphe, and if the rest of the cast in this Phoenix Theatre production had been less uneven. The Feydeau perished almost immediately thanks to Barnes's review, even though all other reviewers, including Kerr, the *Times*'s Sunday man, enjoyed the play thoroughly, and the production, with minor reservations, almost as well. Particularly impressive were Alan Barlow's sets and costumes, and the laughter of both critics and spectators was steady and ringing. This untimely assassination—and David Merrick's, the producer's, refusal to fight the Barnes review—struck me as the year's gravest injustice and loss.

The Repertory Company of Lincoln Center offered, on their big stage, *The Playboy of the Western World, An Enemy of the*

People, Sophocles's *Antigone*, Schiller's *Mary Stuart* (in the Spender version) and Bond's *Narrow Road to the Deep North*. These productions at what is the nearest thing to a National Theatre we have (remote though it be from one) were all fairly disappointing—or would have been if we had expected much from this unfortunate group. The acting always includes some truly hopeless performances, and the directors, not excluding Jules Irving, the artistic and executive director of the company, always come to greater or lesser grief. The reasons for this are too numerous to detail here, but the foremost of them are, surely, lack of sufficient subsidy and Irving's excessive loyalty to members of his original, and somewhat provincial, Actors' Workshop of San Francisco, which years ago took over Lincoln Center from Kazan and Whitehead. Nevertheless, Irving's production of the Schiller had some real merit, especially in the scenic and costume design, not easy to manage on that impressive but not wholly satisfactory stage. Most infelicitous were the revival of Arthur Miller's misadaptation of the Ibsen, and the handsome but unincisive mounting of the Bond play, which, to me, looks and sounds like a feeble bit of Brechtianising.

Lamentable, I say, for both Broadway and me; but *I* can go off-Broadway or to the movies. Where, though, can Broadway go from here? Only up, one assumes. Just wait, however, for next year's chronicle, and see if it does not begin with some variation on the perennial opener, 'It was one of the worst seasons on Broadway. . . .'

Martin Gottfried

Off-Broadway

A year of peril and excellence, reviewed here by the drama critic of Women's Wear Daily.

There may be no theatre event in history to match the sudden, recent and catastrophic collapse of off-Broadway in New York. In a matter of several years a sprawling, thriving collection of producers, organisations and neighbourhood theatres ranging from fully professional to semi-amateur virtually disappeared. In 1962 there were almost a hundred productions on just the basic off-Broadway alone, that is, commercially produced plays with Equity actors, playing in houses of 200–300 seats. This was the theatre arm that introduced Beckett, Pinter, Genet and Ionesco to New York —something Broadway simply never would have done. By 1970, that quantity had declined, but it was supplemented by even more *off-off*-Broadway organisations (the difference between off-Broadway and off-off-Broadway is that the latter uses non-Equity actors, does not pay them and plays to smaller houses; it is not a matter of location). In addition, there were the producing companies in the Grotowski-Living Theatre movement (The Open Theatre, The Performance Group, and so on).

Abruptly, New York's stage world quaked. The pillars of the off-off-Broadway movement—Café La Mama, Café Cino, the Judson Poets Theatre, Theatre Genesis—either cracked or crumbled altogether. The actors' collectives of Joseph Chaikin, Judith Malina, Richard Schechner *et al*, grew so involved in life styles (or legal troubles) they forgot about the theatre entirely, leaving the city,

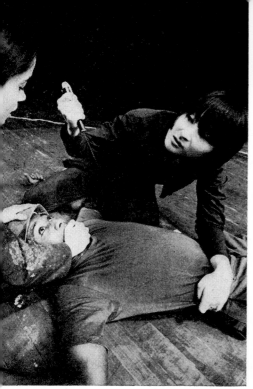

LEFT: '*A tribute to an ordinary, mediocre, simple boy*': Pavlo Hummel
RIGHT: '*Myth and countermyth*': Sticks and Bones

LEFT: '*Ginsberg's death prayer for his mother*': Kaddish
RIGHT: '*Superb and genuinely daring*': The Ride Across Lake Constance

even the country, and Tom O'Horgan—La Mama's leader—was lost, or lost himself, to Broadway. As for the old, commercial off-Broadway, activity became minimal and the work itself is now little different from Broadway's.

In the light (or dark) of this calamitous series of events, one might well ponder the task of describing a 1971 off-Broadway season, and yet, not only *was* there such a season but in fact it was a superb one. The answer to this paradox lies in the unexpected birth and flourishing of several small but first-class institutional theatres, built away from midtown areas.

One of the most gratifying aspects of these new institutions is that one seemed to take up the slack for the others. If the American Place Theatre is having a thankless season, the Chelsea Theatre Center might be enjoying a banner year. In 1971, it was the turn of the Public Theatre—the bee-hive of auditoriums that serves as the winter quarters for Joseph Papp's New York Shakespeare Festival (somewhat like the Aldwych season of the Royal Shakespeare Company).

The Public Theatre's good season was more unlikely than overdue. In the several years of its existence, this organisation had presented a parade of agit-prop plays that criticised bureaucracy, racism, totalitarianism and other social evils beloved of old line liberals. These plays were invariably well produced and heavily written (generally by Middle European intellectuals like Nabokov and Mrozek). There was no reason to expect anything different. Mentalities tend not to change. Yet, in 1971, this one did. No longer were the plays killingly and irrelevantly *relevant*. No longer were they scratching for a *now* style. Mr Papp apparently had one of those revelations about which general directors only dream. He found the clear light that reveals a play's final, onstage value. It suddenly seemed as if the Public Theatre could make no mistakes. Every extraordinary production followed on the heels of another, and one looked forward to each opening as to the next, unexpected course of a fabulous meal.

I would trace this sudden *rightness* of the Public Theatre to Papp's recent sojourn as a professor of directing at the Yale Drama School. Not only did he meet young actors and directors there; he was exposed to new *ideas* and the most important of these was a rejection of Grotowski-style collective theatre and a return to the word—to a literary theatre perhaps more concerned with production and movement than its predecessors; a literary theatre dealing with stylised reality; but a literary theatre nevertheless. Just as the absurdism of Genet and Ionesco was first greeted and then rejected as a be-all modern style, so now was the non-verbal dance theatre of the Grotowskis and Malinas and Chaikins rejected, as well as the god of *relevance* worshipped by America's middle-class revolutionaries. Though Papp still produced some non-verbal, movement works (*Blood, Iphegenia in Concert*), they seemed but incidental stabs for another *Hair* (which still subsidises the Public Theatre through royalties).

Oddly enough, such another moneymaker did arrive, but of all places it came from the summer Shakespeare Festival. A musical, bowdlerised, multi-ethnic version of *Two Gentlemen of Verona* proved so delightful a success during the 1971 summer that commercial producers clamoured for its Broadway rights. The Shakespeare Festival decided to produce the show on its own, but not until the free performances in New York's ghettoes were given as planned.

This success, however financially gratifying, was not the Public Theatre's main work. The personal, spare, surreal play now interested Papp—a play with words and characters; modern, yes, but recognisable as *drama*. Such a play was *Subject to Fits*, which began the Public Theatre's extraordinary streak in February of 1971.

The play was written by a recent Yale graduate—Robert Montgomery—who described it as a 'response' to *The Idiot*. In dealing with Dostoevsky's story and characters, Montgomery found a musical, dreamy, poetic, cinematic style that lapped verbal imagery against physical episode. Though the play had its faults, the production had few and the sum was doubtless the best serious work of New York's season, at least until May, when *The Basic Training of Pavlo Hummel* opened at the Public Theatre.

Between these two dates, the Public Theatre danced through the season: a production of *Slag* that in no way equalled the one at the Royal Court, but nevertheless revealed David Hare's fascinating script; a one-woman show (*Here Are The Ladies*) by Siobhan McKenna, followed by Jack MacGowran's tremendous evening from the works of Samuel Beckett; the fabulous, radial,

Bread and Puppet Theatre; *Blood*, a sophomoric adaptation of the sophomoric techniques of *Orlando Furioso*, but set to a wonderful score of country rock music. Mind you, nearly all this work was happening *simultaneously* in the four separate theatres carved out of the old Astor Library on Lafayette Street in lower Manhattan.

It was *The Basic Training of Pavlo Hummel*, however, that culminated and exemplified the Public Theatre's sensational run for last season. The play not only introduced a new playwright—David Rabe—but made it clear at the outset that he was destined to be a major American writer.

Pavlo Hummel is a classical tragedy whose hero is unheroic. It is a tribute to an ordinary, mediocre, simple boy—the least in everyone—and his basic humanity—the most in everyone—set into the ritual of American basic military training and thrown upon the war machine. Like Mr Montgomery in *Subject to Fits* (and most any playwright today), Mr Rabe's style is cinematic, his realism is poetic and his concern is for personal realisation rather than social righteousness. Although *Pavlo Hummel* does deal with the Vietnam war, its concern is rather with the man than the war and, in any case, Rabe blames the Viet Cong and the Peace Movement for that miserable mess as much as he does the warmongers.

The Public Theatre produced his next play (actually, his first) but five months later, running the two concurrently. Like *Pavlo Hummel*, *Sticks and Bones* found myth and countermyth in the American identity. It is about a young man who has returned, blind, from the Army in Vietnam. He and his family are named for a popular American television series, *Ozzie and Harriet*, and the play is written in laughless satire of the brainless, every cheerful home unit that Americans choose to believe is accurately reflected on television. In the play, this made for a heightened reality akin to the most valid of pop art. The confrontation between such plastic reality and plain truth—the forcing of Ozzie Nelson's face to the mirror—was frightfully effective, made artful by Rabe's consistency of style, deliberation over words and concern for structure. He stands on the threshhold of greatness, restrained from international prominence only by America's disquieting lack of a major theatre to present his work. For however successful the Public Theatre may be, it plays to limited audiences and publicity.

This is even more true of the Chelsea Theatre Center, located in Brooklyn, which, for New Yorkers, might as well be Madagascar. Although Chelsea's location has kept audiences, publicity and even critics away, this theatre has established an exciting reputation because of the ability of its director, Robert Kalfin, to create *production strength*; because of his uncanny play choices and because of his willingness to let each play dictate the production style and even the shape of the auditorium.

Although overshadowed by the Public Theatre's extraordinary streak of successes, the Chelsea still managed to share major credit for the excellence of the 1971 off-Broadway season. Its production of *Tarot*, a mime and rock music rendering of the Tarot card mystique, went on to a commercial production. It offered New Yorkers their first taste of truly mixed media theatre with Heathcote Williams's *AC/DC* though, despite the abundance of television monitors and cameras, live and videotaped, the play seemed more related to LSD than to the McLuhanism it claimed to have on its mind.

In May, the Chelsea began its Paper Bag Project—workshop productions of difficult plays, named for the paper bags filled with background material that are distributed to the audience. The first production in this series introduced Peter Handke to New York with *Self-Accusation* and *My Foot, My Tutor*. Whether Handke's notions about audience response, isolated senses, words and anti-words could be forged into a theatre sensibility remained unproved. but the exercises were among the most interesting on the season's stages.

Some months later, Chelsea finally provided New York with a production of Jean Genet's *The Screens*, a shameful ten years after it had been written. Though the play remains physically unproducible, Chelsea's limited resources were used so inventively by guest director Minos Volanakis that the production was easily superior to Roger Blin's original in Paris. Moreover, Genet's script was more faithfully rendered at Chelsea than it had been in Paris, where Blin had sensationalised and aborted it. *The Screens*, for whatever its flaws as a production, and however much it revealed Genet's limitations, was a major event of the season.

It was followed by still another powerful production—a stage version of Allen Ginsberg's poem, *Kaddish*, adapted by the author and staged by Kalfin with a use of videotape that proved lessons learned from *AC/DC* as well as progress beyond. *Kaddish* is Ginsberg's death prayer for his mother—a lady who tried to leap from bohemianism to middle-class convention, plunging into a chasm of insanity and death. Ginsberg blames circumstance and human bottlenecks for this death as much as he does the mediaeval, electric shock practices of *modern* mental hospitals. The play itself, an objective reality played against the videotapes that open a window into an electrically deranged mine, was of staggering compassion and exquisitely written.

Between Chelsea's inspiration of working with Ginsberg and the Public Theatre's flawless turn toward new American plays, thunder was being stolen from an older, equally valued New York institution—The American Place Theatre. This organisation produces only new American plays. For ten years it had been standing alone in defence of playwrights, throughout the period when the communal theatre groups had been waging war against the written word. The American Place alone had recognised the classic quality of Robert Lowell's *The Old Glory*. It had discovered a superbly artistic young writer in Ronald Ribman. It had encouraged novelists such as Robert Penn Warren, Bruce Jay Friedman and Joyce Carol Oates to turn their abilities toward the stage, even if it sometimes seemed as if membership in the East Coast writing establishment seemed more important than playwrighting ability.

Now, with both Chelsea and the Public Theatre in competition for new plays, the American Place went sailing through rough seas. Its faith in the written word and the writer never faltered, but its rewards were fewer. Writing quality dropped, as did audience subscriptions. Sloppy, propagandistic, faddist plays such as George Tabori's *Pinkville* marked the start of its 1971 season. And ironically, in the midst of this downslide, the American Place was to be opening a new, handsome, no-nonsense theatre in midtown Manhattan—a house beneath a skyscraper, thanks to a special construction ordinance that Mayor Lindsay had sponsored to spur such theatre-building.

The new home was opened well enough in the autumn of 1971 with a one-act play by Mr Ribman that recalled the classicism and poetic depth of his earlier *Harry, Noon and Night* and *Journey of the Fifth Horse*. This was called *Fingernails as Blue as Flowers*, a rare example of artwork though it was not recognised as such by most New York critics. Critics pass, art remains.

But otherwise, the American Place had apparently lost confidence in its own judgement and continued choosing poor scripts. A workshop level one-act play shared the bill with the Ribman play and the next production—*Sleep*—proved Jack Gelber still unable to fulfil the promise that made him a *discovery* ten years earlier with *The Connection*. This theatre and its productions remain of high quality, but in terms of plays produced its value lies more in memory, reputation and potential than in the present.

Still another newly thriving off-Broadway institution in 1971 New York was the Forum, the miniature thrust stage nestled in the bowels of Lincoln Center's Vivian Beaumont Theatre. Throughout the pressure-ridden, overpublicised, overproduced and generally incompetent history of the Repertory Theatre of Lincoln Center, the Forum had lain forgotten. Other problems were too pressing and nobody knew exactly what to do with it anyhow. In 1971, it was suddenly catapulted into the eye of a public hurricane with the revelation that it would be razed to make room for mini-cinemas that would hopefully relieve the financial strain at Lincoln Center (America has no formal system for governmental subsidy of the arts; such theatres, as well as orchestras, dance companies and museums, must fend for themselves. It is a national disgrace, but a separate subject).

The threat of the Forum's extinction evoked greater public response than any play ever produced at Lincoln Center, indicating only that the New York public is more interested in social causes than the theatre. Perhaps that is unfair, since little worthy of response had yet been produced at the Forum *or* the Beaumont. With the Forum's reprieve, the theatre director at Lincoln Center —Jules Irving—found a courage previously unsuggested by his appeasing, anything-for-survival style. While the main stage upstairs continued its overblown productions of warhorse semi-classics, the Forum below began a series of fascinating plays, simply and well done. A set of sketches of the American provincial personality in A. R. Gurney Jr's *Scenes From American Life*. A revival of Duerrenmatt's surprisingly playful satire, *Play Strindberg*. A superb study of human isolation despite an overliterary, overnaturalistic approach in Athol Fugard's *People Are Living There*. And finally, a superb and genuinely daring production of Handke's

The Ride Across Lake Constance (which I doubt that *any* of New York's other institutions would have had the nerve to do).

These four producing organisations—the Public Theatre, the Chelsea Theatre Center, the American Place Theatre and Lincoln Center's Forum—gave New York a 1971 off-Broadway season worth respecting and then some. They emerged unexpectedly and, as luck would have it, just when they were desperately needed. Nor were they the only off-Broadway institutions in town.

The Negro Ensemble Company is handicapped by the time and nature of its birth. This company originated when America's black movement was in its early stages. It soon found itself trapped between old liberalism and the new black militance. Busily adjusting its racial stance, the NEC never duly concentrated on the theatre itself. A theatre essentially concerned with the race of its actors, directors, writers and subject-matter is doomed to be artistically second rate, not to mention inherently prejudiced (in favour of blacks, inversely, and against whites, directly). It puts race ahead of art.

Obviously, then, New York's off-Broadway had an abundance of exciting institutional theatres during this period. Unfortunately, none of them was a full-sized, powerfully professional and nationally recognised producing organisation. None of them had the prestige, publicity and artistic brawn to influence America's theatre, its playwrights or each other. They are 'off-Broadway' in the sense of being not-quite-major. Moreover, none of them presents revivals and that is New York's greatest lack. Without a constant, living reminder of classics, a country's theatre is crippled. Without a past, the present has no mooring, no point of departure. Such theatre is relegated to throwaway capitalism. A play is 'used' once and then discarded.

Nowhere is such disposable theatre more discouragingly practised than in what remains of commercial off-Broadway. Most of these productions during the 1971 season were trivial pieces that in years of lower costs would have been done on Broadway: musicals hoping to capitalise on rock music's popularity (*Love Me, Love my Neighbour*; *The Ballad of Johnny Pot*); the Jesus revival (*Godspell*; *The Survival of Saint Joan*); nostalgia (*Grease*); the last shreds of the fondly forgotten rage for nude and homosexual plays (*Nightride*); sporadic revivals, sometimes rewarding (*One Flew Over The Cuckoo's*

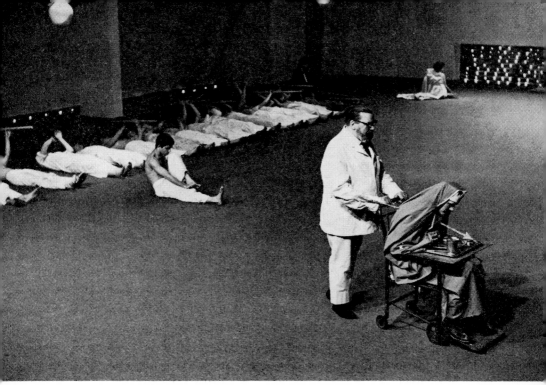

ABOVE: *'The most extraordinary theatre work to be seen in London, Paris or America in 1971':* Prologue to a Deafman

BELOW: *'A revival of Duerrenmatt's surprisingly playful satire':* Play Strindberg

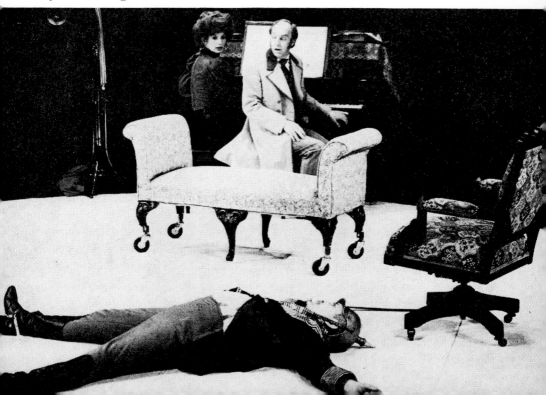

Nest; *The Homecoming*); sometimes unworthy (*Johnny Johnson*; *Woyzeck*; *The Dance of Death*).

Occasionally there was a reminder of the past, when off-Broadway did present a commercial alternative to Broadway. *Six*, for example, was an ambitious experimental chamber musical by Charles Strouse—a show whose ambitions were perhaps too musically esoteric and not very theatrical. *F. Jasmine Addams* was a quiet (too quiet) attempt at musicalising Carson McCullers's *A Member of the Wedding*. *The Cockettes*, a company of San Francisco transvestites, brought hopes of sexual extravagance crashing against the reality of sloppy conception and shabby execution.

The Cockettes opening in November at an abandoned movie palace in the East Village was perhaps the most spectacular event of the 1971 theatre season. There were flamboyant costumes, an infinity of sexual variations, people ranging from the pop underground to hippies to artists to show business celebrities to the chic and would-be chic; lots of staring and wanting to be stared at, a great hullabaloo, floodlights, television cameras, wigs, fringes and spectacular chaos. Unfortunately, this was all due to the audience. On stage, *The Cockettes* only recalled memories of their superiors at the Play-House of the Ridiculous and its successor, The Ridiculous Theatrical Company. Those sexually addled, gloriously baroque, legendary companies are all but extinct, with their by-gone productions of *When Queens Collide* and *Turds in Hell*. Expired, too, are almost all the stalwarts of off-off-Broadway. Café Cino is dead. Theatre Genesis is virtually out of business. The Judson Poets' Theatre has cut back its activities. Café La Mama has grown funded and staid. These were the stalwarts of off-off-Broadway. There are still numerous companies tucked away in lofts, cellars and churches, but the heart has gone out of the movement. Off-off-Broadway blossomed as an alternative to the commercial theatre. With the commercial theatre all but buried in New York, there seems no reason for an alternative. Who needs Communism if there are no Fascists?

Curiously enough, the most important off-Broadway event of 1971 did not occur in New York, nor even in the United States. During the summer, a young man named Robert Wilson was brought to Paris to stage his production, *Deafman Glance*, at Pierre Cardin's *Espace Cardin*. Wilson found Cardin's theatre too small for his vast pageant and mounted *Deafman* instead at the Théâtre de la Musique. As a satisfaction for Cardin, he created *Prologue to a Deafman* at *Espace Cardin* and this was the most extraordinary theatre work to be seen in London, Paris or America during 1971, so far as I could see.

Though Wilson is American, he is virtually unknown there. He has created three works shown at the Brooklyn Academy of Music, each limited to two performances. His style knows no influences. It is dancelike, mystical, drugged and vaguely Eastern. It is visually spectacular and almost always silent. It is programmed but the story is subordinated to Wilson's sense of a time warp. Wilson talks of 24-hour plays (*Deafman Glance* runs six hours and its *Prologue* another three). Such theatre is a far cry from the structured, poetic drama of Bullins and Rabe and Ribman in America, or similarly modern British playwrights such as Pinter and Storey. But it is patently foolish to demand a single trend of the theatre and Wilson is gratifyingly original and, by my definition (which is the capability of conceiving the previously unconceived), a genius. His work is also unmistakably American and so—like The Living Theatre—no matter where he works he is part of the American theatre.

What, then, is 'off-Broadway'? To some it means the group of 200–300-seat theatres hiring Equity actors for commercial New York productions. To others it means anything physically away from Broadway but within New York's limits. To still others, it means a state of theatre mind in opposition to the commercial and conventional. By the first definition, 1971 was a useless season. By the second, it was a good and solid one, thanks to the new institutions. But by the last—and, I think, the best definition, Robert Wilson's *Prologue to a Deafman* was the season's masterwork. Any theatre year with such a centrepiece is a year to be reckoned with. Considering the abundant and satisfying professional and creative productions that were otherwise available in New York, the style and artistic size of the theatre was expanded. That must be the final standard for measuring any theatre season, and by that standard 1971 off-Broadway was excellent.

Michael Behr

'The Success Syndrome'

A profile of Albert Finney in the year which saw his return to the West End after an absence of almost a decade.

Blue-eyed and tousle-haired and firmly packed into a snappy fawn two-piece for a luncheon date with the beautiful Anouk, to whom he's now been happily married for two years, Albert Finney was looking like a man Fate could not harm—not even the particular fate, that's been hanging over him for years, of becoming our greatest actor: 'The last few years I've had kind of doubts about what I want to do with my life. And what I'm supposed to "be". And perhaps I've been denying that I'm an actor, because I didn't feel that I was "just" an actor. Or at any rate I was worried about it. But I feel now that being an actor is—well, doing this play has reminded me how *marvellous* being an actor can be . . .'

He cradled his office-mug of Nescafé in both hands like a champion, taking slow victorious swigs. In a few days he would open in the West End in E. A. Whitehead's *Alpha Beta*. The play had run—and the box office been overrun—just recently at the Royal Court, on a month's try-out. They hadn't expected this huge wave of approval, and now the air had a special feel to it at Memorial Enterprises, his headquarters in Sackville Street.

After six years away from the London stage and nearly ten away from the West End, Finney was back—and already some-

'The hushed, sweet smell of theatrical success': Albert Finney as Frank Elliot in E. A. Whitehead's Alpha Beta

thing was stirring, half-felt like a richness along the nerves—the hushed, sweet smell of theatrical success.

Since the beginning of his career, Finney has been measured against the greatest: 'Half an Olivier—and he's only twenty-one' said the *News Chronicle* of his *Macbeth* in 1958, and with his first film in 1961, *Saturday Night and Sunday Morning*, he was placed firmly up alongside Olivier and Brando by the critics. They've usually praised him more unreservedly than the works he's appeared in: *Billy Liar* was thought to be 'insubstantial', *Saturday Night* was 'inconsequential', *Luther* was 'insufficient', *Tom Jones* was 'indiscriminate'. Or the other way around. But no one doubted that in Finney a whole new generation of actors—Peter O'Toole, Tom Courtenay, Tom Bell, Alan Bates, Frank Finlay, John Stride, Roy Kinnear, had found their leader. And he has shown an unusual facility in keeping one hunch ahead of the public, his fellow-actors, and most of the critics; an ability to generate capacity-runs merely by consulting his own personal promptings.

These have seldom let him down—when they do, he takes off on long sabbaticals to explore his 'possibilities' (a favourite word), returning only when the answer is clear. After the disappointment of *Night Must Fall* (1964) he went round the world for a year: the answer turned out to be a season of classical and modern plays at the National that won him the Best Actor of the Year Award for 1966. He couldn't collect it—he was too busy directing his first film, the haunting and funny *Charlie Bubbles* (1967), about which John Russell Taylor said in *The Times*, 'It is the most exciting, personal and accomplished début by a British director since Lindsay Anderson's *This Sporting Life*.' The film's ambiguous reception by the movie-men and by some of the critics, and his less than successful *Two for the Road*, led to further prolonged think-outs in Corfu.

In 1968 he appeared triumphantly but briefly on Broadway in Peter Nichols' *A Day in the Death of Joe Egg* (of its ten-week run, the American writer and critic William Goldman said in his chronicle of Broadway, *The Season*: 'The best thing to hit Broadway in years . . . *Joe Egg* is what it's all been for . . .'); he made *Scrooge*, and collected a New York Golden Globe award for it, and he recently starred in Neville Smith's wittily-scripted *Gumshoe*. Not really a great deal for someone who is—perennially and inescapably—Most Fashionable Actor of them all.

Had he read one of our senior star-actors' remark about him in a recent interview? Saying he should buckle down to more work in the live theatre? A non-committal 'No'. Then, as though developing a well-reflected theme: 'Yes, but anyway, I'm 36 in May. I think the best years of an actor are between 35 and 55–60. I don't see the rush. If I go to a health farm, and lose a bit of weight, I can still play *Hamlet* for the next four years. And get away with it. No, I don't see any kind of rush. I've just felt I've had to sort of kick my heels, and lay around a bit. I'm an artist, whatever I may be actually *doing*.

'Even if I'm on a golf-course—which I don't play particularly well—the artist in me is breathing, living, thinking. I don't have to be continually practising my art, or my craft. I don't ever feel that I get rusted-up. I don't think I could have done this play if I'd been rusted-up.

'The first eight years of my career I never stopped. And I loved not stopping. I loved *doing*. And then I went away. And I realised for the first time that I was sort of looking at myself, outside the activity. And it's possible to see yourself clearer, to see what you *do*, from a distance. You can't see *how* you do if you're *still doing*. So I would call these "fallow" periods. Not really inactive periods...

'I don't think anything's a waste of time—even wasting time! And maybe five years of indecision and worrying have been necessary, in order for me to become *reassured* by this play that acting is one of the things I love doing. That I *need* to do. But maybe I needed that five years, in order to be convinced so strongly . . .'

There has been plenty for him to digest. The bulky press-library file reads like some show-biz novel to end them all: the houses and horses, the girl-friends and wives, the gear and the globe-trotting; the Rolls and the rôles, the Royals and the royalties; Roman springs, Aegean summers, autumns in Paris; the Lenten withdrawals, the comebacks, the surfeits of prizes. He's won almost as many awards as a racing-driver or a matador—if he was either he'd be bald or gored by now. In fact, he's looking remarkably good. The face is now interestingly dented, the manner graver, but there's still more than a glimpse of young *Tom Jones*—the likely lad who conquered the big city: 'I've had no pressures on me to be "formed". The life I've led has kept me *unformed*. But I think maturity takes longer than 21 years or 35 years—you should mature in the wood!'

I thought of the first time we'd met. It was in the lavatory at RADA, actually. Summer of '53. We'd both just taken our scholarship exams, and the climate was one of magnificent relief. I saw an easy young athlete of around seventeen, with an astronaut's haircut, who told me amiably, 'My headmaster said that as I was no good at lessons, I'd better go to RADA. I had to ask him what RADA was. I've just been acting the Emperor Jones in the school play. That's why my hair looks funny. Do you think we've got in?'

We became classmates, if not intimates; fellow-cadets in the somewhat Prussian splendours and miseries of academy life. He maintains that in those days he was a sort of Tony Lumpkin, awkward and abashed in the presence of superior graces. I don't think he was, but in any case that was how we all felt—the Academy liked it that way. He had a North country accent then, of course; but there again, vocal embarrassment was general (mine was Oxford Prissy).

His unbroken sunniness made him a great favourite. I admired his talent, and he was amused by the sedentary clutter of newspapers and scarves I carried into class (reading hadn't yet become a habit with him). We shared a romantic but respectful attachment to a beautiful and promising young actress called Patricia Cronin, who gave up everything—us included—to go away and get married.

It was a hard-working time, and some happy prodigals of today, who were our contemporaries, must feel a certain curiosity when they look back on such an innocently arduous period of their lives.

There were later encounters in London. He had arrived auspiciously, gaining the most-promising actor award, and marrying at twenty-one the most alluring of the younger classical actresses, Jane Wenham. With his shock of thick-cut marmalade hair and scuffed suède jacket (a prized theatrical trophy that he loyally wore to baldness), he was a welcome sight around the saloon bars and cafés of St Martin's Lane; a happy initiate, exuberantly reporting on the adoption-rites of his chosen tribe ('Last night at supper Charles Laughton and Tony Franciosa both tried to grab the bill, and ended up pelting each other with *fivers*!')

For a year or two he paused on this plateau; and then he was off, moving steadily towards the high peaks. His departure was light-hearted. He hailed me for a moment in Piccadilly, on a winter afternoon, to explain his latest project: 'We've been filming in a factory. Working and living together up North for twelve weeks. It was fascinating. The most enjoyable thing I've done. I wonder how it'll turn out. Hope you like it. It's called *Saturday Night and Sunday Morning*.'

Twelve years later, he smiled at the memory of his breakthrough. 'Of course the first success *did* feel terrific. I mean, when *Saturday Night* opened in 1960 I was in fact twenty-four. So it's very young to notice how you felt. But I did notice!—and I felt very, very elated. Of course, success isn't so hard to handle over here as it is in America. It's more difficult to balance yourself there. The blessed inhibition of the English saves you. Or at any rate makes it easier.

'It's not that *I* felt, "I want to be a success" just like that. But what I was concerned with was *proving* myself. To prove myself by being successful at what I did. And the danger in our society is: "then *what*?" I sometimes meet young actors now who want to be successful, but they don't know why. Well, it isn't necessary to know why you want to be successful. But it becomes important to know why if you then *are* successful. A lot of us are conditioned to be successful—in fact that's often all we're conditioned *for*. Not, in what way? Or how? Or with what end in mind? Or anything, really—it's the sort of success syndrome. And I made *Charlie Bubbles* just because it's right to question success. And not just to say, "Smashing! I've done it!"

'The film refers to the time about a year after I did *Billy Liar*, and had first played in *Luther*. The year after *Saturday Night* came out. I was separated from Jane by then. I was having a very good time, but it was all rather . . . *desperate*. The *reality* of my life had got lost in it. And after I came out of that tunnel, I wasn't clearly *aware* of coming out of it . . . Sometimes you don't realise you've been *in* a tunnel until afterwards. Because no tunnel is the same . . .

'Success has never turned *sour* on me. It's just that I wanted to question its values. And what I might *do* with it. And what it might give me. In a way—it sounds almost arrogant to say so—but in a way I expected success. I anticipated it. It just seemed quite a natural thing.'

How did it feel to be back in the theatre? 'Well, I love doing the play. I feel that I'm able to act in it in a way that I've been struggling towards blindly, most of my time. I think that the way the play's written, and its subject-material, enable that to happen. I like to feel when I'm acting that *I've never been there before*. Now I know subconsciously, of course, that I *have*. And that I've rehearsed the play rather a lot. But the *future* of the character— his next statement or his next move—that has to be absolutely an unknown quantity. Through being buried as much as you can be in the Present Tense. The Future Tense will be "discovered" . . . And it's very hard to do it, because all kinds of things keep imping- ing. There's somebody with a cough out-front, or one of the lights is glaring too much, or there's a door banging somewhere in the wind, or I can hear somebody backstage, whispering . . . The outside world, around the periphery of the created environment of the play, keeps trying to break in. So does your personal "self". And all the "selves" in the audience. And that's why I try to be as much *within* the play, and acting *now*, as I possibly can.

'And *Alpha Beta* enables me to do it more than I've been able to do it before. It's to do with the kind of play it is. It's contem- porary. I'm playing a modern person. It's also to do with the fact that there's only two of us in it, and Rachel Roberts and I work very well together. The concentration between us is quite enormous.

'I'm finding it literally exciting, acting again. I mean, I'm rather "high" after a show. I'm light-headed for about an hour and a half, and I gag rather a lot in the dressing-room, and get a bit silly. But this just does reveal the sort of exhilaration of playing in the theatre. And playing in something that has a degree of *danger* in it. Which I do like . . .

'The amount of adrenalin that stage-acting (that you *enjoy*) produces is considerably greater than you ever produce on a film- set. Because just filming—the actual progression—is a sort of "hiccupping" creative process. So that the amount of adrenalin you use for any of the one hiccups is relatively small. And even with an eight-hour shooting-day, because it's produced over a longer period, its intensity is not felt to the same extent.

'I used to be aware in *Luther* that the anti-Pope sermon could give great offence to Catholics. I was half expecting interruptions or demonstrations. And the risk of offending people with Ted's play is of course there. But that's one of the things I really like about theatre acting. One of the adrenalin-producing elements. The sense of danger. And doing this play has made me realise how much I do enjoy it.

'When I first read it—and I read quite a few new plays that people send in—I had to finish it at one sitting. And I knew by the end that I wanted to do it. First of all, I realised that it was a very good acting part. But I did feel also a sort of affinity and sympathy for the dilemmas of the people in the play. And that it was an interesting view of morality. Of people who for one reason or another cannot *simplify* their life. Who remain locked in some domestic arrangement that is in reality no good for either of them.

'I don't think the theme is necessarily new. Strindberg has been there before. But I feel that a bad marriage in this particular class of our society hasn't been explored to this extent. We've had middle-class marriages breaking down. But I don't think a "bad" working-class marriage has ever been looked at so clearly or so vividly.

'The play has been criticised for a lack of expression of the woman's point of view. But I feel that it's showing the tragedy of what people do to *themselves*. It doesn't matter if she's right or he's right. The play's about the ruination of two *potentials*. She at the beginning is evidently a very good nest-builder. And if she'd got with the right man, she could have created a very good, comfortable, well-aired, clean nest. And he at the beginning indicates some kind of imaginative power. And if this relationship hadn't continued to *use up* his emotions, he *could* have done something a little more interesting with his life. But they're both drained of energy. By the demands of a crippling relationship.

'I've not been keen on naturalistic plays previously. Because, by and large, I do feel that the theatre is another kind of place than one for just naturalism. But if a play in *any* style is a good play, then it doesn't matter what style it's in. It's still theatre. And with this play it's the life on stage—the life within that room —that one's really got to plug into. If some night one's concentration is a bit loose, then one's got to become quieter somehow, and listen more attentively, to draw oneself back inside that little world. It's the kind of acting that almost turns audiences into "voyeurs". So they're half saying, "Oh, maybe we shouldn't be here!" at times.

'And again with the comedy. It would be very easy for me to play it purely for laughs. Maybe it's the feeling I give people when I come on. I don't know. But one could allow the audience to laugh *much more*, and make them feel that it's a working-class comedy. If Frank—Mr Elliot—was just played as a very rough, coarse man, swearing and cursing at his wife, and if I didn't—as I think I do—make the audience aware of his sensitivity, it could seem hilarious. Ted is a witty writer, and during the weeks of rehearsal we hoped that the wit *would* come through. We felt that that laughter was important, to relieve the audience's feelings. But we didn't know. They might have been so worried by the violence of it, and by the attack on our morality, that they couldn't laugh at it.

'On the other hand, one doesn't want to bring out the humour *too much*. To encourage them to say, finally, "Oh, well, it doesn't create any problems for me because I've been able to laugh at it!" To allow them to keep the play at arm's length. Because I *have* found people coming round afterwards who don't want to be drawn into it. And they're often progressive, artistic bohemians who don't wish to be reminded that they're as bourgeois in their guilts as the next man! Other people, of course, find relief. A kind of relief of recognition. They've experienced domestic problems similar to the Elliots, and because they aren't creative or expressive they're often in greater danger than the artist of saying to themselves, "Nobody else feels like I do about this."

'Because it is about *us*. It's saying that we ought to look at the things that are conditioning us. If we were doing a Strindberg play about marriage, you could say, 'That's not really about our society!', if you were worried about the way it was affecting you. "I live in modern, permissive London, and Strindberg's got nothing to do with me!" But with this play you *can't* shelve the guilt . . . I would hope that in fifty years' time this play would be looked on as a piece of historical documentation that amazes and surprises people. Because of the problems the characters talk about. I suspect that it *won't* be the case—which would be a pity—but I'd like it to be very out-dated in fifty years' time!'

'Open to developments': Albert Finney 1960–72

Did his present enthusiasm mean that he would do more live theatre?

The reply came wrapped, carefully but good-humouredly: 'It could well mean that . . . Yes, it could well mean that . . .' Then, disarmingly, 'Maybe I tick over in a slower way than other people. I can cut right off—read a bit, relax a bit. I've learnt to do nothing, very happily. I slip into a marvellous sort of somnambulant state of non-activity, which I find rather pleasant. Oh yes, I get up—I don't actually become bed-ridden! But I think of certain things to do about the house, and maybe note them down. And then put them off for a couple of weeks.

'We're setting up two more films at Memorial Enterprises, but I don't come in regularly. I own the company, I don't run it. I read scripts and attend meetings. I'm not saying that the thoughts are considerable, but I do rather enjoy thinking and dreaming . . . and I don't mean in a fantasy way . . . The fact that I've not been interested in coming back into the theatre until now may not be so much a comment on the plays I've been offered, as on myself. Maybe I've not been able to respond before. I think Ted's is one of the most original plays I've read in that time. That's obviously true. And I'm enjoying the response it's brought out in me. The feeling that acting is a marvellous job.'

I saw him by chance, the evening before the play opened, arriving at his stage-door. A tepid wind came off the streets, and in the dusk his skin looked stale and sore. With the collar of his camel-hair coat turned up against the night he seemed an unenviable, even sacrificial, figure, But he waved no less easily, and two days later the papers recorded a triumph.

And then I remembered a long morning's talk last year, when he'd discussed the necessity of this very vulnerability—placing it carefully in the context of an actor's life and work.

He'd talked with fascination of Lindsay Anderson's production of *Home*, which he'd recently been to see, and of the performances of John Gielgud and Ralph Richardson . . . 'Seeing two of the heads of one's profession doing something so extraordinarily well and movingly . . . but above and beyond the great acting and the splendid play and the accurate production, seeing those two men still showing, still revealing, some quality of human weakness . . . *their own* frailties and sensitivities. They've not—over the years their careers have gone through—they've not isolated themselves. Which is one of the dangers, I think, of being a performer. Your sensitivity can become wary. And therefore you grow a few layers of varnish over it. And if you don't watch that, I would suppose that you can shut yourself off. You feel you're too bruised to reveal yourself, after a number of years. So you stop doing it. Because it's dangerous. And it hurts. I think any actor gets hurt, inevitably, in his career—and [laughing] I think probably great actors are in danger of being hurt greatly!

'But seeing *Home* . . . it was wonderful—the fact that those two great talents are still open to being hurt. They're still that adventurous—they're that alive—they're that contemporary. And for a younger fellow-professional to see that . . . it's staggering . . . it's marvellous. . . .

'And that's where the theatre is immortal, because you can't —you *don't*—get any of it "again". You can take a bit of it away with you, and talk about it, and maybe share it with somebody in a conversation. But that's all . . . I felt present at something very, very rare and unique . . .

'Vulnerabilities—imperfections—I think it's important to accept these as part of one's work. I learnt that particularly when I directed my film. You've got this conveyer-belt of industry asking to be served, and you sometimes dislike its insistent pleas for attention. So it's inevitable that the creative juices inside one, which some days are flowing strong and good, on other days are absolutely as thick as—as—as yesterday's porridge! But I feel that those aspects of one's work are a *part* of it. The good and the bad. They're like night and day, black and white. They make it a whole. So the thing is rounded off, if you like, by the imperfections. You strive to make them as unnoticeable to the layman's eye as possible, perhaps. But they're inevitably there. In fact, they're an essential part of your work. A statement of how you *were* at the time that particular project evolved out of you. So I think it's right that nothing should be too "perfect".

'And playing in a run you get this happening. I think almost the worst thing for an actor, especially a young one, is the evening when the whole thing "comes together", as it were, and he *flies*. His performance is a good six feet off the ground. It all works. And he can't reason why it's all worked. But the young actor (if he's interested enough!) perhaps thinks, "Why was it like that last night?" And that's bad for him. Because the next night he will try and go through the same motions, before the play starts, as he did the night before. Or touch the same stick of make-up in the same way, or come down the stairs holding the same banisters. Feeling that there's something mysterious in the Gods. Some button he touched, that if he touches it again, it'll "happen" tonight. So when he gets on the stage he's continually striving to fly—and what the audience sees that night, if he's inexperienced, is the struggles of a day-old chick to take wing. Instead, he should be saying, "That was marvellous—and what did I learn from it?" And remembering that tonight's performance is in the present. Not in the past. And even if he *cannot* fly, nevertheless still trying to *use what he has with him that evening*. Because that's all the audience have got with *them*. They didn't see it the night before. The actor may be doing the same old play, but he is really experiencing *another* one.

'Your concentration should go into opening yourself to the possibilities of that particular evening. If you *think* about re-experiencing, you're closing yourself. You're tensing yourself up, in the effort to reproduce something "finer", that you felt in the past. That's wrong. Not beneficial. And my experience in the theatre has now brought me to this philosophy of simply saying: "How am I—how is it—how are *we*—going to be tonight, together? The other actors, the play, the audience, and me?"

'When I left the Royal Academy of Dramatic Art, I got a little handbook given to me. It was the *RADA Graduate's Keepsake and Counsellor*. And there were various little chapters on professional do's and don't's, and a section of questions and answers. And one of the questions I remember lovingly was: "Does a bad dress rehearsal mean a good opening performance?" And the answer was: "This is often the case, but should not be relied upon!" And of course there are some nights when *nothing happens* —when you feel nothing. But I think you notice this to a far greater extent than the audience does. Because your Reference Book is a lot thicker than the audience's, on what the evening should be *about*. Your familiarity with what the play *is*, and how experiencing it should *feel*, is much greater than theirs. So inside one's head, the differences in eight successive performances of one's *Hamlet* are considerable. But if a member of the public saw all eight, he really wouldn't notice the differences to the same extent. So a too-great intensity regarding the *regulation* of the performance can actually get in the way of the actor. He may worry that evening that he's off form, and make himself worse.

'I don't know how you keep to the possibility of being "splendid" every night . . . how you stay open . . . I think it's just trying naively to believe that tonight is *open to developments.* It's a sense —within a carefully rehearsed performance—of the unpredictable.

'You know, in bad theatre the most alive moment is when somebody forgets their lines! Dries. Because then you suddenly feel *unpredictability.* You feel danger. I remember when I did Pirandello's *Henry IV* at the Citizens, Glasgow, there was a moment when I had to suddenly lose my temper, and all at once switch my focus. And it worked as a theatrical shock for the audience if I didn't think of the moment until it happened. And if, even for a split second, I thought about doing it, or getting ready to do it, it didn't work. Because I was not *unpredictable* enough. I only managed it by absolutely concentrating, and almost trying to surprise myself with it. Forgetting its existence. Which can be very hard.

'I would have thought that in all good theatre this *intensity* of feeling is something to be aimed for. On the other hand, of course, if you have excitement going on for *too* long, it becomes the Norm and is no longer exciting. So you have got to judge it; to pace it; to *ration* it, if you like. And again, I think you are only open to the possibility of nightly change on a very special esoteric level. By having been as thorough, and worked-out, and having done as much homework as possible beforehand. Because if you haven't, then your insecurity steps in the way, preventing you leaving the well-worn path. Your background—your foundation—has got to be pretty solid, before you can allow yourself a proper freedom.

'I feel that unpredictability is a law of life. And in spite of all our striving and planning and life insurance, insecurity is really a ground-rule of Nature. As a young actor I turned down two film contracts before I even left RADA. At the time it was because I didn't want to *do* that—I wanted to go into rep., and that is what I did. But one of the reasons that I turned them down was that I didn't want to know what I was going to be doing *that far ahead.* And I encourage changes to happen in my life, because I don't

want to feel *ever* that I can predict what I'll be doing in a year's
time. I like to keep the future as open as possible (which doesn't
mean to say that I don't have life insurance!). And I think that if
this spontaneity exists in my work, it's because it also exists in my
life. I mean, I couldn't ever work in a bank! Because knowing for
certain "*That's* what my environment's going to be" would horrify
me!'

I said that I thought he was very fortunate in having enough
talent to live dangerously—had he ever wondered what things
would be like with a little less talent?

'Yes, often! [laughing—then seriously]. It's conjecture from
another position. But—what would I be like in those circumstances?
Well, I like to feel that maybe I haven't started to really "set" yet.
So because of being *desirous* of courting unpredictability, I like to
feel that if the circumstances change, I would *adapt*. And cope. And
still find something beneficial in the situation. In New York, when
I told people I was going to travel, they said that this was madness:
"You're *hot* now—they'll have forgotten who you are." But that
never worried me. I said, "Well, if they have, and I can't get a
'grand' job in the West End or in a big film—well, I feel that I'll
be able to get a job *somewhere* as an actor in Great Britain! Even
if it's only the Outer Hebrides!" That *somebody* would employ me
to do what I enjoy doing.'

'So it never seemed to me a threat that they would forget all
about me. Anyway, I don't feel that's the nature of my business.
What *I've* got to do is explore my possibilities—whether or not it
means they'll remember me, forget me, or be indifferent to me.
It's *my* possibilities I've got to explore, not anybody else's version
of what they may be. So if I was *less* successful—I don't know, I
think I'd be quite content really. If I had to accept a very imposing
limitation of ambition, I'm sure that I would adapt . . .

As a young actor, one wanted to be a Great Actor. Not knowing
really what that meant. Just wanting the word "great" to be
applied to one. Rather nice. Like you might have thought, "Why
doesn't someone call me a genius! Even if it's not true!" It's such
a nice word to be called. When you're 17, or 20, or 24, of course
that's there. But in a sort of non-specific way. You just vaguely
want to be Great. And in fact I got a bit worried at one time, because
it seemed to me that my theatrical ambition had atrophied. Or

gone. I don't think it had, but at the time I felt rather flat and empty.

'It was just after I'd finished *Charlie Bubbles*. It had been a very extraordinary experience for me. And I felt that there was nothing else much that could match that intensity . . . And I questioned whether after all acting was worth it? Because directing that film was the most enormous creative experience of my life.

'It was not only about a certain period of my life—I suppose it also incorporated something of the year and a half I spent making it. The script conferences took over a year. Shelagh Delaney and I would work in periods of a few days anywhere I happened to be living at the time: a mews house in Marylebone, then rented houses in Chichester, in Windsor, and in Ladbroke Grove; in the South of France during *Two for the Road*, and then in Paris. I do feel that it's not just the actual time that you're sitting down with a pen in your hand that gives results. The pressure always is to hurry up and get on with it. But in actual fact it's the activities that seem to have nothing to do with it, really, that are all terribly important.

'Since then I've wanted to direct again, but I haven't. It could be lack of courage, lack of belief in myself; it could be that I had so much trouble getting the film shown that I thought, "what's the point?" But I think the main reason is that there's nothing at the moment that I really want to spend a year of my life exploring. There may be other experiences of my own I shall use for a film, as I did in making *Charlie Bubbles*, but as yet I don't think they're in perspective enough. Or maybe I don't feel I've come to terms with them enough to be able to talk about them.

'I feel there's something I want to do that's connected with *today*. All the art forms are being questioned, aren't they? So in this mood of general questioning, I'm questioning too. So I feel it's as important for me to do nothing, as it is to *do* . . .

'But now and then, theatrical possibilities are flirting with my conscience. . . .'

John Percival

Tradition and Revolution

The Times *critic reflects on a year of ballet.*

The adjective 'provincial' is not one that would normally be applied to the Royal Ballet, but it came into the stinging mid-1971 assessment of Kenneth MacMillan's first year as artistic director which Clive Barnes wrote in the *New York Times*. His argument was that, from being on a level with the Bolshoi, Kirov and New York City Ballet companies, the Royal Ballet was becoming more closely comparable with, say, the Stuttgart Ballet; in other words, still important on the international scene, but no longer in the first rank.

This view, with which many of the company's regular audience would have agreed, was based partly on the quality of the new creations, partly on the standard of performance, which had sunk alarmingly. Luckily, the published criticisms by Barnes and others seemed to provoke a fighting response, and the homogeneity of the corps de ballet began to return after a period when you could be fairly sure that some of the dancers would be out of line or out of time.

But even if the dancers are at their best, a ballet company is no better than its repertory allows, so a lot depended in MacMillan's full-evening *Anastasia* which, after a long period of preparation,

'Hauntingly tragic': Glen Tetley's Rag Dances *created for the* Ballet Rambert

had its première in July, shortly before the summer closure. MacMillan had already staged a dramatic one-act ballet in Berlin about Anna Anderson and her claim to be the surviving heir to the Romanov dynasty. This was incorporated into the new work as its last act, preceded by two acts supposed to show the background to this claim, although the version of Russian history which MacMillan presented was fanciful, to say the least. The incongruous dramatic structure was underlined by a corresponding disparity in the musical basis, a very apt piece by Martinu being abruptly tagged on to a couple of Tchaikovsky symphonies. The atmospheric setting by Barry Kay for the first act (a picnic by the Imperial family on the eve of war) and some strong individual characterisations, most notably by Lynn Seymour in the title role, ensured the ballet at least some success with the general public, but the première was heartily booed and reactions were divided, so that *Anastasia* could by no means be said to have restored the prestige MacMillan lost with his two previous disastrous productions in London, *Olympiad* and *Checkpoint*. It was not until early in 1972 that he was to begin to rehabilitate his reputation with a short, simple work *Triad* which, although slight and somewhat ambiguous in its intentions, at least showed a return to his old ability to invent interesting new movements for his dancers.

What helped to save both the popular appeal and the artistic prestige of the Royal Ballet's season at Covent Garden were the contributions of a Russian-born dancer and two American choreographers. Jerome Robbins's *Dances at a Gathering*, the big hit of the previous year, remained the work which people were most anxious to see, and was joined by another Robbins ballet, *Afternoon of a Faun*, in which he used Debussy's music to make a modern variant on the theme of sexual attraction first choreographed by Nijinsky. Robbins's version, set in a ballet studio and paralleling Nijinsky's faun and nymphs with a sensuously self-absorbed dancer and his remotely involved partner, provided roles with a more contemporary feeling to them than Covent Garden audiences were accustomed to. Even more startling to audiences inclined to assume that ballets must necessarily involve toe-shoes, tutus and artificial wings was Glen Tetley's *Field Figures*, created in autumn 1970 for the Royal Ballet's touring group but brought into the large company's repertory in the summer of 1971. The Stockhausen music,

ABOVE: *'Life as a kind of purgatory'*: Geoffrey Cauley's Ante Room

BELOW: *'An amusing piece involving two couples, an odd girl out, and a couple of pieces of inflatable furniture'*: Games for Five Players

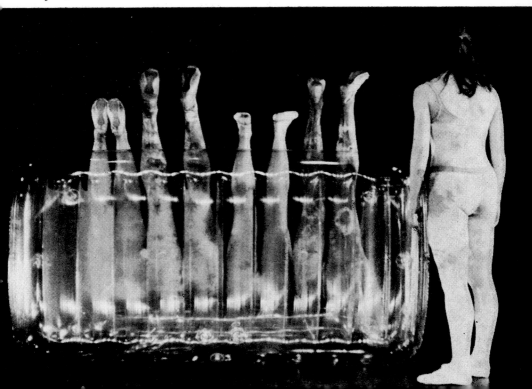

abstract development and mixture of modern-dance elements with classical ballet steps, not to mention Nadine Baylis's unusual setting of metallic rods, demanded a quality of attention and imagination from their audiences which met with a surprisingly sincere and whole-hearted response. In all these ballets, and also in an otherwise entirely undistinguished revival of Balanchine's *Apollo*, Rudolf Nureyev (alternating with dancers from the resident company) had the opportunity to reveal a range wider than his London appearances had sometimes shown. Thanks to these elements and to the work of some of the resident principal dancers, among whom Antoinette Sibley and Anthony Dowell were at last being recognised as stars of the first magnitude, the season at Covent Garden survived its early setbacks and achieved at least a degree of real success.

To some extent, of course, the Royal Ballet's large company could coast along on the impetus of past achievements. With the small touring company, which had been completely reorganised, immediate achievements were more crucial. And with this company, the strong American influence which has so far been one of the most prominent features of the MacMillan regime proved less strikingly beneficial. True, Joe Layton scored quite a hit with his first ballet, *The Grand Tour*. This successful choreographer and director of Broadway musicals had long wanted to work with a ballet company, and when given the opportunity he seized it to realise also another long-held ambition, that of creating a work based on the idea of a ship's cruise. The resulting work, *The Grand Tour*, with its score based on some of Noël Coward's most famous songs and its characters mainly based on celebrities of the period around 1930, had a great initial impact. A cast list including (as characters, not performers) Gertrude Lawrence, George Bernard Shaw, Mary Pickford, Douglas Fairbanks, Theda Bara, Gertrude Stein and Coward himself, most of them rather cleverly imitated or parodied, ensured a gasp of surprise and pleasure from audiences at each fresh entrance, and even if this effect eventually wore thin, there was a neat sub-plot to give both comic and romantic interest.

Layton's other contribution to the programmes, however, a curtain-raiser to the overture from Leonard Bernstein's *Candide*, had a more perfunctory appeal, and the reception for two works by another American creator, Herbert Ross, was altogether equivocal. A few people admired his work based on Genet's *The Maids*, although without a prior knowledge of the play it was virtually incomprehensible. *Caprichos*, based by Ross on some of Goya's pictures, was given without any of the sharpness and vicious definition which made the ballet memorable when shown in London by American Ballet Theatre in 1956. It was difficult, in fact, to see why these two old works had been resuscitated for the touring repertory.

MacMillan's only contribution to the new productions for this smaller Royal Ballet company was a revival of his melodramatic *Las Hermanas*, based on Lorca's *House of Bernarda Alba* (a popular subject among choreographers, for some strange reason). Strong performances from the dancers and the very non-balletic look of Nicholas Georgiadis's heavy, built-up setting play a big part in the work's popularity. Two other British choreographers, each of whom had been nurtured over the years by the Royal Ballet's previous management, were both allowed to stage one more work. These proved the best they had so far produced. Geoffrey Cauley's *Ante Room* was an abstract treatment of a theme suggesting life as a kind of purgatory. Although many people found it puzzling, the striking visual effects (Cauley designed his own pale setting and costumes) and unusual dance images proved fascinating to others. David Drew's *St Thomas' Wake* was based on music by Peter Maxwell Davies and made a vivid impression of the period of Scott and Zelda Fitzgerald, with jolly foxtrot episodes interrupted by a loathsome masked intruder personifying the grim decade that was to follow the 1920s. Another proposed creation by Drew, however, *Impressionist* (based on the life and work of Monet), was cancelled a few days before its première. The two new works were both quickly dropped from the repertory, and Drew and Cauley were left with no doubt that the Royal Ballet would not be requiring their choreographic services again in the near future.

So it came about that the smaller Royal Ballet, intended to develop new talent and provide opportunities for experiment, was doing very little in either of these directions. Also, the ambitious plans attempted the previous season for exchanging dancers between the two Royal companies (meant to provide the best circumstances for artistic growth) were virtually abandoned and the two companies remained as distinct as they had ever been. The small company, in short London seasons and on tour, did enjoy a considerable public success, largely because of the fine spirit of the dancers in the older works from the repertory. Quietly, the much boosted reforms which the new management was to bring were put aside, and the company relied for its momentum very much on the achievements of the old regime.

Fortunately the picture elsewhere in British ballet was much brighter. For Ballet Rambert in particular it was a year of great achievement. Outstanding among the five new works presented was Norman Morrice's *That is the Show*. The inspiration of this work was the music, Luciano Berio's *Sinfonia*, which in the couple of years since its première had established a popularity and grip on the public imagination like no other serious piece of modern music since Britten's *War Requiem*. Written for orchestra and voices both speaking and singing, its structure is that of a collage, and to go with it Morrice produced a similar choreographic form, containing recognisable dramatic incidents but without a specific plot. The main theme, however, is clear enough: it is the intolerable burden which the public puts on the shoulders of those it chooses as its heroes, and the even greater tragedy which can come to a woman whose husband or lover dies a hero's death. The theme could hardly be more topical, and it could hardly have been more elo-quently expressed than it was by Morrice and his cast. Sandra Craig, in the leading part, finally proved herself to be a great dancer (the modern-dance equivalent of what would be in classical ballet a ballerina) but her performance was only the outstanding one among a perfectly tuned ensemble.

A musical crisis nearly sabotaged the best of Rambert's other productions during the year. Glen Tetley had created his *Rag-Dances* to Messiaen's *Quartet for the End of Time*, but shortly before the première found that the composer would not allow this music (which had strong personal associations for him) to be used for a theatrical production. A new score for violin and piano was specially composed by Rambert's assistant conductor Anthony Hymas to fit the already completed choreography, and far from being a makeshift, this music shared the impressive impact of the whole ballet. Tetley's characters were a group of people all in some

'A perfectly tuned ensemble': That is the Show

way afflicted, the drop-outs and cast-offs of society, and the dances he devised for them had a hauntingly tragic quality, heightened by the contrast with a deadpan satirical representation of a typically glamorous waltzing pair of old-time stars.

With these two works alone, the creative pre-eminence of Ballet Rambert among the British ballet companies would have been secure, but they had more to show besides. Morrice's *Solo* (which in fact involved John Chesworth and a shopwindow dummy as well as the soloist, Sandra Craig) was a minor work, a brief but effective essay in movement about the effect on a woman of a man's attitude to her. Christopher Bruce, the company's intense young male star, produced *Wings*, a rather frightening ensemble work using movement-images drawn from birds to create a strong atmosphere; and another of the male dancers, Joseph Scoglio (who also very ably took over some of Bruce's roles while he was temporarily absent through injury), invented an interesting set of dances to electronic music. Some additions to the company's special programme for children, *Bertram Batell's Sideshow*, established that the Rambert choreographers could also work in a lighter mood.

The *Sideshow* was in fact only one of two programmes the Rambert company had jointly devised for young audiences. This one was intended for children of any age, but with a bias towards the youngest (and with the thought always present in the minds of the directors that ideally, when opportunity permits, they would like to be able to afford different programmes for different age-groups). The other introductory programme, which could serve equally well for older schoolchildren or for adults with no previous knowledge of ballet and modern dance, was called *Dance and Dancers*. This included a demonstration of the dancers' daily classes, with a commentary on the different techniques they use, as well as some shorter works from the repertory.

Started simply as an experiment for school matinées, this programme grew increasingly popular and was consciously used in an attempt to build up new audiences. In this, Rambert was beating a path on which they were soon joined by others. Scottish Theatre Ballet devised a special schools' programme in which a work from their repertory for the week was analysed: the parts played by music, costume, mime and dance explained; the scenery erected with the curtain up so that the audience could see how everything was done (very popular, this); and finally one act of the complete work was danced straight through. Festival Ballet devised a different way of arousing interest, by sending dancers, singly or in pairs, to talk informally about their work to schools, clubs or any other group who wanted them. London Contemporary Dance Theatre put an Experimental Group on the road, consisting of senior students and apprentice dancers performing specially created works—mainly in colleges and similar institutions. Dancers from the London Contemporary company also participated in one of the programmes of the long-established Ballet for All group, which toured continually to awake interest in ballet generally, but with a strong bias of concentration on works performed by the Royal Ballet.

All this activity was a heartening indication that British ballet had woken up to the fact that the days when it could sit quietly and wait for people to clamour at the box office were over. The need to sell itself gradually sank in. The ways in which the different companies sought popularity were, of course, as varied as the companies themselves. Festival Ballet followed a policy of playing safe. The new productions for the year in which it celebrated its twenty-first anniversary were all revivals of works previously given. Audiences for the programmes of popular classics were good, but some of the dancers found the limited range and absence of creative work rather stultifying. The company's two stars, Galina Samtsova and André Prokovsky, felt this so strongly that they took leave of absence to form a small group of dancers for some guest appearances in Italy, for which they commissioned a new ballet by Peter Darrell on the *Othello* story. The success of this venture, undertaken at their own expense, led them to plan further similar engagements for which they would gradually have more works created.

At the other extreme from Festival Ballet was London Contemporary Dance Theatre. Their year began with a London season in which were mounted five new works by members of the company and one work by an outside choreographer, Talley Beatty (his *Road of the Phoebe Snow*, previously danced in London by Alvin Ailey's American Dance Theatre). At the year's end they were about to start another season with five more premières, only one by an outsider. In between, the company's artistic director had produced

T.72—I

a full-evening work, *Stages,* using both electronic music and jazz, with spectacular production effects and gymnastics (taught to the dancers by the British Olympic team's coach, Pauline Prestidge) mixed in with the dancing. Not many of the new works would necessarily stay long in the repertory, but one of the aspirant choreographers, Richard Alston, showed evidence of a really individual talent, and the company's policy of constant experiment attracted a whole-hearted enthusiasm from a regular audience of mainly young people.

However, some of the most interesting work during the year came from companies of an outwardly more conventional nature and based in the more conservative regions. Against stiff competition from larger and wealthier companies, for instance, Scottish Theatre Ballet's *Giselle* proved by far the most rewarding of the year's classical revivals. This was partly because its producer, Peter Darrell, had the idea of reverting to the score as originally written by the ballet's composer, Adolphe Adam. Since there had been some extra numbers interpolated even before the first night in 1841, this was probably the first time Adam's score had ever been played as he intended it, and the effect was far more dramatic than other productions which make cuts and additions more or less *ad lib.* The traditional choreography needed some slight adjustment (but surprisingly little) to fit this leaner, more muscular musical support. The most important aspect of the production,, however, was the fact that Darrell (much aided by his designer Peter Cazalet) found a credible motivation for every character and every incident by setting the ballet firmly in a recognisable village square in a specific period (mediaeval), instead of the usual vaguely romantic rustic location at an undefined point of time.

Darrell's other production during the year was a small work *Four Portraits* for a special tour undertaken by a group of dancers from the company to small towns throughout Scotland which lacked proper theatres. This tour, under the title (or slogan) Ballet for Scotland, was evidence that Scottish Theatre Ballet was taking seriously its responsibilities towards its adopted country; and for a similar expedition at the beginning of 1972 the associate director, Stuart Hopps, produced the company's first work based on Scottish themes and music, *An Clo Mor,* inspired by songs of the western isles. For the main autumn tour, Ashley Killar staged *Arriving*

Bellevue Sunday . . . (inspired by the film *Theorem*), an ambitious but only partly successful dramatic work. Given with it, however, was a welcome new new production of *La Fête Étrange*, Andrée Howard's evocative work drawn from an incident in Alain Fournier's novel *Le Grand Meaulnes*.

Scottish Theatre Ballet had been born with ready-made traditions and standards when the former Western Theatre Ballet was transplanted to Glasgow. In Manchester, Laverne Meyer had started Northern Dance Theatre from scratch, but already in its second season it was achieving notable results. John Chesworth (from Ballet Rambert) created *Games for Five Players* for them to music by the contemporary Japanese composer Toru Takemitsu: an amusing piece involving two couples, an odd girl out, and a couple of pieces of inflatable furniture. Although light-hearted in mood, the work had some serious insights into human behaviour to give it depth. Walter Gore, who for some years had worked mainly abroad, staged his *Dance Pictures* for the company, a divertissement with dramatic incidents, in which his wife Paula Hinton (an exceptional dramatic dancer too long absent from the British stage) appeared at the opening performances, to be followed, with almost equal success, by the company's own leading dancer, Suzanne Hywel. Meyer himself contributed only a modest curtain-raiser, *Introduction Piece*, but another of his dancers, John Haynes, made his choreographic début with the pleasant but rather slight *Towards Night*. The really surprising new work was *Quartet*, created by Jonathan Thorpe to the first five movements of Beethoven's B flat quartet op. 130: an audaciously difficult piece of music for a young choreographer, with only one apprentice work behind him, to attempt, but inspiring Thorpe to a work of genuine invention and some real emotional content.

In addition to these home-based companies, there was a constant succession of visiting troupes. Folk-dance ensembles came from Burma, Ceylon, Czechoslovakia, Greece, Hungary, India, Jogjakarta, Jugoslavia, Korea, Russia and Spain; there were three Czech mime companies at different times in London, and even a group of whirling dervishes. A small modern dance group from Paris failed to make much impact; the Cullberg Ballet from Stockholm and the City Center Joffrey Ballet from New York both ran into rather more severe criticism than reception at home had led them to expect; and even Alwin Nikolais, the wizard whose clever lighting effects seem to move more than his dancers do, failed to repeat on a second visit to Sadler's Wells his first immense success.

The big hits of the year among our dancing visitors were the Royal Danish Ballet at the Edinburgh Festival (their programmes were the first in the whole festival to sell out) and Maurice Béjart's Ballet du Vingtième Siècle from Brussels at the London Coliseum. The one company is as staunchly traditional as the other is deliberately revolutionary, so it would be hard to define any trend from their success; but it is significant that both had a clear, strongly defined policy, and both offered dancers of exceptional quality. The comparative success, among other visitors, of the young Ballet Théâtre Contemporain from Amiens, which at its more modest level could make similar claims, serves to reinforce the moral.

One fringe event of the year demands to be recorded. Richard Buckle, ballet critic, author and exhibition designer, announced The Greatest Show on Earth, to be given at the Coliseum to raise money to help buy Titian's *Death of Acteon* for the nation, or failing that to provide funds for Buckle's pet brainchild, the Museum of Performing Arts. After furious rumours, counter-rumours, alarms and excursions the Greatest Show was called off but a Répétition Générale for it was held, at which tickets printed with the price £100 were sold off at £10, and others in proportion. Some people dressed to suit a seat priced at £10 (or £100); others wore the old clothes they thought appropriate to a dress rehearsal. For our money, we saw two rather quaint new ballets dreamed up by Buckle, and a rather marvellous collection of dancers doing their party pieces. Whether anybody actually benefited financially from the occasion, and if so who, and by how much, seems not to be recorded.

And I ought to mention the biggest ballet success of the year, which took place not on stage but on the wide cinema screen where Frederick Ashton's *Tales of Beatrix Potter* played to enraptured houses up and down the country, and made the Royal Ballet's Michael Coleman, in his frog costume as Jeremy Fisher, the pin-up hero of a commercial poster that was eagerly bought to decorate thousands of nursery walls. How many other performers appearing on stage today could make such a boast?

J. W. Lambert

Non-Stop Juggling

The Chairman of the Arts Council's Drama Panel, who is also literary and arts editor of The Sunday Times, *explains the mechanics of theatrical subsidy.*

All institutions need to be kept under constant scrutiny; their principles should somehow combine consolidation and flexibility and must never be allowed to set. One vital element in this process is constructive criticism from the outside. Unfortunately constructive criticism of the Arts Council is very rare. What criticism there is tends to be blinkered by personal grievance, understandable but seldom helpful, or vitiated by ignorance and thus bombinating in realms of fantasy.

The Arts Council is an institution which deserves to be taken seriously; its worst enemy would hardly deny that its influence on the fabric of life in this country, even in its brief and formative twenty-five years' existence, has been considerable. And I don't imagine there is a single reader of this book who has not at some time or other cursed the Council's stupidity, or, more mildly, wondered what on earth it thought it was up to, in the field of theatre.

Contrary to what some disgruntled voices believe, when criticisms are made, attention is paid. But since most adverse comments are so divorced from the practical business of organising such a body as to be virtually useless, I am writing now in the hope that an account, as clear as I can make it, of the Council's machinery, and in particular that of its Drama Department, will give future attacks more relevance to real life. I recognise of course that to some, especially journalists in search of a damaging story, a knowledge of the facts is a severe handicap. But they can, and do, ignore them anyway; I address myself to those who genuinely wish to change things for the better.

First, a basic point. The Arts Council exists, in the terms of its charter, to improve the availability of the arts to the people of Great Britain, and to give encouragement to the arts and artists— in that order. Artists are of course benefiting from the steadily increasing availability and appreciation of the arts; some artists, in all fields, will be at least temporarily ahead of even informed public understanding, and it is the business of the Arts Council to give some help to them if they ask for it; but it is not the business of the Arts Council simply to support artists, and it does not do so, except in a few isolated instances in literature and the visual arts.

A second basic point, equally often forgotten or not realised: granted that availability of the arts is a prime concern, it is not the business of the Council to ram them down people's throats. The Council exists to respond to local initiative. It does not try to force, for example, theatre upon an area with no local enthusiasm for it (though it will certainly do all it can to encourage and help sensible local enthusiasm, within its own severe financial limitations and a national perspective). It did once set up a company in a theatrically deprived area, in the hope that local enthusiasm would build around it, but this did not happen. Except in the case of art exhibitions, the Council is not a promoting organisation. It is in intention a pump-priming body—though more often than it would wish it has to fill most of the tank as well. It does not believe that an artistic enterprise in need of subsidy should get all its financial assistance from one source, and a central London-based source at that. It never stops cajoling local authorities to spend more of their permitted $2\frac{1}{2}$p rate on the arts, and sometimes—especially in the context of theatre—has in its eagerness to encourage, or to keep something worth while alive, landed itself with heavier continuing burdens than it should be called upon to bear.

So much for its underlying principles. But when it comes to the point, what do people mean when they speak of 'the Arts Council'? Even more important, what do people understand by the words when they hear them or see them? Experience has made it plain that most folk have only a very blurred image.

The picture is perhaps best clarified by the analogy of a limited company, with a board of directors, which in turn has a number of subsidiary companies, each with their boards of directors, though in this case the directors are unpaid and in some circumstances advisory rather than executive. At any given moment nearly four hundred people, in England, Scotland and Wales are serving, for free, on the Council, its Panels and its Committees. The work of actually running the Council's activities is done by about eighty salaried officers.

To carry on with the analogy, the holding company, the Arts Council of Great Britain (not including Northern Ireland), has two virtually autonomous subsidiary companies—the Arts Councils of Scotland and Wales respectively—and six subsidiary companies under its own hand: Drama, Art, Music, Literature, Touring and Experimental Projects. All these manage their own affairs, but their policies and proposed expenditure must be ratified by the Council itself at its monthly meetings; in practice the Council very seldom interferes or quibbles.

The money which the Council distributes comes from the Treasury, by way of the Department of Education and Science and under the eye of the Minister Responsible for the Arts. Such a minister is of course a very recent innovation. Our first was Jennie Lee, appointed by Mr Wilson; our second is Lord Eccles, appointed by Mr Heath. To what extent is the Arts Council's own independence threatened by all this governmental background? So far, not at all, though it is an area in which the Council maintains an electric sensitivity—'eternal vigilance is the price of freedom'; and it would be idle to pretend that down the years an atmosphere of unruffled harmony has prevailed between the Council and the Civil Servants, not temperamentally equipped to grasp the hazards and uncertainties of artistic enterprise.

Once the Council knows how much it is likely to get from the Treasury, it sets about dividing up the spoils. Up to now, this has been possible only very late in the financial year; it has therefore been impossible to tell 'clients' what they were likely to get until a most inconveniently late hour. Literally years of persuasion by Arts Council officers have now produced a modification—inelegantly known as the Rolling Triennium, a three-year guarantee—which should mean that everybody's planning is less hampered, that some degree of adventure need not be quite so precarious. In dividing up the total Arts Council grant from the Treasury the cost of the four national institutions, Covent Garden, Sadler's Wells, the National Theatre and the Royal Shakespeare Company are first deducted; then the Scottish and Welsh Arts Councils get a fixed percentage of the remaining basic sum. The four major English departments then put in bids for their share of the remainder once allowances have been made for Touring, Experimental Projects and a substantial reserve—against, mainly, disasters, which are bound to occur to some of our clients during the financial year. All this takes place at a meeting of what is called the Estimates Committee, at which interested parties are all present and jockeying for position.

When they have fought to a finish—and the infighting, believe me, is often pretty tough—off they go with their prizes. Off, in our case, goes the Drama Director to draw up, in consultation with his officers and his advisory Panel, the best approach possible to an equitable allocation of funds for the theatre. The total available, it may be worth mentioning, has increased from £95,000 (divided between just over a dozen companies in 1951–2) to £2,600,000 in 1972–3 (divided between some seventy companies as well as writers, training schemes and much else). Let me try to describe the administrative machinery which makes its allocations possible, and the human elements—of the Drama Department and the Drama Panel —who try to make it work.

The Drama Department, looking after the theatre in England (not Scotland or Wales), has a total staff of fourteen, including secretaries, plus three more who are concerned entirely with touring and also work closely with the Music Department in connection with opera and ballet. Seven officers, in practice, administer the Arts Council's service to seventy-odd companies and a good deal of other activity as well, which I shall outline in due course. What, though, is actually involved in that easily written word 'administer'?

The Drama Department's share of the Arts Council's total grant, divided up in turn by the Drama Director and his officers (no light task) among the assorted companies and projects, is then submitted to the Drama Finance and Policy Committee, which consists of members of the Drama Panel—all members of the Panel, in fact, are encouraged to attend the monthly meetings of Finance and Policy Committee. Throughout the year this Committee combines decision-making of an immediate and practical nature with a broader consideration of gradual changes in emphasis: do we want to spend any more money in London? Is the experimental theatre showing enough vitality to justify a marked increase in the money made available to it?

Thus when the Drama Director puts before the Finance and Policy Committee his suggestions for a new financial year he does so in full knowledge of the way the Committee's, and by extension the Panel's, corporate mind has been moving. Indeed, for the purposes of discussion the officers of the Drama Department are simply regarded as exceptionally well-informed members of the Panel and the Committee. All officers, unless they are out of London visiting a theatre, attend all meetings, a procedure which adds to the burden of their work but is of great benefit to the discussions. Similarly it is a firm principle of Dick Linklater, the Drama Director, that although naturally enough each member of his staff has areas of special responsibility, all of them are kept aware of what everybody else is doing. Apart from the fact that they all seem to get on remarkably well, and never stop talking, in or out of office hours, about their various preoccupations, they have their own regular staff meetings, and the day-file, as I believe it is called, of all letters to all officers is regularly circulated.

As I am here concerned to describe the *machinery* of the Drama Department I shall not expand its policies, or the various considerations of size, catchment area, geographical location, enterprise, local authority support and much more which influence the Panel in its recommendations to the Council—indeed to spell all that out would require a sizeable essay to itself; but obviously the Panel, whose members come from all over the country, while relying to some extent, in its formation of an overall perspective of theatre in England, upon the local knowledge of its fellow-members, depends much more upon the first-hand knowledge of the officers.

The Board meetings of every company assisted by the Arts Council are as often as possible attended by one or other of the officers, as an 'assessor', or observer, to give advice when asked for it but certainly not to tell the boards how to run their own theatres. There is some feeling, especially among younger, more authoritarian or more impatient theatre people, that the Arts Council positively ought to throw its weight about much more; but as the Council itself demands a high degree of autonomy, of freedom from interference by the Government, so it feels that its clients too should have a high degree of freedom to run their own organisations—even though the way they do it often causes us acute dismay.

Before I was associated with the Drama Department I had vaguely assumed that the subsidised theatres would regard visits by the Council's representatives as a nuisance at best, or even as a disgraceful intrusion by a *rond-de-cuir* snooper from London. I soon learnt that the reverse was the case; that most of our supported theatres up and down the country positively look forward to an officer's visit—which is at the least a splendid opportunity to work off accumulated frustrations; and if they have a grievance, it is that the Arts Council doesn't visit them often enough. Even so, it will be clear that with seventy companies to pay attention to, seven officers are kept pretty well on the trot. In practice, the Drama Director is likely, over the year, to be out in the Regions at least one night a week and the other six two or three nights a week. This involves working in the office (or attending a meeting) until the last possible moment before catching a train which will get to its destination in time for the board meeting and/or that evening's performance; after the performance, talking to those who run the theatre, acting as a constructive safety-valve, or sometimes as a buffer in internecine quarrels, encouraging—or sometimes restraining—ambitious plans (to avoid excessive identification any given theatre will not always be visited by the same officer); snatching a few hours' sleep; and the following day, having formed as clear a picture as possible of the prevailing standards and morale, either moving on to another regional theatre, or catching an early train back to London and the maelstrom of correspondence, reports and urgent telephone calls which are common form at the Arts Council's headquarters.

In some leisurely employments this might well seem in itself an adequate programme for a week's work; but the Drama Department's officers have much more upon their plates. One is wholly concerned with the manifold activities of Young People's Theatre,- and the intermittent emergencies of the Drama Schools—so shamefully denied any support from government or local authority, in glaring contrast to the proliferation of art schools. Another, though involved in all the Department's activities, is particularly concerned with experimental companies, and yet another with new drama—these two used to be grouped together, but there is now so much of both that they had to be separated. Training schemes, touring, computer booking, seat prices, other professional bodies . . . sometimes there seems to be no end to the aspects of theatre demanding close attention and expert knowledge.

What is required of these officers, in short, is a flair for theatre as such, a crisp administrative mind balanced by an understanding of the stresses (and the chicaneries) of the creative mind, and—without which all the rest will go to waste—the ability to like and cope with a wide diversity of difficult human beings, from baffled town councillors by way of niggling academics and chilly accountants (there are many splendid people of all three kinds, but one must be ready to face the worst) to power-mad directors, whimsical designers and embittered actors. As a set of ideal qualifications this is perhaps daunting; only their 'clients' will know how far the Drama Department officers are able to live up to it. One thing is certain: they are all inadequately paid. Although they are not and never have been civil servants—the theatre itself has been their nursery—their salaries are judged by some system of civil service grading which slots them in with dim functionaries who have no craft knowledge and need hardly speak to, much less understand, another human being in the whole of their working lives. When I made this point to a senior member of the present government he replied, with rubicund joviality and total indifference, 'Well, they enjoy their work, don't they? Why should they expect to be well paid for it?'

On that cheerful note, let us turn to those who don't get paid at all—the Panel and its associated committees. The Panel has at the moment twenty-eight members, and its associated committees a further thirty-six. Their function in both cases is to supplement the officers' expert knowledge with their own. They are the most frequently and most virulently criticised of all the Arts Council's outward and visible signs. Their Chairman and Deputy Chairman are members of the Arts Council itself, appointed by the Minister responsible for the arts. Experience down the years has suggested that it is desirable to establish some continuity in these roles; they are not therefore subject to any statutory time-limit, though in

Composition of the Arts Council Drama Panel
as at January 1st 1972

practice so demanding of time, thought and energy, and so strikingly lacking in glamour or acclaim, that few are likely to hang on for an excessively long run. Ordinary Panel members are appointed for three years or less. Thus the composition of the Panel is continually changing. Nobody is invited to join the Panel as a representative of an organisation, though many are of course prominent in organisations; they are invited specifically for their personal qualities and qualifications, though we do try to keep a certain range of reference by asking individuals who have different backgrounds and concerns: members of theatre boards, artistic directors, designers, company administrators, actors and actresses, dramatists, critics, a senior TV drama man, one very experienced regional local government expert and an academic with a wide knowledge of the arts in society are all currently members. We also try to ensure a wide geographical spread, an age-range which means that at the moment six members of the Panel are under thirty, and rather more who, whether or not personally engaged in it, are keenly sympathetic to what for want of a better word must be called the experimental theatre.

Given that these are the sort of people who make up the Panel, how are they chosen? Is the whole thing in practice just a cosy club, basically concerned to look after its own interests, and devil take the hindmost? Obviously it could be precisely that, and it is easy to understand that in the light of disappointment some of its decisions must look decidedly fishy, even to those who don't feel that all its priorities are hopelessly wrong and that it should, shall we say, abandon the National and the Royal Shakespeare and give all that money to street theatre. Equally obviously I, as Chairman of the Panel, and its spokesman on the Council, don't feel that it is anything of the kind. At any rate I can acquit my predecessor and myself of the charge of having packed the Panel with yes-men; nobody who sits on a committee with, to choose a few examples from many, James Saunders, Oscar Lewenstein, Kenneth Tynan or Jennifer Harris of the Combination could possibly regard them as acquiescent nonentities—or, indeed, at times as anything but confounded nuisances, and a very good thing too. Even as Chairman I feel that there is something not merely undesirable but, worse, positively boring about a meeting at which all present appear to be of one mind. And as for the selection of Panel members being only the operation of a handsome old-boy network—well, any member of the Council, and of the Panel, is entitled to suggest new members. In fact, come to think of it, it's a free country, anybody at all, anywhere, can send in a suggestion.

The resulting list of candidates will not of course be elected after a nation-wide ballot. To ask thousands of people to vote for candidates they've for the most part never heard of is to make a mockery of democratic procedures in a manner currently popular only with large capitalist enterprises on the one hand, and on the other extremely stupid doctrinaires and extremely clever nihilists. The Arts Council itself will invite people to join its Panels, choosing from the list of those suggested in accordance with the guidelines of age-range, geographical scope and professional knowledge. I should be the last to deny that at this stage I as Chairman of the Panel have a considerable say in the matter; but it is also true that rather more than half of those invited have been personally unknown to me, and to many of the rest of the Panel, before their first appearance at a meeting.

For better or for worse, it is before this body that the officers put their reports on the present and their suggestions for the future. To this body report the sub-committees, made up of Panel members and co-opted outside experts, each serviced, as the saying goes, by one of those hard-pressed officers: the Young People's Theatre Committee; the Experimental Drama Committee, which deals with the extremely vigorous cellar-attic-pub-arts lab theatre, many of its companies continually on the road, rushing in groaning old vans, from one-night-stand to one-night-stand and the New Drama Committee, reading scores of desperate scripts in the eager hope of unearthing a new genius—these two Committees mopping up, by the way, £80,000 a year between them; the Theatre Administration Training Scheme—which, encouraged by the Council, has developed into a much bigger, and in our view vitally important, Arts Administrators' Training Scheme; the Experimental Projects Committee, made up of representatives from all the Council's departments, to help ideas which cannot be categorised; and the Training Committee, which in turn has sub-committees, or working groups, working for future technicians, drama students, directors and designers, all concerned to find out what form of training is most needed and how it may best be supplied (and which keep pretty busy people of the calibre of Richard Pilbrow, Carl Toms, John Bury, Ralph Koltai, Ian Albery, William Gaskill, Val May, Vivian Matalon, Janet Suzman, Michael Elliott, Martin Esslin, Stuart Burge . . .).

The Panel, in short, does its best to perform a non-stop juggling act, trying to keep buoyant at the same time the most miniscule and the most majestic enterprises; and what's more, trying all the time to add new ones as fresh and worthwhile applicants appear in, it seems, numbers which increase much faster than the money made available. This, incidentally, is hardly twice as much for the whole of England as the Schillertheater in West Berlin gets for its mere three companies; but here is an argument which must be used with care, since if some hard-faced realist asks 'Then I suppose the Schillertheater is infinitely better than any of our under-nourished theatres?' one is forced to admit that, indeed, money isn't everything. Furthermore, the Drama Panel has less freedom of action than might be supposed, in that what are known as historical reasons have imposed a ramshackle pattern upon the English theatre over which the Arts Council could at no time have exercised much control unless it had turned itself into a brutal, centralised administration imposing its own rational grid regardless of local iniatives and enthusiasms. That it has never even thought of doing, and I hope never will do. Anomalies, inefficiencies, absurdities, even injustices are infinitely to be preferred to a juggernaut master-plan. And little by little, community by community, the pattern is in fact changing.

The Arts Council and its Drama Panel still aim at flexibility both in ends and means. In a stormy sea a ship's head will yaw from port to starboard and back again. A skilful helmsman will check the swing at the right moment (he cannot possibly prevent it altogether) and ensure that, despite the turbulent upheaval all around, the ship in the long run drives ahead on the right course. If the Arts Council's Drama Department and Panel is the helmsman of the subsidised theatre as a whole it must expect a lot of advice from the rest of the crew, to say nothing of the hundreds of passengers. I hope that these notes will have given some of these at least a rudimentary notion of how we set about our job.

Raymond Mander & Joe Mitchenson

Posters of the Actor-Managers 1891–1920

From originals in the Raymond Mander and Joe Mitchenson Theatre Collection. Photographed by Robert Primmer.

From the earliest times theatrical entertainment has been advertised by posters, literally a printed announcement to be displayed on a post, that is 'posted' and so a poster!

For many years during the eighteenth and nineteenth centuries a playbill (we would now call it a programme, with information of the evening's proceedings) sold or given in the theatre itself did double duty both as programme and poster.

With the advances in printing machinery and commercial lithography, coloured posters began to make their appearance on the London hoardings in the 1860s, but it was the influence of the French poster artists of the eighties and nineties which transformed the 'pictorial' into an art and made the hoardings into the poor man's Academy.

The 'Double Crown' size was for outside theatres, bill boards, sandwichmen or general advertising. The smaller 'Folio' was mainly used for the ticket booking agencies, both in shops and hotels.

Often the London posters were printed blank at the top to allow the insertion of the theatre to be played on tour, or unlocated posters printed to do duty, with a big success, up and down the country. Some of both these types are included in the following pages, while some are the West End originals, but they all give a good idea of how the actor-manager sold himself but how seldom his leading lady!

A typical hoarding, 1898.
*An actor-manager
announces his arrival with
an imposing display—
incorporating posters of
several sizes*

Frank Benson, on tour,
1891. *A two-colour poster,
à la Walter Crane,
which must have seemed
very 'modern' in its day*

Poster designed by John Hassell for The Only Way *at the*
Lyceum Theatre in 1899 and used by Martin Harvey both in
London and on tour for many years

Poster for a late revival of W. G. Wills's version of Goethe's
Faust *for Irving at the Lyceum in 1902*

Poster for a comedy by R. C. Carton in 1909, with Katherine Compton (Mrs. Carton) and Weedon Grossmith, leaving their audience behind them

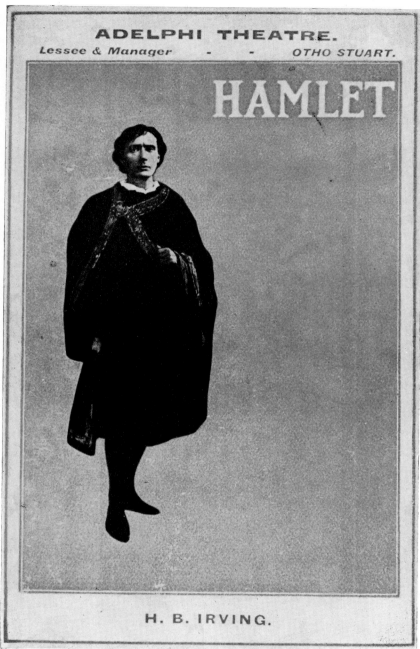

H. B. Irving following in his father's footsteps, under the managerial banner of an old Bensonian, 1905

*A Charles Buchel poster for Beerbohm Tree with Lily Brayton in
a Michael Morton adaptation at His Majesty's Theatre in 1903*

A poster by Ritz for a melodrama at the Strand Theatre which starred Matheson Lang with Lilian Braithwaite in 1913. It was later toured for many years by Lang under his own management

ABOVE: *Albert Morrow's poster of the Elders of the Kirk in Barrie's play as first produced at the Haymarket Theatre in 1897, under the management of Cyril Maude*

BELOW: *A long forgotten Gilbert fantasy with Bourchier and his wife, Violet Vanburgh, at the Garrick Theatre in 1904*

ABOVE: *George Alexander and Irene Vanburgh in a play by Cosmo Gordon-Lennox at the St. James's Theatre in 1907*
BELOW: *Justin Huntley McCarthy's play for Alexander at the St. James's Theatre in 1902. Later to become a musical* The Vagabond King

Poster by George Story for the revival in 1911 at the
Criterion Theatre

Original poster for the first production of Shaw's play in 1914, on which both the author and leading lady, Mrs Patrick Campbell, were unnamed!

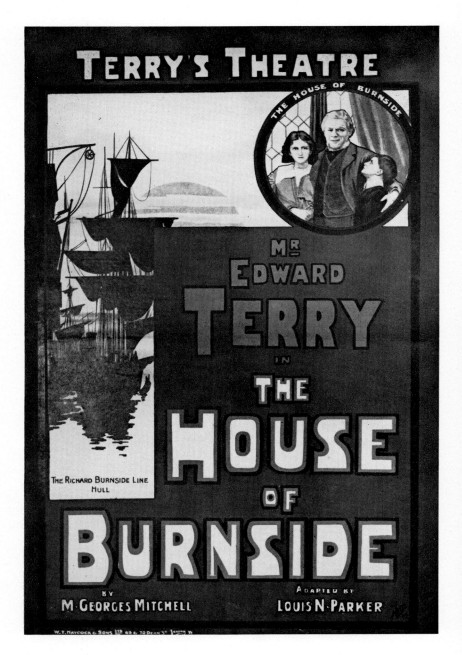

A poster by Nibs for a long lost theatre in the Strand (now covered by Woolworths) in 1904. One of the few theatres to bear the name of its actor-manager and builder

*Poster by Albert Morrow for Mollison at the St. James's
Theatre (misspelt on the original!) for his Christmas season
in 1905, of a play by James McArthur and Augustus Thomas*

A Buchel poster for Waller at the Imperial Theatre,
Westminster (its site now covered by the Central Hall) in 1904,
advertising a play by R. N. Stephens and E. Lyall Swete

Poster by J. M. Dowd for Ainley's venture into management in 1920

London Life 1905: A newsvendor and a sandwichman

Andrew Porter

In Triumph through Persepolis

Peter Brook's Orghast *was the principal event in the 1971 Arts Festival of Shiraz-Persepolis; it is described here by a critic on the* Financial Times.

The sun rose at six. I was at the top of Naqsh-i-Rustam, the sacred mountain behind vanished Istakhr, into whose sheer cliff-faces are hewn the hypocaust tombs of Darius, Xerxes, Artaxerxes and Darius II. Marvellous place at any time, overwhelming as sunrise formed the climax of an experience which had begun twelve hours before, four miles to the south at Persepolis: Peter Brook's *Orghast*, public first-fruit of his International Centre for Theatre Research which had been working for a year in Paris. At the foot of the mountain Man walked a cow to pasture along the path which a little earlier Kings and Heroes had trod. From a dozen crags the Gods were calling and chanting sacred *Avesta* texts in the old magic language of Zoroaster. As light flooded the plain a flock of goats, their bells mingling with the ritual chime from the mountain, passed across the scene: unplanned but ideal close to the drama. The King had been burnt in the fire-temple, Prometheus had been unbound, Salamis fought and lost, and on the Persian plain the people's day began once more, as it had done for unchanging centuries.

Orghast is a drama—opera, ritual, ceremony, theatrical action —with its roots in many things: myth, history, the sites of its performance; Brook's preoccupation with the nature of theatrical communication, his researches into what bodies, voices and lights can achieve when deployed before an audience; his knowledge of contemporary music with its spatial effects, counterpoints of random detail under large-scale control, and free juxtaposition of speech and song (from *Titus* onwards Brook has shown himself an accomplished composer; and a 'concert performance' of *Orghast* would grace an ISCM Festival); also, I think, his experience of Persian *ta'azieh,* which is so profoundly impressive and affecting even when no words are understood. *Orghast* was played in tongues unknown (*orghast,* and that of the *Avesta*) and little known (classical Greek, Latin) to its audiences. Immediate sources were Aeschylus, Calderón, the *Tempest* exercises, and Seneca's *Oedipus* at the Old Vic in Ted Hughes's translation.

To share in the first part we pass through portals and palaces and climb a steep mountain track, flare-lit, to the tomb of Artaxerxes III, a huge open cube cut into the mountain behind Persepolis, three sides and its floor of living rock, the fourth open to the palaces and the great plain. The actors are already disposed on the dim empty platform; we line the sides. High above us Prometheus is chained to the crag. A mystic chant swells from all sides. The voice of Zeus, of Ormazd in Old Persian, rings from the skies. Earth answers deep in the cave. Light, personified, silhouetted against the sky, cries an invocation. Prometheus sends fire to man, and a globe of fierce fire descends from above, past the relief of Ahura-Mazda, past sculptured Artaxerxes upheld by his two tiers of subject races before the fire-altar, to be received by Man below.

But Man, as even Prometheus who loves him admits in Aeschylus's play, is an imperfect creature; fire is at once a boon and a force for destruction. Krogon, the King, advances, and his attendant, Strength, seizes and appropriates the fire for royal power. The tyrant father fears the son who may overthrow him: Krogon's first son is murdered; the mother, a sad, mad shadow of grief and revenge, will pursue him to the end of the play. His second son, Sogis, is caged in a cave (Calderon's *Life is a dream*); grown, he is dragged forth painfully to pursue his destiny. Prometheus lights his reason: in thick animal tones Sogis echoes the Titan's ringing lines, 'O $\Delta\iota o s$ $\alpha i\theta\eta\rho$. At a feast Krogon, driven mad by light, kills all his current family; recovered, in the light of sanity, he blinds himself.

The rites of Orghast

Winding through the action, leading, coaxing, restraining, cradling the child, freeing the chained youth with a touch of his torch, is Furorg, who seems to personify human instinct, at once tender and fierce, unreasoning. Furorg leads Sogis to the blind father he must kill, but—and this is where *Orghast* departs from the murderous old myths—the youth cannot do it. Krogon stumbles out into the night. The platform grows dark but fires leap up on the lower terrace, and after a silence we feel our way past the actors still sitting or standing there to the plain below.

The rites of *Orghast* are chanted from the *Avesta* in a Zoroastrian language of singing vowels, ullulating portamentos, and sudden sharp cut-offs with a steep rising inflection to a glottal stop. No one could speak it except one scholar, Mahin Tajadot, who determined a pronunciation and taught it to the cast. Passages from *Prometheus* are declaimed in an open-vowelled ringing, singing Greek (*oo dee-os a-ee-theer*) as if from an opened heart. The Latin of *Hercules furens* (when the family is murdered in madness) strikes a high rhetorical note. But most of *Orghast* is performed in *orghast*, a dramatic language invented by Ted Hughes, an attempt to find the sound most directly communicative of ideas (light, darkness, death) and even of specific objects (skylark, fish, the whirling dust-clouds which are *flota falluttu*), sounds which carry an emotional and dramatic sense even when the listeners do not know the precise meaning of the words.

Hughes and Brook began the work in English. A scene was written, and then the poet found himself blocked by what he called 'literature'. He tried an experiment in syllabic sound, another in which the international cast declaimed charged words for their sense rather than their pronunciation: of *murder* a Japanese actor made a sound in which murderous intent was clearly recognisable though the original word was not. From such research *orghast* was born. Essentially it is a development from English, but an idealised dramatic English, 'clear-eyed, resounding, with strong teeth', whose vowels sing clear and true into the night, blaze fiercely, or shine like the steady moon (*luna*, or *moan* in *orghast*) which played over the drama. The consonants are craggy (fire is *gheost*, while *orghast* itself is the sun; agony, *dagon*, acquires that initial stab so that it can be cried out as the English word cannot). *Eorda* is earth, *man* is man, *ladda* is son (Hughes spoke of the Yorkshire influence).

When English does not supply evocative sounds, Romance roots are called into play. *Palom* is dove, *narga* is nothing, *ombalom* womb. *Lugh* is light and so *glittalugh* is star.

On paper a little basic *orghast* is easily acquired. *Datta ma ladda lugh* means give my son light, and *bak opp eorda* return to earth. Persians might find it harder, though their sounds are evocative too: *amurdaad* (immortality), *Dadhv* (the Creator), *spandarmad* (holy submission) are names of the Zoroastrian months, not yet *orghast*, though they very well might be. But learning the language is not the point—in fact precisely not the point; the intention was that the audience should respond instinctively, not set themselves semantic puzzles. Hughes suggested a simile of music which had been buried for centuries until all sophisticated developments had decayed from it, and only essentials remained. My peek at some pages of the script was unauthorised—and undertaken only after I had seen the piece several times. The 'plot' as outlined above needed no verbal crib (only the proper names are supplied from subsequent knowledge). Response was direct enough to, say, the three different words for darkness: *bullorga*, which is plainly active, teeming darkness, the kind Mark sings of in Tippett's opera *The Midsummer Marriage*; *blott*, the removal of light, blindness; and the *narga* of nothingness. On returning to the performances my understanding remained instinctive, for it is not the meaning of the words on the page which matters, but the sense of the sounds in the context of the dramatic action. When Furorg croons over the baby, or sings his *lohorn* song leading Sogis, and in part 2 the pilgrims, into the distance, his meaning needs no translation.

Yet I was not sorry to have seen some of the text in black and white. (Brook often insists that a play exists only while it is being acted, and has no life except that which players and audience together provide: too extreme a view which does not allow for the imaginative reader, of text as of musical score, who can experience a performance—can be producer, players and responsive audience in one—while he reads.) On the simplest level, perusal dispelled some unnecessary etymological mysteries which had been spun. Reading *Orghast*, aloud, proved a curiously stirring experience; pronouncing the lines one could understand, sensuously rather than rationally, why they had fired acting of such openness and force. Hughes has a marvellous ear, and here commands a language free from all sound-limitations. Root sounds, stems, syllables, break apart, reshape to make new senses. *Boda kagaock, boda scrord*, something laughed, something screamed—and though we may not know the exact meaning of the words we can hear clearly enough what kind of laughter, what kind of scream was heard. Far from Persepolis, beside a sunny Mediterranean sea, I cried *urgith*, trying to fill the word with the meaning I knew it bore. I asked my listeners what it meant. *Death* was the unhesitating, and correct, response.

The sacrifice of normal verbal comprehensibility (to at least one part of a multi-tongued audience) in order to achieve a new openness, a more direct kind of communication, was one object of the research. Another, the effect of this on the performance of an international cast with no language in common, playing to a similarly international audience. Discovering our, and their, changes of response to the four languages, the varying degrees of specifically verbal understanding (following, on this semantic level, none of the *Avesta*, a few words of Greek, rather more Latin, in time a little *orghast*), were part of the endeavour, which became an adventure, a voyage of excitement and instruction, for the play-goers as well as the players. Brook had discovered, he said, that some episodes seemed to 'need' Greek, or Latin, that the sound-pattern of those languages expressed more perfectly, more directly, certain ideas or states of feeling. In early rehearsals other languages and other juxtapositions of idiom had been tried; and in late rehearsals there were some curious fortuitous effects of theatrical interest: as when through the flaming funeral rites there cut Irene Worth's voice in English demanding to know whether the fires were safe, or when, in a visual parallel, an assistant on a bicycle hastened after the Messenger from Salamis to take him the torch he had forgotten.

★

Naqsh-i-Rustam is a long line of cliffs, part of the mountain bounds which circle the plain of ruined Persepolis, sacked by Alexander in 330 BC, of vanished Istakhr sacked by the Arabs in the seventh century and now buried in desert dust, and of thriving Marvdasht whose industries are powered by the increasing output of the Darius dam. High on the rockface are the huge Achaemenian tombs, cut deep into the mountain; below them, the reliefs of Sassanian triumphs, including Shahpur I's capture of Valerian in

Two scenes from Orghast: ' a drama—opera, ritual, ceremony, theatrical action—with its roots in many things: myth, history, the sites of its performance'

AD **260**. Over the centuries dust dunes have built up at the foot of the cliff. The Achaemenian fire-temple (let us call it that, though the purpose of the building has been disputed), excavated to its base, rises now from a deep square pit. In preparation for the October Festivities the cliff-foot had been levelled to a huge parade-ground—less picturesque than it was, but a noble setting for theatrical action which formed part 2 of Peter Brook's *Orghast*.

Things began at 4.30 in the morning, so that they should end at dawn. The only light came from huge bowls of fire which blazed on the crags. The audience thronged the site, free to follow the action wherever it moved. From a rock by the tomb of Darius II a Vulture —the Vulture which had rent Prometheus, and dragged Sogis from his cage—screamed a summons; from a fiery pit below, Furorg the light-bearer led *Krogon geblott auld*, the old blinded King, on the last stages of his journey. He felt his way painfully up the rocks, followed ever by the pale, mad, chanting figure of the wife whose child he had killed, long ago. From the distance came a call from the voices of Hercules and Sogis. Sogis's mother heard it too, and came forward to greet the son who was returning. Reunion; and slowly, chanting, singing and murmuring in *Avesta* and *orghast*, the main characters from part 1 made their hour-long pilgrimage down the central path which runs the length of the site.

And the movement of their minds, their memories of deeds, battles and strife, took visual shape and verbal form in an enactment of Aeschylus's *The Persians*, done with violence and much movement, in hectic torchlit chase across the full site, zigzagging across the slow processional path and scattering the onlookers. The two actions coincided when the pilgrims had reached a space below the great central tomb, and joined in the choral invocation:

> King of old days, Our Sultan! Come, appear!
> Stand on your tomb's high crest, King of our King!
> Darius, Father, Lord, Preserver, hear!

When from the darkness of Darius's tomb-mouth the solemn shape stepped forth, the effect was overwhelming, and the impulse to fling oneself to one's knees along with the actors proved hard to master. What could have been just melodramatic became thrilling and awe-ful. Darius chanted his great speech in periods whose pitch rose step by step. (Only later, much later, did the analytical mind recall Hector in Berlioz's *Trojans*, and wonder whether the influence was conscious.) Atossa now joined Krogon to lead him to his final adventure in life, to a deep fiery cleft in the mountain face, an encounter with Mage and Sibyl. And then, while Xerxes advanced with his grief, and the Messenger from Salamis progressed and passed along the full stretch of the site with his long speech, Krogon was carried to rest in the fire-temple amid a counterpoint of solemn funeral chorus. Dawn was at hand. A steep path led straight to the top of the mountain, where already the gods were calling. The survivors went upward to greet *orghast*, the sun, irresistibly drawing the more involved members of the audience with them.

Instinct, intellect and genius, months of hard study and sudden late moments of inspiration (faculties of both creators and on-lookers made keen by sleeplessness, by the stimulant climate, and by the extraordinary spell of the sites), went into the making of *Orghast*. I saw it five times, under varying lights, from different places, choosing different aspects of the drama: one night never straying from the pilgrims while the actions surged back and forth, another racing to Persian assemblies on the hills and running to meet the messenger from Salamis. *Orghast* part 2 is, among other things, a 'spectacular', which makes stunning use of cleft and crag, plateau and sculptured platform, and also such chance things as the archaeologists' scaffolding round part of the fire-temple. No light except from fires and flare, and nature's. Electric sound at times, to fill the place with omens, and carry voices from cliff to cliff with strange resonances. The critics who saw only a moonlit pre-performance, with few people there, stressed the visual beauty of the show; but it reached its dramatic climax only on the last morning of the festival, at the single public performance, when the site was thronged.

Part of the Paris Centre's research concerns the interaction of different cultures. Krogon was played by a Japanese, Katsuhira Oida, Noh-trained, samurai film-experienced, with power and passion, jaw muscles of fine-tempered steel, a classical tragedian with a flame of violence whose emotions blazed in face and body. Furorg, Malick Bagayogo, came from Mali, soft-stepping, gentle-fierce, instinctive and beautiful; sometimes a grown Puck, some-times a grown Ariel, as he carried his torch through this world of dark complex feelings; a deep croon in his tones. Bruce Myers,

Sogis, tore thick animal cries from somewhere deep in his body, shaping them to words, and in the arch of his straining back could make us share the agony of a beast-intellect being dragged to the light of wisdom, to accept his destiny.

Irene Worth, Moa, divine Earth-Mother-Wife of the God-King, rang through her deep-based vocal spectrum. Natasha Parry, the voice of Light, shone like a bright star. Paloma Matta, but more eagle than dove, screamed the avian summons in tones which set the scalp pricking. Fahime Rastkar's grave gentle beauty as Moasha, Sogis's mother, brought the element of human tenderness to the fierce tale. And so one could go through the long cast—Michèle Collison's grandeur, of voice and bearing, as Atossa; Robert Lloyd's noble voice in the heavens; Pauline Munro's obsessed mother, following the King like a pale steady flame: Nazar Azadi's clear, heroic Hercules; the *Persians* chorus led by the free-voiced Darius Farhang; many others. Vocally and physically this international company had been brought to a rare degree of expressiveness.

Orghast will never be seen anywhere else. It is 'the product of the work done in Iran, and of the effect of Iran itself on the work'. The musics of its drama, the wide-flung counterpoints of speech, speech-song and song, the elaborate patterns of dramatic and sonic densities, to some extent the language itself, were all dictated by the spaces and acoustics of its sites. The western-based dramatic tongue which Ted Hughes has invented, the Greek mythology, the elements of Greek, Latin and Spanish plays, have all taken new root here, in this drama of darkness and light. 'From Zoroastrian times,' Arthur Upham Pope writes in his *Persian Architecture*, 'the beautiful was integrally associated with light. It was an essential component of the divine personality. Physical light in Persia— intense, palpable creative—persuasively expounds the role conferred on it by religion.'

Orghast was claimed as no more than experiment, a research-project, 'work in progress'. My surrender to it was not instant, but by the end it was total (except for details, such as feeling that the electrical amplification, recognisable as such, struck a jarring note). The playgoer who entered deeply into *Orghast* passed through fire, and can never be the same again.

Benny Green

Soothing
the Savage Breast

In the era of the non-musical musical, the lyricist and critic who script-edited London's current revival of Show Boat *reports on its re-launching.*

In the opening weeks of 1972 Mr André Previn was interviewed on television about his voluminous musical past, vaulting as always with consummate ease from the conservatoire to the night club to the sound stage and back again. It is often forgotten, even by those who praise him, that in the context of modern music, Previn is unique. He is unique because he is the only man in the world to have built bridges between all the self-supporting principalities of musical life. Even more remarkable, having built the bridges, he has then proceeded to cross them one by one, from concert hall (the Cello Concerto) to Broadway (*Coco*) to Hollywood (*It's Always Fair Weather*) to jazz club ('Shelly Manne Plays *My Fair Lady*').

Having established himself as the only musician, so to speak, to have circumnavigated the musical world in this way, Previn has succeeded, quite accidentally, in placing all his opponents out of court. When Sir Francis Drake returned from his world tour and described conditions in the Pacific Ocean, there were many who took exception to what he said, but it was quite impossible for them to argue. Drake had been there. And so has Previn. (Whenever I define Previn as being unique in this way, there is always somebody to ask 'What about Leonard Bernstein?' to which I always reply, scrupulously correct as always, 'What about him?') For this reason, Previn's televised interviews comprise the best con-

versation currently available to music-lovers, and are of special
importance to those who are fascinated by the question of relative
merits in modern music, with particular reference to the musical
stage. And in his first interview of 1972 Previn paid passing tribute
to three gentlemen called Henderson, de Sylva and Brown. The
fact that perhaps 98 per cent of those active in British musical life
have never heard of that trio only underlines Previn's uniqueness
as a man able to encompass so broad a view of music.

Henderson, de Sylva and Brown are the unholy trinity of the
song-writing profession who once perpetrated on a lamentably
quiescent public an outrage called 'Sonny Boy', an act which has
enshrined them in memory as the Three Musketeers of the tear-
jerking ballad, Bathos, Pathos and Onerous. Indeed, posterity is
so embarrassed about 'Sonny Boy' that it has usually sought refuge
in obscene lampoons of the original lyrics of the song. Even the
stereotyped witless bio-pic which was eventually tossed on to the
corporate grave of Henderson, de Sylva and Brown in 1956 had to
pretend that its execrable lyric had originally been written in jest.
(In which case it would not be very surprising that Al Jolson
took it seriously. Nothing Al Jolson did would be very surprising.)
But 'Sonny Boy' notwithstanding, Henderson, de Sylva and Brown
remain of some considerable interest to those disenchanted cus-
tomers who discover themselves time after time emerging from
West End musical theatres dolefully whistling the price of the seats.

Ray Henderson (1896–1964) was the team's composer, while
Buddy de Sylva (1895–1950) and Lew Brown (1893–1958) shared
the lyric-writing. (One fact which might just conceivably explain
how Brown came to use the language of Shakespeare as he did in
'Sonny Boy' is that he was born in Odessa.) For most of their
career, the three men concerned themselves with the cliché plots
of their era. There was the one about the two college football
heroes contending on the gridiron for the hand of the campus
queen ('Good News'); followed by the one about the two prize-
fighters contending in the ring for the hand of the working girl
('Hold Everything'); followed in turn by the one about the two

*'. . . and I can't explain why he should be Just the one, one man
in this world for me.' Cleo Laine as Julie with Ray Cook in* Show
Boat

lady golfers contending on the links for the hand of the men's champion ('Follow Through'); succeeded in the fullness of time by the one about the two aeronauts contending in the air for the hand of the working girl ('Flying High').

But before we start indulging in derisive laughter at the trio's expense, it may be as well to record the fact that from out of this welter of self-perpetuating garbage, Henderson, de Sylva and Brown came up with 'The Best Things In Life Are Free', 'You're the Cream in My Coffee', 'Button Up Your Overcoat' and 'You Are My Lucky Star', that in their flirtation with Hollywood the Three Musketeers disarmed criticism with 'It All Depends On You' and 'I'm a Dreamer, Aren't We All?', and that among their other exploits together there stand 'Birth of the Blues', 'I'm Sitting on Top of the World', 'Life Is Just a Bowl of Cherries' and 'Bye, Bye, Blackbird'. To sum up, Henderson, de Sylva and Brown had the elusive knack of producing melodies, and Mr Previn, knowing, like all true musicians, how rare that ability is, had been duly impressed.

Now it is certainly true that nobody in the 1970s can afford to laugh at a song-writing partnership capable of producing melodies. Indeed, if our own era can be said to have contributed anything original to the conception of the stage musical, which is doubtful, then it can only be that type of show which we all know so well, the musical without any music. It is usually accepted that the working definition of a failed musical is one which closes quickly. But there appears to be another, equally applicable definition, which is a show which runs for a long time without establishing in anyone's mind a single scrap of melody. Why should there be this paucity of melodic inventiveness? How come that Henderson, de Sylva and Brown, submerged as they were in a sea of half-witted characterisation and papier-mâché plots, could endow their scores with grace and inventiveness, while the modern composer, buttressed by respectable novelists and playwrights, weighty themes, and even weightier scenery, can still be dumb enough to create instantly forgettable music?

The problem of the non-musical musical and the attempt to solve it were both to be seen on the London stage during 1971 in several places at once, and may be symbolised by what were perhaps the two most commercially viable shows of the year, *Godspell* and

Show Boat. The success of *Godspell*, which was taken in conjunction with the promise of *Jesus Christ, Superstar* to herald the dawn of a new age of evangelical hysteria, is in fact a simpletonian sort of affair whose only genuinely sophisticated stroke is to crucify Jesus on a familiar-looking length of garden fence at the same time as it crucifies the audience on an equally familiar-looking length of musical wadding. The fact that there were those actually prepared to accept *Godspell* and kindred works as a sign that Nietzsche was wrong and that God is not dead after all, only slumbering at the back of the stalls, perhaps gives some indication of the depth of thought lavished on the musical theatre today. The truth is the precise opposite. The success of *Godspell* has about as much to do with a return to the Church as *Ben Hur* did with a return to the Roman Empire. Only when a received philosophy has no further relevance to the workaday world do the English ever permit the reduction of its most sacred tenets to knockabout farce. I assume that if Christianity really were about to enjoy a renascence, the first act in the drama would be to take those responsible for *Godspell* and *Jesus Christ, Superstar* and hand them over to the Inquisition. Oh, Torquemada, why are you sleeping now?

The revival of *Show Boat* represents a different approach to this problem of tiding us over until the arrival of a new wave of accomplished melodists, and that is to return to the old wave. It could be said that the revival of *Show Boat* was a retrograde step, but only in the sense that it is retrograde for the legitimate theatre to keep harping on Shakespeare all the time. The tactic of looking to the past for a good tune has been gathering popularity for some years now, on Broadway as well as nearer home, and the news that the New York musical theatre was performing an act of the most gallant and extravagant self-abasement before the dancing feet of an old lady called Ruby Keeler should not have come as quite the staggering surprise it did.

One of the most fascinating radio talks of the year was the 'Letter from America' where Alistair Cooke theorised about the Broadway revival of *No, No, Nanette*, the show in which the indomitable Miss Keeler, like some real-life incarnation of a faded Gilbertian blossom, was dancing her way to stardom all over again. Cooke very reasonably suggested that in a world in turmoil it was natural that the bewildered middle-aged should turn in desperation to a past so distant by now as to appear positively serene. After all, current intimations of Armageddon have lent the old bootlegging era, with its quaint old gang murders and pineapple bombs, the retrospective charm of an old-fashioned English garden, and it is that garden through which Miss Keeler has been tripping so daintily. But that is only half the story, the extra-musical half. It is perfectly understandable that the Class of '26 should confuse Ruby Keeler's immortality with its own, perfectly excusable that it should, as Evelyn Waugh once nearly said, take great healing draughts from the well of Jazz Age certitude. But there are two other very precise reasons why *No, No, Nanette* has been able to sustain a revival. Those two reasons are 'Tea for Two' and 'I Want to be Happy', either of which songs, if they were to grace a modern musical production, would be enough to keep it running indefinitely.

The fact that it often requires no more than one song of this calibre to ensure a successful run has now sunk in so deep that critics have become dangerously addicted to the phrase 'A one-song score', and tend to exhibit all the symptoms of acute musical indigestion the moment they are confronted with a two-song score, which, fortunately for them and unfortunately for the rest of us, isn't very often. *Hello Dolly*, which enjoyed a long and prosperous life culminating in the *folie de grandeur* of the last sacraments administered by the taxidermists of Beverly Hills, thrived purely on the strength of its title-song, which itself looked back, as so many of Jerry Herman's songs do, to the harmonic innocence of Prohibition. But its successor, *Mame,* was a slightly more complex affair, dismissed at the time of its London production as a 'one-song score' by critics who most selflessly left to their readers the task of deciding which song that was, 'Mame' or 'If He Walked Into My Life'.

But having nodded in the general direction of the no-song show, the one-song show and the two-song show, we arrive at *Show Boat,* the multi-song show whose revival has been dazzling if only for the way in which the extreme richness of its music has exposed the poverty of so many musicals since. There are, of course, many factors which contribute to the current triumph of *Show Boat,* several of which have already been pointed by Alistair Cooke in his disquisition on *No, No, Nanette.* But *Show Boat* swept the field largely because it contains one of the most remarkably variegated and prolifically inspired scores ever composed for the musical theatre. (The fact that I was involved in its revival does not, I feel, endow me with the privilege of hiding Jerome Kern's light under a bushel.)

For those who are interested in such things, *Show Boat* comprises a remarkable compendium of musical styles in the theatre over the last hundred years. Kern (1885–1945) was an American by birth, an Austro-Hungarian in early musical influence, a cosmopolitan by temperament, and an American once again in the eventual outcome of his style. He was, in fact, the man who rescued the American musical from the turgid protocol of non-existent Habsburgian Grand Duchies, and who earned from Richard Rodgers the observation, 'Kern was typical of what was and still is good in our general maturity in this country in that he had his musical roots in the fertile middle European and English school of operetta writing, and amalgamated it with everything that was fresh in the American scene to give us something wonderfully new and clear in music writing in the world. Actually he was a giant with one foot in Europe and the other in America. Before he died he picked up the European foot and planted it squarely alongside the American one.'

It is hard to know which to admire most, the relentless syntax with which Mr Rodgers embellishes his own prose, or the remarkable acrobatic dexterity with which he endows Kern's feet, but the point he is trying to make is well borne out by the score of *Show Boat,* which very nearly comprises a romp through the pantheon of the twentieth-century operetta. In the wedding scene climaxing Act One there are unmistakable traces of the buoyant rumpty-tump of Gilbert and Sullivan, while the verse to the show's first ballad, 'Make Believe', positively steams with the Ruritanian passion so widely popularised in 1908 by Franz Lehar's '*The Merry Widow*'. 'How D'Ya Like to Spoon With Me' is a distinct throwback to Kern's days as a jobbing apprentice in the London Edwardian musical comedy theatre. And with 'Ole Man River', which, with its uncomplicated line is curiously untypical of the great baroque masterpieces of Kern's maturity, 'Smoke Gets In Your Eyes', 'The Song Is You', 'All the Things You Are', we see the composer arriving at a style which might be described as indigenous American.

T.72—M

But there is a further, more personalised sense in which the score of *Show Boat* is a revelation to all students of the art of popular song-writing. It is always assumed that Kern composed the score in 1926 and that all subsequent revivals have involved the presentation of a period piece, also that any representations in the score of the old pre-Jazz Age are attempts by Kern at pastiche. All these assumptions turn out to be untrue. So far from having written his score within the compass of a single year, 1926, for one producer, Florenz Ziegfeld, Kern may be said quite literally to have lavished his time as well as his affections on the score of *Show Boat* throughout his working career, which, as it stretched from 1905 to 1945, encompasses a period when the evolutionary movement in live productions of musicals was remarkable both for its pace and its scope.

My first intimation that there might be more in *Show Boat* than at first met the eye came with my rediscovery of the fact that 'How D'Ya Like to Spoon With Me?' was a far more ancient item than the show itself. (I say rediscovery because at the time of Kern's death I remember having read in one of the obituaries that he had interpolated the song into a later show.) 'How D'Ya Like to Spoon With Me?' is used in *Show Boat* as a duet for the boy-girl comedy leads in a scene supposedly taking place in the Edwardian era. In 1904 the young Kern had spent some time in London, contributing occasional songs to revues and musical comedies for impresarios like George Edwardes, and incidentally knocking out one or two patter songs with an obscure dramatic critic of the period, P. G. Wodehouse. 'How D'Ya Like to Spoon With Me?' had been an indirect outcome of this period, which means that so far from being an attempt at pastiche, a calculated experiment in creating a period flavour, the song was the real thing, an authentic example of music-hall writing at its harmonic wittiest, which somebody like Marie Lloyd might well have sung had she only known of its existence.

There were much odder things about *Show Boat*, and the oddest of all was the way in which Kern had had no compunction about incorporating into his score the work of other popular composers where the action or the characterisation demanded it. He had, for instance, included in the same scene as the 'How D'Ya Like to Spoon With Me?' episode the old tear-jerker from the 1891 season, 'After the Ball', composed by Charles K. Harris, an ex-pawnbroker

ABOVE: 'The success of Godspell was taken to herald the dawn of a new age of evangelical hysteria'

BELOW: The shape of musicals to come? Donna McKechnie, Larry Kert and Annie McGreery in the London production of Company

and banjo player whose activities in those two strictly non-musical fields had so damaged his sensibilities that he died convinced that 'After the Ball' was a great masterpiece. For good measure Kern had also thrown in a snatch of somebody else's hit from 1904, 'Goodbye My Lady Love', composed by a man called Joe Howard who is remembered today only because his life was so relentlessly bowdlerised in the movie named after his biggest hit, 'I Wonder Who's Kissing Her Now'.

All this meant that by now there were no fewer than four lyricists to be credited in *Show Boat.* for in addition to Oscar Hammerstein, Kern had collected Howard, Harris and Edward Laska, the early partner of Kern who had contributed the words of 'How D'Ya Like to Spoon With Me?' But there remained a fifth, and it was this last collaborator who frankly interested me more than the other four put together, and who unintentionally helped me to realise that *Show Boat* was really a compendium, a musical holdall into which Kern never stopped thrusting his choicest musical fragments.

In 1915, Kern, at this time involved in composing the scores for a series of mini-musicals known to theatrical historians as the Princess Theatre shows, met one of his old partners from London days, P. G. Wodehouse, now in New York on a short vacation which was destined to last, with interruptions, for the rest of his life. Kern and Wodehouse had always liked each other, and now they quickly resumed their old relationship. Among the melodies Kern threw at Wodehouse was one which he had composed back in 1909 and had never named or seriously tried to find a lyric for. The prolific Wodehouse soon obliged, and in his book of reminiscences, *Bring On the Girls,* has since told of the extraordinary vicissitudes of fortune which this song suffered. It was dropped from two shows and finally, after Wodehouse and Kern had parted professional company, Kern to work with Hammerstein, Wodehouse to expand that phenomenal variation on *Burke's Peerage* which was to occupy him for the next half-century, was left in Kern's bottom drawer to moulder with all the other musical might-have-beens.

But in 1926, by which time Wodehouse, already deep in that summer dream of Blandings from which he was destined never to emerge, had drifted away from the musical theatre, Kern and

Hammerstein were suddenly confronted with the opportunity of planting into the score of *Show Boat* any old song they pleased. It happened that because in her last appearance in the story Julie, the mulatto ex-star of the 'Cotton Blossom', is rehearsing in a Chicago night club, clearly neither the lyric of her song nor its melody need conform to the pattern of Julie's personality, or indeed anyone else's. This was, in fact, one of those very rare occasions when the insertion of extraneous musical matter into a score, or to put it another way, when the return to the bad old days of interpolated songs, need outrage nobody's aesthetic morality. At which point the intuition of the actress performing the role begins to impose itself, showing how intangibles of technique and temperament may transform the nature of the raw material, restoring to it the integrated purity which is every librettist's dream.

Some years before the revival of *Show Boat* I had enjoyed a fascinating and highly educational correspondence with that delightful man, Mr Ira Gershwin, and had asked him about the inclusion of 'Bill' in a show for which it had never originally been intended. In his reply he pointed out quite correctly that 'Bill' was:

> a speciality number introduced in a nightclub scene, wherein any blues or torch song could have been used. After all, had Julie been singing in character and in a completely integrated score, the title of the song ought to have been 'Steve', the name of her erstwhile lover.

The interesting thing is that technically there was no reason why Kern and Hammerstein should not have performed in deadly earnest the amendment which Ira Gershwin mentioned in jest. 'Bill' is so constructed that a change to 'Steve' would disturb no rhythms, amend no stresses, disrupt no rhyme-schemes—except that for no particular reason 'Bill' is a more romantic-sounding song title than 'Steve'.

The role of Julie was played by Cleo Laine, who, remembering that she was succeeding Helen Morgan and Ava Gardner in the part, pointed out to us that she was at least the first Julie ever to be racially right for the role, and might therefore define herself as a Julie 'who was no pigment of the imagination'. More to the point was that when Cleo as Julie sings 'Bill' in the Chicago night club, it becomes two quite different songs. The first chorus is what

Kern and Hammerstein must have intended it to be, and what Ira
Gershwin meant by 'any blues or torch song'. But there follows a
second verse and chorus, and it is towards the end of that second
verse, on the words, unusually poignant and expressive for a writer
like Wodehouse:

> . . . and I can't explain why he should be
> Just the one, one man in this world for me.

that 'Bill' suddenly becomes as deeply embedded into the score of
Show Boat as 'Can't Help Loving That Man', 'Make Believe' and
all the others. For by projecting her grief for her own dead life into
the lines of the song, Julie flings to the back row of the circle the
fact that although she may be talking about Bill, she is thinking
about Steve, and that what began as the impersonal recital of a
vocal exercise has become transmogrified by the intensity of the
performance into a subjective expression of romantic despair. For
this reason it is the apparent non-runner 'Bill', and not the far
more famous 'Ole Man River' which is the musical climax of *Show
Boat*, and it just happens to be one of the curious ironies of that
most empirical of all sciences, the architecture of the musical, that
Kern should have crowned his masterwork with a melody he had
composed nearly twenty years before he had even heard of Edna
Ferber's novel, and more than sixty years before Cleo Laine's
remarkable re-creation of Julie. Indeed, it all happened so long ago
that in the autumn of 1971, after *Show Boat* had settled into what
looked like being an indefinite run, Wodehouse, approaching his
ninetieth birthday in a blaze of world publicity, told the *Guardian*
interviewer:

> I love writing song lyrics. I've had more than 300 copyrighted,
> I think. Everybody asks me about 'My Bill', which Helen
> Morgan sang in *Show Boat*. You know, I can't remember now
> whether Jerry Kern wrote the music to my words, or that I
> wrote the words for his music. Generally with Jerry it was me
> writing words to his music.

But on his own authority twenty years earlier, in *Bring On the Girls*,
Wodehouse explains in detail how for so many years 'Bill' lan-
guished untitled and with no words.

There was one last flourish to the score for the 1971 version of

Show Boat. On November 5, 1945, Kern was walking down Park Avenue on his way to a rehearsal for the first Broadway revival of his show. He collapsed in mid-stride and died six days later, on which President Truman maintained the unblemished record of politicians all over the world for saying the wrong thing in the wrong way, by describing Kern's output as 'simple songs'. The fact that when he died Kern still regarded his music for *Show Boat* as an open issue is proved by the fact that he had composed a new song for the revival, 'Nobody Else But Me'. It was the last song of his life, and somehow it seemed in order to achieve a final absolute symmetry by incorporating it into the Adelphi production, so that the score, without violating any of Kern's intentions, should symbolise his entire career, from its vaudeville beginnings with 'How D'Ya Like to Spoon With Me?', through its gathering maturity with 'Bill', into the start of his prime, with the original songs for *Show Boat*, and ending with 'Nobody Else But Me' and the inspired chromaticism of his late flowering. So far as I know, the current London production of *Show Boat* is therefore unique in the annals of the musical theatre in that it represents the full life-cycle of a composer's career.

Some months after *Show Boat* opened, there arrived in London a new American musical by Stephen Sondheim called *Company*, and in the course of a conversation with me, Sondheim single-handed broached the subject of his own melodic gift, reacted sharply to the general feeling that his score for *Company* possessed no real melodic content, and claimed that as the singers in the cast had succeeded in learning his notes, then he must have produced retainable melody. Overwhelmed by this artistic humility, I omitted to draw the parallel of the stones in your dungeon wall, which are each of them memorable if only someone will be considerate enough to condemn you to ten year' solitary confinement. In spite of the fact that to me many of Sondheim's songs sound like second alto parts, he may well be right about his own endowments as a melodist, although perhaps he is not quite the best-placed person to insist upon them. In any case, I should be very surprised if Sondheim's was the kind of special pleading that Jerome Kern had to bother with. Or Henderson, de Sylva and Brown, come to that.

Poor Johnny One-Note

A dissenting view of John Osborne by the drama critic of New York's Village Voice.

'In a rebellion, as in a novel, the most difficult thing to invent is the ending.'

Alexis de Tocqueville

'. . . Now I am boring. I am quite certainly the most boring man you have ever met in your lives. I see you're not going to contradict me so I won't let you.'

The Hotel in Amsterdam

Once upon a time, John Osborne was interested in the world as well as the private battles of his middle-class soul. He was a fighter whose roundhouse blows had a sinewy wit and hatred-hard logic. His hectoring gave voice to the disenfranchised and aimless younger generation of England in the late fifties and produced a vibrant, uncouth, honest, and abrasive *Look Back in Anger*. The play single-handedly blasted the smudge and blur of Victorian melodrama off the West End stage and earned him a footnote in theatrical history.

What has become the destiny of that seething rage, that call to social and emotional honesty? Audiences shattered by Jimmy Porter's outrage have lived to see its heritage—a sad and confusing

'The English look upon Osborne as their moral weather man'

spectacle. At forty-three, sixteen years after his initial success, Osborne's plays, *Time Present, The Hotel in Amsterdam* and *West of Suez*, are works in which literary muscle is turning to flab and ruthless self-examination is going to sleep. Once, Osborne could dedicate a play (*The Entertainer*) this way: 'To A.C., who remembers what it was like and will not forget it; who, I hope, will not let me forget it, not while there is till a Paradise Street and Claypit Lane to go back to.' But Osborne has forgotten; and there begins the steady decline of his craft, a prophecy which he is willing to chronicle despite its humiliation and encroaching tepidity.

The Hotel in Amsterdam, for instance, is filled with the bric-à-brac of the affluent life. Where Jimmy Porter and his candy store were outside society, Osborne now finds himself within the Establishment. The people who clutter this play are rich, successful, bored, and too tired to fight. Their lives are not a matter of animal survival or even aggressive lust, but one of bourgeois pleasures accompanied by bourgeois civility. Food, accommodations, endless gabble about prices and prestige fill the stage. When Jimmy Porter snarled at a recalcitrant world which took its toll on the spirit and the ambition of the young, the play helped crash class barriers. Osborne has lived to see a national permissiveness. The world has bent to his whims, and the effect is confusing for someone whose best plays explore the anguish of private disgust. If rage is to be valid, it must have a focus. When the targets shift, Osborne must find new ones. 'I see treachery everywhere,' he told Kenneth Tynan in an interview in *The Observer*. 'In my opinion you should never forgive your enemies because they're probably the only thing you've got.' Osborne's disgust, the power which feeds his rhetoric, takes on a smaller focus as he moves away from basic concerns. Comparing *Inadmissible Evidence* to *The Hotel in Amsterdam* illustrates how the timbre of Osborne's voice diminishes with his recognition of the smaller, more compromised circumference of the world he describes. The invective of Bill Maitland, the obsessed lawyer whose world is falling away from him in *Inadmissible Evidence*, gouges a passion and an irony from experience in prose which tries to corner life and punch it to the floor. It is a hopeless fight, but sometimes awesome to watch. Maitland hurls words at his mod daughter.

... But, and this is the but, I still don't think what you're doing will ever, ever, ever, ever, approach the fibbing, mumping, pinched little worm of energy eating away in this me, of mine, I mean. That is: which is that being slowly munched and then diminished altogether. That worm, thank heaven, is not in your little cherry rose. You are unselfconscious, which I am not. Quite rightly. Of course, you are stuffed full of paltry relief for emergent countries, and marches and boycotts and rallies ...

The speech spills on, forged with an energy which makes every conjunction seem a necessity, every word an embodiment of the self-defeating rage which is both the subject and object of the play. *Inadmissible Evidence*, in fact, takes on an apocalyptic dimension (not only in staging but in relation to Osborne's entire work) because it is the last flowering, the final vestige of energy before the suffocation. In *Hotel in Amsterdam*, Laurie—movie producer, husband, court entertainer—is on the weekend trip he and his friends take to Amsterdam to get away from their movie-mogul boss, K.L. Osborne's rage is directed at second-hand experience: press notices, nannies, the kind of burgher household which has sprung up mysteriously around him. Significantly, K.L., the man who feeds his wrath, is present only in his imagination. We never see him. He is not part of the society, but a spectre—perhaps villainous, perhaps not. When Osborne's main character, Laurie, speaks, we hear the words; but, without a tension from the world outside, we no longer care.

But I hope, at least, you will feel alone, alone as I feel, as we all in our time feel it, without burdening our friends. I hope the G.P.O. telephone system is collapsed, that your chauffeur is dead and the housekeeper drunk and that there isn't one con-man, camp-follower, eunuch, pimp, mercenary, or procurer of all things possible or one globe-trotting bum boy at your side to pour you a drink on this dark January night ...

The rhythms are familiar but the language does not cut through to raw experience. It is merely gratuitous rhetoric; the humour of which is lost in the absence of dramatic tension, making every moment swollen and prolix instead of pertinent.

Osborne's world has closed in around him. He has watched with a writer's clinical interest, charting his soul as it runs aground in shallow waters. Jimmy Porter's inability to do anything about his rage is indicative of Osborne's predicament. The playwright and his character are haters, but too cynical about the world and too ruthlessly absorbed in themselves to consider action. Words are a risk, but in comparison to action, talk is cheap. Sadly, *Hotel in Amsterdam* and *Time Present* seem like they were written by the very 'Colonel Blimp' he gave two fingers to in *Look Back in Anger*. Colonel Redfern, a military remnant from Imperial India, explains his reaction to England's waning power: 'The England I remembered was the one I left in 1914, and I was happy to go on remembering it that way . . .'

Osborne reacts to theatrical change with the same bulldog tenacity, disliking change without really understanding what it represents. Theatre must adapt to new worlds, but Osborne has dug himself in for a long siege. 'I think these new forms of theatre may supplant—are supplanting—what I do. There may be a case for them, but I don't see it, and I *don't want to see it*.' Osborne's desire to widen the circumference of his world is matched only by his instinct for standing still.

> TYNAN: Given an unlimited amount of money, what would you buy?
> OSBORNE: I long for space. I'd like to live in a place as big as a railway station. But I don't think I'd buy a jet plane or anything like that, because I never want to go anywhere very much.

Like Osborne, Jimmy Porter saw an ugliness and lashed out at it with a curious combination of charm and venom. Osborne has always been certain of his charm, the brute appeal of his verbal momentum. But the resources of his venom have been another, more mysterious matter. It is Porter who ends *Look Back in Anger,* retreating from the world instead of finding strength to meet it:

> We'll be together in our bear's cave, and our squirrel's drey, and we'll live on honey, and nuts . . . There are cruel steel traps about everywhere, just waiting for rather mad, slightly satanic and very timid little animals. Right?

Having traded on his rancour, Osborne finds himself in a strange, but perhaps inevitable position. He now has very little basis for his barrage of spleen. His sense of the world becomes a victim to his verbal strength, which acts as radar, bouncing off the ugly, intractable facts of life, It also sets up a barrier between him and the experience. Osborne, whose Jimmy Porter spoke to the restless educated 'red-brick' element among England's university graduates, now finds himself talking down students who have surpassed invective and demand justice and action. The world slips away; Osborne dismisses as foolhardy events he has not cared enough to understand completely:

> I don't know any students, and I certainly would not like to see a Negro minority taking over this country. A lot of nice bus conductors running the government isn't my idea of a sensible way out. And student power is a very factitious thing. It always seems to me that 'What am I?' is a much more interesting question than 'What are we?' but now they're all 'we-ing' all over the place. And acting as groups which I find both uninteresting and ugly.

What could be the catalyst for a more flexible, fictive imagination is merely dismissed. Osborne has always been more interested in individuals than society, but he has forgotten—or can no longer see—that a man's identity cannot be separated from a country's history or the men with whom he has to deal. He, like his characters, has cut himself off by the ruthless onslaught of his voice—an emotional, lacerating appendage of self which contains both a longing and an impossible demand for empathy. 'I've worked in the theatre for twelve years, but I've hardly got any close friends,' Osborne told Tynan in their printed interview. 'In fact, they seem to get fewer and fewer.'

Anger can outlive its historical moment. It is an ambiguous passion, criticising the past but rarely building for the future. Because of England's continuing liberalisation, times have changed and the currency of Osborne's wrath seems spurious. Jimmy Porter raged against the American moment—the sense of imperial destiny, of power, of coherence which had passed to America. England, however, has now adjusted to her role. Even though a loss of power may bring a diminution of dignity, there is still a saving grace in sophistication. It is not unusual for rebels to change voices as they move into a more comfortable middle age. Vituper-

ation numbs the mind; it keeps a man at a constant fever pitch.
Osborne has not been able to shake free from the legacy of anger,
although in certain theatrical experiments, like *A Patriot for Me,*
he has tried. The new plays show him finally coming to grips with
his own period of adjustment—one that may prove fatal to his
craft. As John Weightman observed in *Encounter*:

> [Osborne] is not so much concerned to find any general signifi-
> cance in his somewhat disabused acceptance of the fact that life
> is for the most part a series of disappointments; only he notes
> almost casually that he belongs to a generation which grew up
> during the war, and that their anger was largely directed against
> the conditions and the society which made that particular war
> possible. But the war is over and so are the conditions which led
> to it, and Mr Osborne has the wisdom to see that there is very
> little room today for the particular form of anger which they
> provoked in him and his contemporaries. Their anger came gen-
> uinely from looking back, but one cannot go on looking back
> forever, at least not if one hopes to go on creating works of art,
> or creating anything at all, nor is anger a kind of inexhaustible
> fount of inspiration, which can be switched from one subject to
> another with the passage of time.

The voices in Osborne's more recent plays are dyspeptic but
not angry. They are too tired, or in the case of Pamela, the heroine
of *Time Present,* too ordinary to rail against the world with any
precision. Where once Osborne's main characters created an
abrasive liveliness because of their demand to be heard, the main
speakers in Osborne's new plays are assured of a small, attentive
coterie. Laurie has his friends who let him go on about 'El Fag'
airlines and laugh as if he had just uncovered a new social caste;
Pamela has her friend, a successful, strangely masculine woman
M.P., Constance, at whose house Pamela stays after her father—a
famous theatrical actor-manager—dies; Wyatt Gillman, the ageing
and famous expatriate writer in *West of Suez*, has his family and
friends who join him on vacation in his tax haven west of Suez.
Nothing happens in all these plays. Each is essentially a monologue
in which Osborne has casually mismanaged structure and the sus-
pension of disbelief. Everything is tired, verbose, and bathetic.
The canker has been snuffed out.

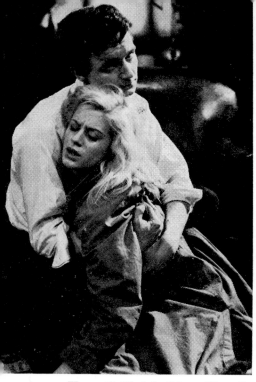

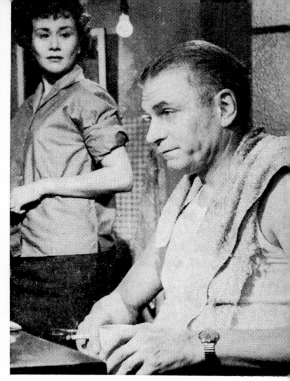

LEFT: *Kenneth Haigh, Mary Ure:* Look Back in Anger, *1956*
RIGHT: *Joan Plowright, Laurence Olivier:* The Entertainer, *1957*

LEFT: *Jill Bennett:* Time Present, *1968*
RIGHT: *Ralph Richardson:* West of Suez, *1971*

Osborne's 'heroes' had very little glory except their obsessed voices which crashed into the world. They were modern figures— failing, unfair, small. But at the core of their personality was a belief in the validity of their rage. Says Jimmy Porter in *Look Back in Anger*:

> Was I really wrong to believe that there's a . . . a kind of . . . burning virility of mind and spirit that looks for something as powerful as itself. The heaviest, strongest creatures in this world seem to be the loneliest. Like the old bear, following his own breath in the dark forest. There's no warm pack, no herd to comfort him. That voice that cries out doesn't *have to* be a weakling's, does it?

Osborne's plays uncover a heroic voice no longer in heroic circumstances. This is the tragedy of his characters up to now, but it is also their dignity. They are chest-beaters, unable to act but always willing to talk. And talk they do. Jimmy Porter, Bill Maitland, and Archie Rice (*The Entertainer*) demand gut reactions from the world. They settle for a good listener.

In *Look Back in Anger*, Alison, Jimmy's wife who suffers the thrusts of his ruthless barbs, explains the curious demands of this heroic timbre: 'He wants something quite different from us. What it is exactly I don't know—a kind of cross between a mother and a Greek courtesan, a henchwoman, a mixture of Cleopatra and Boswell.'

Once, the Osborne hero was seductive, his language precise, bitter, trenchant in its flights of satire. It was a voice which isolated everything and yet demanded impossible sympathy. There was a dignity in that stance, which all of Osborne's characters understood and were all too willing to explain. Archie Rice recollects a moment of beauty—a singer and a song:

> . . . But if I ever saw any hope or strength in the human race, it was in the face of that old, fat Negress getting up to sing about Jesus or something like that. She was poor and lonely and op- pressed like nobody you've ever known. Or me, for that matter, I never even liked that kind of music, but to see that old black whore singing her heart out to the whole world, you knew some- how in your heart it didn't matter how much you kick people,

how much you despise them, *if they can stand up and make a pure
natural noise like that,* there's nothing wrong with them, only
everybody else . . . I wish to God I were that old bag. I'd stand
up and shake my great bosom up and down and lift up my head
and make *the most beautiful fuss* in the world . . .

That gorgeous fuss was honest; it acknowledged a jagged
humanity. Rebellion is a gorgeous fuss, as is anger. But Osborne's
rage seems tepid now; the injustices he fought seem a petty scuffle
compared to the questions of genocide or colonisation which
haunt Western man a decade later. 'My instinct,' he says, 'is to
lower the temperature rather than raise it, because it seems to
me that there's an unreal sort of medium hysteria going on in this
country. If anything, it needs a bromide.' No more muck-raking
then; Jimmy Porter misjudged the effect of his choler. It was
perhaps a call to change, but Osborne in 1972 wants to move backward rather than forward. 'I'd like to see this whole headlong
rush into the twentieth century halted a bit,' he told Tynan.
Perhaps Jimmy Porter, like Osborne, was too easily cast in the
mould of significance. For both Osborne's fictional characters and
his real personality are, for all their rantings, politically unreliable,
combining fiery convictions with a dislike of mankind in particular
—a fascination with the self, unable to reach out to society.

Osborne has given up trying to make his words purify the
world. His earlier heroes tried; his present ones have forgotten
how. Laurie has sold out to the film industry; Pamela is lost between
mediocre acting parts and mundane affairs; Wyatt Gillman, resting
on literary laurels, admits: 'Thing about pain. It changes as you
change. But it doesn't go, does it?' But pain is now more a notion
than a fact. The hard fear behind the words of earlier Osborne
spokesmen has given way to a glibness, as if Osborne knows that
people will listen to him and no longer needs the security of that
relationship. The great fear, of course, was that no one would listen,
that the rage would be vented on deaf ears. Bill Maitland continually barks on the telephone, 'Is that you?' 'Are you there?'
Archie Rice, in his last song and dance, plays to an audience as
dead as the click of the receiver at the other end of the phone.
'You've been a very *good* audience,' he says. 'Let me know where
you're working tomorrow and I'll come and see you.' Even Jimmy

Porter's baiting of his wife is a childlike attempt to arouse another voice to counteract the sound of his own words:

> All this time, I have been married to this woman, this monument to non-attachment, and suddenly I discover that there is actually a word that sums her up. Not just an adjective in the English language to describe her with—it's her name! Pusillanimous! It sound like some fleshy Roman matron, doesn't it? . . . Hi, Pusey . . .

Behind all the voices in Osborne's theatrical rogues' gallery were a style of living and a disguise. Behind the bold, virile braggadocio about women there is a fear of weakness. They protest too much. For Bill Maitland, the sordid, nervous liaisons are sweaty, transient moments of forgetfulness; for Jimmy Porter, burning dissatisfaction. He says:

> I've just about had enough of this 'expense of spirit' lark, as far as women are concerned. Honestly, it's enough to make you become a scout-master or something, isn't it? Oh, I'm not saying that it mustn't be hell for them a lot of the time. But, at least, they do seem to have a cause—not a particularly good one, it's true. But plenty of them do seem to have a revolutionary fire about them which is more than you can say for the rest of us . . .

Osborne's obsession with invective instead of action has always taken control of his plays until with *Inadmissible Evidence* he wrote what is perhaps the longest part (Maitland) in English dramatic literature since Marlowe's *Doctor Faustus*. His next play, *A Patriot for Me,* tried to find a way beyond rage in spectacle. It was an interesting, bold attempt to get beyond his obsessional voice. Whatever the limitations of the piece, Osborne was building—or so one thought—for the future. However, he has returned to his previous pattern, but with a difference. The characters are no longer demonic. Before, his plays, as Mary McCarthy pointed out, resolved themselves in 'a kind of running down, the exhaustion of an impetus, a tire deflating'. There is no longer an impetus; his plays merely trickle past the imagination, occasionally finding a laugh or a moment of pathos, but more often, spilling over into his special brand of verbosity.

Although Osborne claims to respect the word, his texts are

loose and strangely undisciplined. They distort language instead of infusing it with greater clarity. His self-indulgence stifles the ability of his audience to hear clearly. Words spill out so blandly and in such quantity that the mind is numbed. The language of dismissal, the peckishness, which fills so much of Osborne's prose does not make for communication but only for static. Pamela, returning to an old Osborne war-horse, homosexuality, observers:

> Homosexuals? Well, they've mostly given me up. I'm ultimately unrewarding to them. Which is just as well . . . If you're a woman or a moll, you do have to spend quite a lot of energy flattering them with your sympathy and admiration and performing like captured dogs for them . . . Like most sizeable pressure groups, I suppose, and not even poor liberal Constance can really escape the fact, beyond all her Parliamentary recommendations, that as a group they are uniformly bitchy, envious, self-seeking, fickle, and usually without passion.

The language forces every auditor back to the simple question —so what?

West of Suez, Osborne's latest play, focusses more clearly, and with more attention to verbal detail, on his current obsessions with fame and nostalgia and boredom. Wyatt Gillman is visited by a sharp-tongued interviewer:

> MRS JAMES: What do you think about the class situation in England?
> WYATT: I'm very fond of it. It provides a great deal of entertainment, fun and speculation for people who have nothing better to do. Like many of the upper classes, I've liked the sound of broken glass.

The English look upon Osborne as their moral weather man. They expect him to forecast the barometer of their spiritual climate. Since *Look Back in Anger,* Osborne has made it a point to take the nation's temperature nearly once a year. As his predictions get farther from the centre of life—breathtaking in their misreading of the elements—he has begun to whine with a reactionary fervour. Typically, a reporter from the *Evening Standard* asked: 'Our readers would like to know whether you think England is finished?' Osborne replied: 'I think we should go down decently.'

West of Suez is an argument for style. The fossils collected around
Wyatt Gillman—butting into each other, arid, played out—have a
tenacity and resilience that Osborne admires. At the end of the
play, when Wyatt dies ludicrously from a guerrilla's bullet, the
curtain line is not about tragedy but bad form. Wyatt's son-in-law
leans over the body.

> EDWARD: There's an old English saying.
> JED: So? What is it?
> EDWARD: My God—they've shot the fox.

Osborne believes in the autonomy of language; but language
without action is deadly theatre. It belongs on radio, not on stage.
He tries to drum up facile fireworks in the second act by pitting
Wyatt's literary intelligence against the bitchy irrelevance of an
Island newspaperwoman. This is as heavy-handed as using a hammer
to kill a flea. Osborne's apocalypse in *West of Suez* is laughably
arbitrary and raggedly constructed: the kind of violent demise
dreamed of by old ladies at Harrods as they contemplate society's
violence over cucumber sandwiches.

A young American (of course!)—Jed—is asked to dinner; and
afterwards backs out on to the terrace cursing his guests, just
before the guerrillas sweep the stage with their gun-fire.

> '. . . Why we fall about laughing at your people, not people,
> you're not people. We are. But not you. You don't understand
> and why should you because, believe me, babies, old failing babies,
> words, yes I mean words, even what I'm saying to you now is
> going to be the first to go. Go, baby. Go. You can't even make
> love. Do you understand one word, those old words you love so
> much, know what I mean? No. If it ain't written down, you don't
> believe it . . . There's only one word left and you know what that
> is. It's fuck, man. Fuck . . .'

Osborne, bully of the old school, smells another fascist in the
woodpile. But what is astonishing in this scene—besides its haute
bourgeois fascination with rudeness—is Osborne's gross misunder-
standing of the nature of contemporary rebellion. As he told the
Evening Standard: 'Young people produce a lot of self-congratu-
lation. I don't see very much self-doubt.' Osborne advocates angst,
not action; voluptuous guilt not emotional evolution. Cut off from

the young and the disenfranchised, he writes about rebellion with only a foggy notion of its pain and real demands. As a result, Osborne's vision of the culture has as much shock and truth as a banner headline. He has become a victim of his play's universe where everyone talks but nobody listens. His spokesmen are no longer the Jimmy Porters of this world: a 'disconcerting mixture of sincerity and cheerful malice, of tenderness and freebooting cruelty; restless, importunate, full of pride'. Instead, it is the famous writer: posing, hiding, turning that stiff upper lip to conceal —even from himself—*rigor mortis*.

People revere Osborne's craft, and well they should. For many years he has opened his soul for the kind of public exhibition which is both thrilling and often embarrassing. But, no longer believing in the validity of that anger, cut off from the political radicalism which once fed his wrath, his theatrical possibilities seem limited. He is not a thinker, but a talker; he is not even an intellectual, merely smart. The fictional world he created is not one in which people interact and grow; there is only that stunning voice, highlighting everything in its radiance. Osborne has come to know his predicament and his people so clearly that there is no place for discovery in himself. Now he merely reports. His newest plays have no sense of unconscious insight, no mystery, only contrivance. In order to grow, he must be open to experience. He is not.

Osborne will continue to write and rant. People will go to his plays, remembering the embers of an earlier vitality and concern. He has, in his time, given us a theatre which adds to the debate of modern consciousness, which fills the mind with surprise and no little awe. But that variety of language dwindles when his world loses its focus. And Osborne, that grand gladiator of private despair, is in danger of writing himself into the sticky, soft corner which always betrays his heroes. He is already talking in the past tense. 'I think I was rather fortunate to live when I did. That sounds as though I'm talking about myself in the past, and I find myself doing it more and more. I think I lived in the right time for my own talent.' But that time has passed.

Tom Sutcliffe

That Bastard Medium

The current state of opera reviewed by the editor of Music and Musicians *who also talks here to Peter Hall, now director designate of the National Theatre, about his abortive Covent Garden appointment.*

Suppose live theatre really has collapsed with the advent of cinema and television. Just a few houses keep going with massive subsidies in London, New York, Toronto, San Francisco, New Delhi. In the UK there are occasional tours of popular shows to a few provincial centres. The annual diet at the leading house, the Royal Theatre, consists of about forty plays. You seem to get much the same audience all the time there. They see most of the plays once, and like to treat going to the theatre as an occasion. That has been bred into them. Another theatre, showing much the same repertory on about one quarter the subsidy that goes to the Royal, draws a rather more proletarian crowd. Most of the public for this kind of thing seldom goes to the cinema, seldom watches TV.

Last season there was great excitement when Gielgud did his Japanese *Lear*, though the critics said it was not what it had been sixteen years before. Then John Neville revived the original production of *Look Back in Anger*, to give Michael York a chance to do Jimmy Porter. And Gaskill's Royal Court *Macbeth* came back: rehearsed by Peter Dews, with Burton in the title role and Diana Rigg as his leading lady—total production schedule (partly because of Burton's filming commitments, partly because of his cost) six days. Very popular with the regulars was Sidney Poitier's *Othello*, in Dexter's famous production also revived by Peter Dews —the version launched almost ten years ago by Olivier. Strangely, another Olivier-connected piece, *Rhinoceros* of Ionesco, played to half empty houses with Raymond Massey in the lead. It is no news that the public will not go to experimental drama. Even Beckett loses money. Yet John Barton's versions of Goldoni are incredibly popular, even if critics are snooty about his liberal re-writing of the text. Last year there were no new plays performed.

It is an imperfect analogy, but that broadly speaking is the world of opera, a limited, protected isolated world, which may be characterised by the unattributable quote: 'I know it's ridiculous, but I love it.' In 1971 there were no new operas performed in this country apart from Britten's *Owen Wingrave* on television. The Berlin Deutsche Oper's production of Aribert Reimann's *Melusine* had a few performances in Edinburgh, and, at the Cockpit Theatre in London, Focus Opera (an off off company) did the Danish composer Mogens Winkel Holm's *Sonata for Four Opera Singers*. Nevertheless the repertoire in fact continued to age at much the same rate as that small proportion of the public interested in so-called serious music continued to diminish. These are related phenomena. Perhaps those of us who believe, against the evidence, that opera is (or can be) part of living theatre should start accepting this pattern of decay as natural. Yet if the dog is sleepy, and by most critics let to lie, it is still capable—to change the metaphor —of biting the hand that fed it. It can be controversial, it can be effective. While most of the time the opera public tolerates feeble conventions of performance so untheatrical that the general theatre audience cannot accept the art at all, on occasion when everything works it can be the most marvellous experience.

A colleague pointed out to me that I had scarcely written one single enthusiastic notice last year. Fortunately I write infrequently enough to avoid the total depression or Quisling compromise that would otherwise be inevitable. It is true that, from a specifically theatrical rather than musical standpoint, I am usually disappointed. At the same time I know my response to be untypical. The audience around me, which has paid its money and come committed to be entertained, manifests often extraordinary enthusiasm. In these days of publicity and propaganda one cannot rely on the audience's discernment to preserve or demand standards. It is already a running injustice that a sector of the arts patronised by so minuscule a proportion of the people should receive so huge a

subsidy, and those who want (and get) opera are prone to a Pan-
glossian smugness. Most music critics, who seldom get inside a
straight theatre, continue to affirm that everything is lovely in the
opera garden. Star singers, like so many Palestinian guerillas, continue to hijack arts budgets for their ludicrously inflated fees. Their
agents certainly do not object. If the existing audience is to be
satisfied, the auction for the star singers has to be met by larger
subsidies, which are invariably, sooner or later, forthcoming. Who
is complaining?

Any policy for opera which concerns itself merely with satisfying
and maintaining the existing audience is a doomed policy, because
of its manifest inequity. Only a radical change of direction will both
raise the general standard of production and remedy the injustice
of existing subsidy. What is needed is a new audience, a large
audience, a growing audience. Then the medium will become
effective. Then its finances will be secured. To state this now, after
Peter Hall's decision not to take up his post at Covent Garden as
joint artistic director, is like shutting the stable door after the
horse has fled. The Royal Opera, one of the most important opera
organisations in the world, governs our picture of how things should
be. With the Peter Hall episode, which was both a disappointment
and a poor reflection on all concerned, the possibility of radical
change (which would have been, at this house, influential to a
degree) was looked at, and baulked at. Silence reigned. Lord
Drogheda, chairman of the Royal Opera's Board of Directors,
seemed determined to maintain existing well-tried (and in some
views found wanting) policies. The Royal Opera should be not the
last place, but the first, to change direction. Peter Hall lost faith
in the practicability of his having a heavy involvement with the
place because he came to perceive the intransigent nature of the
beast. It should be a warning to us that things are not going to
improve. Opera like all non-folk arts was in origin a plaything of
the rich and privileged. It has not yet been claimed by 'the people',
but one need not be a millennialist to believe it inevitably must
be.

Last year at the Royal Opera there were three new productions.
At the Coliseum there were five. The Welsh National had two,
Scottish Opera four. The Handel Opera Society did *Ottone* in the
autumn, Glyndebourne gave a new *Ariadne auf Naxos* and *The*

Queen of Spades. The Camden Festival maintained its tradition of mounting low-budget productions of little-known works. There was a sprinkling of operas from societies and music faculties. As usual the greater part of operatic activity by the major companies consisted in the presentation of revivals of standard and popular works. The quality of such revivals is entirely subject to fortune. Sometimes everything gells. Perhaps the cast in question is almost identical with the original version, the impossible time schedule given the producer in charge is miraculously coped with. More often the result has as little to do with live theatre as Whispering Glades.

That the regional companies have finally come of age was conclusively demonstrated. The Welsh National mounted the first home-based (and English language) production of Berg's *Lulu* in the U.K. Scottish Opera gave the first complete cycle of *Der Ring des Nibelungen* in Scotland. Although the Royal Opera gets the largest proportion of subsidy of any opera company in the UK, and the London companies continue to perform a larger number of works, the axis between capital and regions is much better balanced. Both Welsh National new productions were by Michael Geliot, who has built up wide experience with this company. His *Magic Flute* attempted to get away from the usual view of the work by shifting its location to a kind of *Royal Hunt of the Sun* Amazonia. It was sung, however, in English. The new *Lulu*, drawing its visual inspiration from the animals of the Prologue, used a constructivist cagelike set. Whether the results were felt to be totally effective or not, they were certainly different. When Ken Russell dropped out as producer of Peter Maxwell Davies's new opera *Taverner* at Covent Garden, Geliot was drafted in his place. Peter Ebert's *Siegfried* for Scottish Opera completed his *Ring* operas in May, and the whole cycle was given in Glasgow in December. The cast contained some of the younger figures from the international circuit (or ring, dare one say), and the whole enterprise—perhaps inevitably, it was unthinkable a few years back—was greeted with more applause than went to the last two revivals, under Edward Downes, of Hotter's *Ring* at Covent Garden. Anthony Besch's English-language *Rosenkavalier* continued the happy Scottish tradition of finding new, and previously unimagined, successful roles for the delightful and histrionically very gifted Janet Baker. Both regional companies demonstrated teamwork of a high order, a fresh view, enthusiasm, qualities sometimes rather lacking in the metropolis.

Of the new productions at the Coliseum in London Glen Byam Shaw and John Blatchley's *Twilight of the Gods*, continuing the build-up of their complete English-language *Ring* cycle, was probably the most successful. If the first act drags rather, that is inherent in the work. But it was not a help to have rather dull designs from Ralph Koltai. The middle act, however, was from every point of view superb, and one readily forgave the untidy handling of the difficult immolation scene. When the problem of translation is properly handled, as it was by Andrew Porter, the rewards are immense. Wagner's operas are all heavy with text, and vernacular performance helps communication no end. If for no other reason than the reinforcement it gives to the opera-in-English faction, the extravagance of two London ring cycles, at the Coliseum as well as at the Royal Opera, has justified itself. Blatchley's modern dress *Cav* and *Pag* (why be pompous about giving the full Italian titles when the old pantomime horse is anyway sung in English?) was greeted with derision by the critics. But the new public which the late Stephen Arlen succeeded in luring to his new London base for his Sadler's Wells company supported it all the same. Perhaps they live on the bleak trading estate that the set was supposed to resemble, according to one Betjemanic diatribe, and found the realism moving. This was a different kind of opera experience from the received (and by the critics preferred) version of Zeffirelli at Covent Garden. But surely it is better to avoid duplication.

The band of working producers in the UK is quite select. None of them handled more than two new productions in 1971 for the major companies. Colin Graham, whose *Tales of Hoffman* was such a success at the Coliseum, came rather unstuck with his *Lohengrin* and fell on his face with *The Coronation of Poppea*. Admittedly it was bound to be hard to expand Monteverdi's delicate masterpiece to fill the vast Edwardian expanse of the Coliseum. Yet the problem with both works seemed to be one of taste. The tinsel crowns were not tongue-in-cheek. Perhaps they reflected the economic rigour of being Covent Garden's poor relation. Or perhaps the management felt that to attract the crowds you had to mount opera with the flavour of Danny La Rue at the Palace. Raymond Leppard's arrangement of the Monteverdi was certainly 'dragged' up, but that tallied with the production style, and the environment.

ABOVE: *Covent Garden:* Figaro *with Eric Garrett, Victor Braun, Geraint Evans, Reri Grist, Kiri Te Kanawa*

BELOW: *Sadler's Wells at the Coliseum:* The Twilight of the Gods *with Rita Hunter and Katherine Pring*

Unlike Scottish Opera, Sadler's Wells did not make good use of
Janet Baker in the title role.

The other two producers to get their hands on two operas were
John Copley, one of the resident producers at Covent Garden who
is having some success breaking out of that mould, and of course
Peter Hall. For those who understand the subtle (and professionally
significant) difference between the titles interior decorator and
interior designer, it will be enough to say that John Copley is
basically, and inescapably, the former. That need not be disastrous,
though it seemed nearly so with his new Coliseum *Seraglio*, which
he overloaded with inspired diversions like a particular kind of
brothel. Well, *Seraglio* is just that, I admit. But for my taste this
sublime piece of Mozart requires a childlike simplicity in its presentation, at least at some level. Selim's niceness has to hurt. Copley's
aesthetic, particularly the vulgar apotheosis imposed on the ending
by him, seemed just out of court. His other effort was honourable,
and greeted with audible sighs of relief by critics who had come
fearing the worst. He took over the *Figaro* which would have
inaugurated the Hall/Davis regime at the Garden. The result was a
competent, and really very good, traditional version. As with the
Seraglio, I was not fond of Stefanos Lazaridis's set designs. But
Copley got the balance of the production right, with some help
from Geraint Evans's old faithful performance as *Figaro* (was it his
1000th?) and a handsome-looking, if under-sung, Count by Victor
Braun. Copley did not succeed in developing very far his immature
Countess—the beautiful and lovely-voiced Kiri Te Kanawa. But
Reri Grist, a hard little bitch of a Susanna, did not have to learn
her role in English, and that, it had been rumoured, was the real
final breaking point between Hall and the Establishment at the
Garden.

A consideration of Hall's two productions—*Tristan und Isolde*
and *Eugene Onegin*—made an interesting follow-up to the exciting
success of his production of Tippett's *The Knot Garden*. The Tchaikovsky opera was not very happily received by critics who wanted
something more grand, passionate and R-r-r-romantic. It was
also sung in English, which offended some people's idea of Covent
Garden as the 'international' house, where you hear the real McCoy
in its original language. However it did have, as one would have
expected, more feel of theatre, almost of Chekhov and Moscow

Arts Theatre, than anything comparable that had been seen at the Royal Opera for a long time. This *Onegin* dealt in real feelings rather than the apology for feelings that usually passes, with a few limp gestures, among opera singers. Hall's *Tristan und Isolde* was remarkable. Again controversy rang out. Critics did not like the way Tristan in the last act tore off his bandages and left his wound exposed. Blood! It was too nasty. At the end, in the Liebestod when Isolde was reunited with him in death, Tristan rose up behind her, his hands stretching out along her spread arms. This, we were told by many critics, would not do. It was director's licence with a vengeance. Furthermore Birgit Nilsson, who took over the role of Isolde for Solti's last two performances as musical director, did not like it. Her solution was to 'just take Tristan away, don't put the light on him, just on Isolde's face. I cannot think of a better solution.' But that's a prima donna for you. In his production Hall followed, within the context of modern theatrical practice, as closely as possible Wagner's intended stage directions. The most impressive fact about this *Tristan* was the way everything worked on stage. In principle. In fact, the first night was plagued with technical problems. But the overall effect was theatrically exciting and deeply moving. The company, including the guest principals, really acted. It was, in terms of theatre, an experience.

1971 was a watershed for opera. Hall's decision not to take up his appointment was the gravest of tragedies. It seems to me the most serious thing to have happened on the opera scene in the UK since the war. During Solti's last year at the Royal Opera, after a successful decade, the intellectual vigour of Hall's approach to the problems of opera production, repertoire, public, gave promise of a notable (though inevitably difficult) time ahead. That promise will not now be realised. The conjunction of talents that we seemed about to witness cannot return. Hall has moved on, fancy free. about ten days after the news of his leaving the Garden broke, he was approached about the possibility of his succeeding Olivier at the National Theatre. Hall is adamant that his disillusion with the earlier post had nothing to do with this development, and clearly his feelings about opera are more basic than his concern for any particular public appointment. Now that his course is set, he seems pretty well lost, apart from the occasional production, to the world of opera. But in order to salvage something from the wreck, in the

way of discussion, opinion, potential, in order also to understand
better what has been forfeited, I raised a number of questions with
Hall personally. He did not want to talk about actual events at
the Garden. 'I made a mistake, and in resigning I let down Colin
Davis and John Tooley—two men I have a very high regard for. I
also think Covent Garden is one of the three best houses in the
world. My strictures about opera are not, therefore, aimed at
Covent Garden but at the system around the world.' However,
generalising inevitably came down to the specific recent experience.

Hall's musical credentials should be a basic factor in any consideration. Of course, he is not a highly skilled professional musician.
At the age of sixteen he opted for literature. But he has always
been musically literate. He regrets not having read music at
university, though those familiar with such courses may not. His
father was a leading light of the local amateur operatic society,
mostly Gilbert and Sullivan, which Hall now 'absolutely loathes'
and finds 'flippant, sexless, pointless, very unoriginal and very
dishonest'. Otherwise his early musical memories were of Salvation
Army bands, and old 78s of dance music of the 20s and 30s. He
started learning the piano at seven, and has never been without
the instrument since. 'I went to opera from quite an early age. I
remember in the early years of the war, about '40 or '41, Sadler's
Wells did one or two seasons at the Arts Theatre, Cambridge. That's
the first time I saw *The Marriage of Figaro*. I had a teacher at
school who had an enormous collection of 78 classical music, and
he used to have evenings of Camp coffee and fruit cake and selections
from his recorded repertory. I had piano reductions of all kinds of
music that I picked my way through. I can't actually remember
when I couldn't read music, any more than I can remember when
I couldn't read.'

His taste in music has remained very catholic. When I arrived
to see him, he was listening to *Jesus Christ, Superstar*, which he
was going to have to write about. The development and variety of
pop music in the last decade he finds very exciting. Particularly
because, unlike the theatre audience or the gallery public, the

PETER HALL: '*If ever you do anything in opera which releases
human reality, opera-goers get frightfully upset—that's not why
they go*'

number of people interested in 'serious' music seems to be, if anything, diminishing. 'I just long for somebody to come along who can take this great fertile mess of pop and use it in a personal way, as Verdi used that bloody old Italian brass band that was wandering round his village. Pop has a size of audience and a language which is all there ready, though you mustn't be self-conscious about it, and you mustn't write down, and that's really why I object to *Jesus Christ, Superstar*. Then maybe modern music will get out of its ivory tower.'

One of the inescapable facts of life about music, and the arts, today, Hall sees as the promotional phenomenon of brand-selling. The great divide between serious and popular comes down to this, which is a kind of class thing. Defined audiences exist and get catered for as such. 'Audiences enjoy getting what they expect to get, although they are slightly resentful when they get what they expect.'

From the first, Hall's response to opera was both musical and theatrical. When he saw that first *Figaro* he was about ten, and 'already hooked on Mozart in a very strong way. It was just unbelievable because I've also always been hooked on the theatre, and to see the two things operating was an extraordinary experience. I didn't miss very much from then on by one means or another. In the last years of the war at the Cambridge there was J. Pomeroy's company which had a good opera repertoire. That's when I saw *Falstaff* for the first time, and *The Barber of Seville, Rigoletto*. My background is not the Carl Rosa. In fact I don't think I ever saw the Carl Rosa. It was the Cambridge Theatre Opera Company, and then the re-opened Covent Garden and of course the Wells. I saw *Grimes* in '46. I was terribly excited by the work. It was wildly theatrical. In actual fact I'm not quite sure about *Peter Grimes* now, if you pin me against the wall. I think the reason why it's entered the repertory in the way it has is because of the basic nineteenth-century way it tells a story. It is in fact a nineteenth-century opera most marvellously done, not a modern opera at all. Another vivid musical memory I have is the Tippett *Child of our Time*. I then spent my national service in Germany, and saw a fantastic amount of opera. In the old stables—the Herrenhausen—at Hanover, and Hamburg where the opera company was still playing on the stage of the old theatre. I mean the whole auditorium was on the stage.

It was very makeshift. I went to Vienna, and Berlin, and I saw pretty much all the repertory. That was the first time I saw *Tristan* actually.

'I was quite pleased as a young man that opera was so special, for me and for this small audience that was sitting there. We were in the know. And I remember a certain smug pride at being there, and *knowing* about it and knowing what happened in the plot when I didn't understand it. That's now what I detest about opera. The interesting thing about opera for me is that all theatrical experience is bent on some kind of disturbance between the performers and the audience, and if the audiences are not disturbed they resent it. It's then a flat evening. If they are disturbed they resent it because it moves out of the convention. There's quite a contradictory tension going on all the time. I think it's supremely visible in opera where convention is so comfortable. I mean if ever you do anything in opera which releases human reality, operagoers get frightfully upset. That's not why they go to opera.

'My experience in Shakespeare has been exactly the same as my experience in opera. In Shakespeare as long as the actors wear the right Shakespearian clothes, and make the right Shakespearian noise, full of sound and fury, it may not actually be a marvellous experience but it's Shakespeare. It's what they expect, and everybody's quite cosy and comfortably a bit bored at it, but they like it. As soon as you start saying this Shakespeare speech is about this or about that, and you reduce it to something nakedly human, in terms of meaning, the majority of the audience is excited, and a minority of the audience (and often a vociferous one) is outraged. They immediately say "that's not Shakespeare". When I did the *Wars of the Roses* some nuts screamed "Shakespeare is not that violent". It was absolutely ludicrous. I couldn't believe my ears.

'In exactly the same way there is a minority in the opera house which wants to be kept comfortable. They don't actually want to know about incest in *The Ring*. They don't actually want to consider the moral values of *Tristan*. For instance, it's quite specific in the libretto of *Tristan* that when Tristan hears Isolde is coming he tears off his bandage thereby releasing his blood, and that is why he dies. That's a physical concrete fact. We know he's been badly wounded in the duel with Melot, and that embracing of life when

he gets so excited and happy that she's coming that he rips off the
bandage is the paradox: that's actually what causes his death.
I have never seen that done on the stage, although Wagner's
stage direction is quite specific. He tears off the bandage and blood
flows out. So I did it. I received an outraged mail. There were a lot
of outraged critics in the press too. This is a perfect case in point of
people wanting to be comfortable. They don't want to go to *Tristan*
and actually consider death. They want to listen to music.
They want to go to Shakespeare and hear all that beautiful language.
They don't want to actually consider that Shakespeare was dealing
with brutality and ambiguity, and horrible things quite often. They
don't want to even consider how coarse Shakespeare is, how bawdy.
It is the same thing, the comfort of Convention. Only opera's
worse than Shakespeare, and it's worse than straight theatre. I
don't think it's got anything to do with the music actually. I think
people hide behind music, but they also hide behind Shakespearean
verse. They hide behind the technique of ballet. They hide behind
just the act of going to the theatre—"I go to the theatre to be
entertained". Well for me there's no point in going to the theatre
just to be entertained.

'The objection to the vernacular for opera performances is
partly due to this, that we don't like the theatre to be disturbing,
we like to be comfortable. It's also partly to do with the snobbism
of opera. Every opera-goer pretends he speaks two languages.
Most of them don't speak any. One gets to the ultimate nonsense
of an entire opera chorus learning an opera in Russian, as if they're
learning Esperanto, and an entire audience sitting there gravely
nodding their heads without understanding one word. Now of
course this discussion about words or music in opera is as long as
the history of opera, and that tension must continue. But I can
hear the words in Monteverdi, I can hear the words in Mozart, I
can even hear a lot of the words in Verdi. I find it difficult to hear
the words in Wagner, but when somebody starts making music in
Wagner in a controlled and human way (as I think Karajan has
done in this whole series of *Ring* recordings) the dynamics are such
that I might actually hear some of the words.

'It's quite clear that the words are important. Yet the problem
is that the words are apparently so unimportant that the singer
doesn't need to know what he's singing, the audience doesn't need

to recognise whether he knows or not, and we're making music. Now this is all nonsense. I am still putting music first. I do want to emphasise this. I think opera begins and ends with music. That's what it is. But it is other things too, and music is not enough. I've got practically every opera I love on my shelves as a disc, and I'd much sooner sit at home and listen to them, than go and see a lot of people making arbitrary moves in silly costumes meaning nothing, in a language that the audience doesn't have the faintest clue about. Or the singer. Now I don't want to hoist my pennant to the opera-must-be-in-the-vernacular party, because I don't believe it. I don't believe in a dogmatic judgement. There are times for translation, times for original language.

'The famous *Figaro* which I didn't do, I very much wanted to do in English. As did Colin Davis at that time. Because we had something to say about it in English. I was going to do the revival in Italian, which seemed to me a perfectly just situation. It was brought home to me by an earlier revival of *Figaro* not very long ago at the Garden, in which that particular pain of *Figaro* was coming off the stage like one-oh; there it was, all that beauty, all that grace, all that wit, all that comedy, but the pain of it, the danger of it, which is something which fascinates me about that opera. And there was row upon row of seraphic faces with a Mozart smile, just bathing themselves in the cadences. This scene was a thing of terror, and they didn't know. Something wrong there, it seemed to me for a moment. At least it would be worth putting it into English to see if you could make them understand.

'It *is* a question of audience engagement. That really is what we're talking about. I don't believe you have any right to put something on the stage that doesn't totally engage an audience. That's all. Whatever medium we're talking about. And I don't want to work in situations where that can't happen. Sometimes one can do opera in the original language and communicate, I think, but you know you just have to judge the circumstances. Of course I am worried that the phrases, the sound of the words that the composer set, are not the same as the translator provides. Of course I'm worried by that.'

As Hall admits, the more subtly a composer sets words, the harder it is to render the stuff to his expression in another language. This is true particularly of Monteverdi, and other composers of

baroque opera which has for the producer versed in Shakespeare
and Jacabethans a special affinity. The time scale of the dialogue
has a natural and easy flow. People say things at the right moment,
theatrically.

Hall would agree with Joan Ingpen, who used to be Controller
of Opera Planning at Covent Garden (in charge of booking singers)
and is now in a similar position at the Paris Opèra—Conseiller
Technique pour la Programmation Artistique—when she said,
'there's too much opera in the world: there's a shortage of supply
of singers for the roles that people want to hear'. As he put it,
'there's a problem in opera because the number of people who can
do the roles is much less than the demand of the world for them. I
would say miscasting is the norm in opera, if I was forced to
generalise. Although they may be able to sing it, very few of them
can *be* it. Now that's not because they're not good actors, because
my experience of first-class singers is that they're just as good
actors as everybody else. They're just as eager to learn. They're
just as eager to work. They're not saying, "let me sing my beautiful
music" and don't bother with it. Not at all. I find them marvellous
to work with. But because there are so few of them, there are errors
of casting committed in the opera houses of the world every day of
the week, which you couldn't support, and wouldn't support in the
straight theatre. You just can't believe that that temperament, that
personality, has got anything to do with that role. Although opera
begins and ends with the voice, if the personality is wrong for the
role, it doesn't matter how good is the music you make.'

One of the major problems, of course, is that operas costing a
fortune to mount in ideal circumstances can only be performed a
very limited number of times because the audience for the medium,
in any particular centre, is too limited to support a run. Hall: 'I
think the opera audience is much too small. I think that is terrible.
I'll never forget during that *Tristan* production I did last year, I
heard somebody in the interval saying, "She's much better than
Tuesday, but not a patch on the last Friday." And I looked at this
fellow and I thought, is he on the staff, is he a critic? No this was
a member of the Covent Garden public, who by whatever means
apparently went every night. He was there doing comparisons. I
found that absolutely appalling, when the world is full of people
who say they can never get into Covent Garden.

'I believe that the future of opera, not just in this country but everywhere, must lie in getting a large enough audience to run a properly prepared piece for more performances. I find it extraordinary that in any house in the world you prepare a piece for five weeks in rehearsal, and you then do it for six or eight performances, and when it returns a year or so later it has eight or ten days to rehearse with a different cast. Now either you don't need five weeks in the first place, or what you're selling second time round is something quite other. Of course the second is true.'

I asked Hall about modern opera. Was the tradition a dead one, in the sense that perhaps the symphonic tradition was a dead one? He said: 'I can't see why it's dead, except that it is. There is no reason why it should be, and people keep on proving that it's not dead, but not quite proving it strongly enough. What alarms me about the operatic repertory is that if you look at the 1870s, the 1880s, there are works tumbling into the repertory which are still there. If you look at the 50s and the 60s, you wonder what the hell's going on. Nothing. Since *Turandot* what do you *have* to have: *Peter Grimes* perhaps, *The Rake's Progress* perhaps, *Capriccio*, *Intermezzo*, not really—you don't *have* to have them. The repertory is ageing at a colossal rate. It's all very well for opera buffs like me to go and say "lovely", but it's not going to get any new audience in. There are two problems about modern opera. One is the gap between the public and serious music. We no longer have a situation in which a whole country has Wagner fever or Verdi fever. It seems to me opera is landed with a shrinking musical tradition, but also I think modern opera's got to justify itself, because it's got to put on the stage something which cannot be a film, or a television play, or a straight play, or a piece of music. It's got to be necessarily an opera, and only an opera, and this is why I was so very attracted by and admired and enjoyed working on *The Knot Garden*. Because it couldn't be anything else except an opera. It was the only way you could express that theme. It was trying to open some new doors, and it was important for that reason. It was about now, and it was about what is in people's heads now. It wasn't in fancy dress, and it was essentially a musical concept.

'I do get excited by a lot of modern music. If I can follow it. I'm a reasonably sophisticated person musically. Sometimes I get lost, but all right I'm prepared to try. The trouble is that one thing music has not required of singers for many a long year is that they should sing. Just that. Now you can't really blame an opera singer who doesn't want to do a modern opera because he cannot detect the essential singing quality. He wants to sing. When you really reveal *Wozzeck* or *Lulu* and you cast them with people with voices who want to sing them, as opposed to clapped out singers or ladies with acid voices who can't do anything else except modern music, you suddenly realise that Berg's strength is that he did write to sing. Those two operas are fantastic, for me, because they're about singing. In many a modern opera, on the other hand, there is too much reliance on a dry dramatic leaping-about-from-note-to-note, and there is no feeling just of that basic human instinct of singing its express emotion. Now opera singers over-react, and many of them who ought to be helping the modern repertory say, "I'll ruin my voice". I can understand it though.'

Other problems Hall sees stem in part from an over-reliance on the theatrical model. Caution and a certain self-consciousness often lead the composer to use as model a stage play which is quite satisfactory as it stands. Creating new operas, like producing them, is an endeavour to make an experience both individual and necesary in that form. It should not be a matter of mere circumstance, that the inspiration ends up in operatic form. Most composers try their hands at the art, but sometimes it's really hard to see why they bother, or want to bother. Why do they want to write operas? Hall: 'Because there's something about that bastard medium, which when it's good it's just better than anything. It is to me, I'll tell you. I've spent my life in the theatre, and why do I break my heart in opera from time to time? Because when opera's good it's better than anything to me. Absolutely a more complete experience. Most of the time it's awful.

'The reason for that is largely economic. I actually believe that in the present circumstances of world opera, with the demand there is for singers and the amount that they can call the tune, with the quantity of routine and rubbish that audiences are prepared to accept in the name of opera which I think is fairly horrendous, I cannot see how an opera house anywhere can work outside festival conditions. That's my mature reflection. I think Covent Garden does an extraordinary job. But I still think it is ridiculous to ask a theatre to put on twenty-five productions a year of top quality.

There aren't enough hours in the year. It's not a question of anything else. It's a basic fact. But the audience size is such that you have to give them twenty-five operas a year. The singers' ability to go to other places and whizz round the world is such that they don't want to stay for long runs anyway, so it's a vicious circle. I only want to work in opera now, if it is in controlled festival conditions. Meaning that the given series of performance is special, and it's being done specially, and it will not be put on again in a routine way. There's nothing new in this. Opera workers have felt it for centuries—it's why Wagner started Bayreuth.'

In the aftermath of Peter Hall's resignation it has looked as though the job which existed for him had suddenly disappeared. The partnership with Colin Davis had fantastic potential. When Davis was, as he put it, 'left at the altar', or as Hall admits—with deep regret—'let down', his answer to questions about a successor for Hall were that he wasn't contemplating another marriage. 'If you're left standing, you think twice before you try again.' Well, he's had time to think. The pressures on a theatrically orientated Artistic Director would be, in effect, heavier than on a Musical Director who also conducts. Davis bears joint responsibility, with his Board of Directors, for policy. He bears sole responsibility for performance only when he is in the pit with his baton. A producer isn't in charge in the same way, but he is held just as, if not more, responsible. The Musical Director can be away half the year, running a symphony orchestra. The Artistic Director needs to be at it all the time. If there is a successor to Hall, a man of the theatre to balance the musical side, he will have his work cut out. Until there is such a successor appointed, it must be assumed that the management at Covent Garden has still not regained the nerve it lost when confronted by the phenomenon of Peter Hall. We must wait in hope.

Richard III:
A Production Diary

An associate director of the Royal Shakespeare Company, Terry Hands was the first Englishman invited to direct at the Comédie Française where he worked early in 1972.

January 9th: Arrive Paris. Settle in. Eleven weeks to go.

January 10th: Talk to Hirsch* about Richard. Ideas? Problems? Questions? He explains that he works simply from the text and what happens in rehearsal. No problems therefore, no questions.

January 11th: Prearranged date for first meeting with cast. Nobody warned. No meeting.

January 12th: Succeed in starting. Read prepared first talk. Try to explain Elizabethan background to the play, cruelty, energy, Renaissance idealism. Look for reactions. None. Ring of friendly faces more interested in the processes of speech than the content. Me too—for different reasons. Try a joke. Mistake. Get bogged down in description of English Morality Plays. Should have worked in La Fontaine instead. Essentially the purpose of this first talk is to explain the English 'tragi-comic' form. French classical drama tends to be compartmentalised. You don't normally laugh during tragedies, nor weep at comedies. Shakespeare on the other hand puts a fool into *King Lear*, Malvolio into a dungeon, and Richard laughs his way to eleven murders. Equally, at the Comédie Française 'tragic' and 'comic' actors tend to be divided. You are one **or**

* Robert Hirsch, the distinguished French actor who was to play the lead.

LEFT: *Robert Hirsch as Richard*
RIGHT: *Ludmila Mikael as Lady Anne*

BELOW: *'Cruelty, energy, Renaissance idealism': Richard with Buckingham (Jacques Charon)*

the other—the long nose pointing toward tragedy, the retroussé toward comedy. The cast is made up of their top comic actors: Hirsch, Charon, Gence, Samie, Duchaussory. To them *Richard III* is a tragedy.

Some reassurance is necessary. Try to explain Shakespeare's freedom. No rules. The only discipline his text. We communicate his words. If they're funny the audience will laugh, if serious fall silent. We must embrace the unity of his imagery and the disunity of his style. Act III Sc 7 is virtually Vaudeville, Act IV Sc 4 Greek. Shakespeare appears to be more revered than liked in France. French productions tend to make him consistent: unrelievedly tragic or fairy-tale romantic. Experimental productions appear to maintain the process more grimly. 'Richard III is a kind of evil El Cid'. First reaction. '*Richard III* is a tragedy played like a comedy, or a comedy played like a tragedy'. Second reaction. Both puzzled. In desperation: 'Richard III is like a Racine hero shot by a Feydeau heroine'. Great joke. They don't believe it—but at least they're intrigued.

Hand over to Farrah, who explains in immaculate French the model and costumes. All changed from Stratford. Wish directors had something one could look at. Two hours pass. Ideas? Problems? Questions? Apparently they like to work simply from the text and from what happens in rehearsal. No problems therefore, no questions. Half the cast leaves. They have other rehearsals. 'But the Richard cast was to be free.' 'Yes, but it's been changed.' The day finishes.

January 13th: Matinée at Champs Elysée, matinée at Richelieu, evening shows Champs Elysée, Richelieu and Odéon. No cast. Can't rehearse.

January 14th: Start proper rehearsals in the Foyer de Public. It has a red carpet, mirrors, chandeliers, busts of Molière, Racine, Corneille, red velvet curtains and the chair Molière died in. There is no proper atmosphere the actors can use, and insufficient acting acoustic. The alternatives are the Foyer des Artistes, similar but smaller, and an over-heated salle named after Mounet Sully. Nowhere is there a space large enough to mark out the stage, nor neutral enough for the actors to imagine the world they inhabit.

The system consequently is to rehearse half the rehearsal period in these rooms and then on the stage itself. The Comédie Française has always rehearsed this way. The result is a withdrawn working process. You can't fight chandeliers and velvet so nobody tries to. Moves are demanded, lines learnt. A kind of polished ballet develops. Little contact, less energy. Everybody waits on the move to the stage. But here they are forced into performance before they're ready. Exploration is halted. Moves are polished; lines are polished —to the point where one can almost see the paper they are being mentally read from. No risks are taken and the plays remain consistent and safe: Shakespeare is neither.

Rehearse first two scenes. Start round the table analysing and clarifying the text. Refuse to give moves. Paralysis except for Hirsch who instinctively moves with the thought. Try improvisation. Total paralysis. Clearly there's no point in trying to change an established system. Try to use it. Start giving moves— varying each move with the change of thought. Scene one between Clarence, Richard and Brackenbury takes a shape. Go back over the scene changing every move. The scene takes another shape. Actors remain perfectly happy. Some kind of method develops. A sort of protracted improvisation, bringing the concentration constantly back to the words. The process is cerebral but over the weeks leads to instinct.

January 15th: Rehearse Lady Anne scene. Enjoyable day. With their conservatoire training neither Hirsch nor Mikael find any difficulty in understanding that emotions can be passionate and articulate. Above all they accept simply and easily that motivation can be subordinate to rhythm.

ANNE: *Tu n'as de place nulle part, qu'en enfer.*
RICHARD: *Si vous le permettez, peut-être ailleurs . . .*
ANNE: *Un donjon!*
RICHARD: *Votre lit.*
ANNE: *Que l'insomnie hante le lit où tu couches!*
RICHARD: *Elle le hantera, Madame,*
              Jusqu'à ce que j'y couche avec vous.
ANNE: *Je l'espère.*
RICHARD: *Je le sais.*

ANNE: And thou unfit for any place but hell.
RICHARD: Yes, one place else, if you will hear me name it.
ANNE: Some dungeon!
RICHARD: Your bed-chamber.
ANNE: Ill rest betide the chamber where thou liest!
RICHARD: So will it, Madam,
             Till I lie with you.
ANNE: I hope so.
RICHARD: I know so.

In England the question inevitably arises: 'Why doesn't she spit at him when he mentions bed?' In France no problem. 'She's not thinking. She responds automatically. She needs time to think and Richard doesn't give her any. The rhythm continues to: *Je le sais.* In any case going to bed with him would be nothing to marrying him. That's where she ought to spit. Where Shakespeare puts it.'

In general this kind of scene turns out to be the easiest for the French—to understand anyway. Like the scene between Richard and Elizabeth. They accept debate. In England the danger is either that emotions are generalised and swamp the lines or detailed motivations are sought which introduce 'bridge passages' where none are written. On the other hand crowd scenes like Act I Sc 3 or Act II Sc 1 are relatively easy with English actors. They accept the life of reaction and concentration, responding to the speaker but maintaining their characters. At the Comédie Française both scenes become nightmares. As Marguerite starts to speak everybody, save Hirsch, freezes. Every attempt to emphasise 'situation' as opposed to 'blocking' meets with the same response —or lack of it. The problem lies partly, I think, in the classical tragedy training—long speeches are arias, you pose and wait—and partly in protocol. *Pensionnaires* are less important than *Sociétaires.* Charon is the *Doyen*, and very important. His name is inscribed in gold on a marble plaque going back to the seventeenth century. He may also park his car where a proper rehearsal room is finally being built, while the others, including Hirsch who is merely the *Vis-Doyen*, trundle all over Paris looking for space. So when he speaks all fall silent. They also stop acting. We try improvisations and simple Stanislavsky exercises. They respond politely, but half-heartedly. It turns out, also, that they don't like liquid in goblets they're supposed to be drinking from, physical contact or 'real' props.

Directing Act I Sc 3 and Act II Sc 1 becomes painting by numbers. 'When she says that, you go yellow; when she says that, you go blue.' Dutifully they go yellow and blue. It isn't until the last week of rehearsals that the company finally comes alive to these two scenes, and begins playing with the richness and detail that no director can give. They are over-worked. They put on twenty-five plays a year (before Dux, the present *Administrateur Générale*, it was nearer sixty), most of them revivals. Like an opera house they are used to learning lines and moves in a fortnight and reproducing them exactly. Consequently they find Shakespeare's rhetorical discipline easy, his freedom difficult. After a month I have seen little invention, received five questions (three of them from Jane Shore, who doesn't feature in Shakespeare's cast list) and no ideas. The atmosphere is calm and reverent. Over-reverent—particularly towards directors.

February: Hirsch learns the entire role in two days. Having adopted a method of 'move with the thought', discover that the thoughts expressed in French often lack the intensity of the English. Suggested reactions over-ride the power of the line. The translation is already in its fourth draft after nearly a year's consultations with the translator Jean-Louis Curtis. But it still doesn't sound right. We can understand Shakespeare perhaps because the language appears to have developed naturally from the mediaeval through to today. An augmented rather than broken tradition. French on the other hand seems enviously to have lost touch with the language of Rabelais. It can be understood but doesn't seem to be of use for translations. It's as though a purifying influence has been at work from the eighteenth century on clarifying ambiguity, abolishing inconsistency. No clusters of adjectives, therefore, few foreign words. The translation works in phrases. The basic form the Alexandrine—less pungent than Shakespeare's iambics. The words come in a regular order and at a regular length. For instance Lady Anne in her monologue talks of her husband: *'Poignardé par celui qui te porta ces coups'.**

In English the word 'wounds' can be long or short. Lady Anne

* 'Stabb'd by the self-same hand that made these wounds'

can be repelled by the idea, or relish the horror. She can also indicate the corpse of Henry VI by stressing *these*. In French, '*ces coups*' is a phrase, and consequently indivisible by stress. And '*coups*' is a short word. It cannot be stretched. While the English Lady Anne is free to elaborate—or over-elaborate—the French is tied to acceptable pronunciation. All the more difficult in a monologue which rises on a wave of emotion, above a corpse which audiences resolutely misconstrue as that of her husband. On the other hand where Shakespeare flows the French can flow too:

'I pour the helpless balm of my poor eyes.'
'*Je verse le baume impuissant de mes pleurs.*'

The problem of stress remains. For a start personal pronouns. 'We wait upon your Grace'—Buckingham's line at the end of Act II Sc 1. Edward is dying, Clarence is dead. At Richard's instigation the other lords leave to comfort Edward. Buckingham and Ratcliffe choose to remain. It appears deliberate. One can therefore stress the we. '*We* wait upon your Grace.' The beginnings of a link-up between Buckingham and Richard are at once suggested. Alternatively the other lords can remain with Buckingham and Ratcliffe, and one can run the line on its iambics.

In French there is no choice. 'Nous *suivons Votre Grâce*', is not permissible. '*Nous*' and '*suivons*' have to be linked. One can double the pronoun: 'Nous, *nous suivons Votre Grâce*'. But it makes the suggestion a certainty. To retain Shakespeare's ambiguity Buckingham has to do something: smile, offer a hand, something. The moment comes perilously close to 'wink and nudge' acting. The problem is at its worst in Richard's last soliloquy. He examines the idea of himself, contemplates suicide, in effect debates with himself about himself. The soliloquy is full of words like self, myself, I.

'Richard loves Richard; that is, I am I.'
'*Richard aime Richard. Je suis moi.*'

The one word you cannot stress is '*Je*'. The totality of Richard's statement and all that it implies after four acts of the play is limited to a rule of French grammar. We try doubling the phrase: '*Je suis moi, je suis moi*', and stress the second '*moi*'. But again a gesture has to be used to maintain the force of the English.

Further problems with adjectives. Particularly in active phrases— the famous ones. 'Relenting fool and shallow changing woman'—

the contemptuous rhythm, each word prancing after the other towards the dismissive balance of fool and woman—can't be done. 'A jolly thriving wooer'—('stress each word, relish the trampoline effect, bounce off towards your bride'). *'Un joyeux vert galant.'* Can't be done. *'Vert galant'* is one phrase. Instead of three stresses we have to settle for two.

The French Classical Tragedy makes great use of *la tirade*—a long rhetorical speech controlled, often with great subtlety, toward one basic point on the basis of one emotional state. Shakespeare rarely uses it. A long monologue contains any number of different thoughts. The effect is perhaps less sonorous than the French, on the other hand the changes—and their swiftness—are perhaps the source of Shakespeare's energy. Working with English actors one is aware of them searching for meanings of words, how to stress, how to catch a particular flavour in a general phrase. Working with the French actors one finds them looking for where to breathe. The phrase is all important; the individual word generally subservient to the whole.

With such major differences in language and technique there is little hope of retaining exact literary parallels with the English. Nor perhaps any need. The theatre isn't an intellectual medium. The actor has a wealth of meaning he can communicate with pure sound alone. We start concentrating on rhythms. If we can catch the rhythms of the English text perhaps we can convey emotionally the English meanings. 'Relenting fool and shallow changing woman' —starts as *'La folle, elle a fléchi! Pauvre gironette'*—progresses to *'Pauvre gironette, elle a fléchi. Femme futile et changeante'*—and ends up: *'Pauvre gironette, futile et changeante femme.'* It's not good French but the rhythm's right. We start to get somewhere.

'Joyeux vert galant.' Can't do anything with the words, but Hirsch throws his sceptre twirling in the air, catches it, slams his good foot on to the stage, and sets off for the wings. The spirit is caught and we've got the third stress. The actors join in the game. What's the line in English? What can it convey? What should it convey? They suggest changes, different words. Curtis keeps up an unending supply of synonyms, and together with Charon becomes a kind of *arbiter elegantarium*. Duchaussory wanders off with:

'Soudain il m'a semblé que Gloucester trébuchait
Sur les planches branlantes du tillac,
Et qu'en tombant il me poussait par-dessus bord,
Alors que je voulais le retenir,
Et je chois dans les vagues déchaînées de l'Océan'—

As we pac'd along
Upon the giddy footing of the hatches,
Methought that Gloucester stumbled; and, in falling,
Struck me, that thought to stay him, overboard
Into the tumbling billows of the main.

and comes back with:
'En marchant sur les planches branlantes du tillac,
Soudain, il m'a semblé Richard trébuchait
Et qu'en tombant, alors que je voulais le retenir,
Il me poussait par-dessus bord,
Et je chois dans les vagues déchaînées de l'Océan.'

The actors cease to worry over-much about blocking. They
move when the thought changes, even if the move is only a change
of weight from one foot to the other. Business is invented to catch
the rhythms of the English, when the French words can't do it on
their own. Everything and anything is used to communicate the
changes of mood that Shakespeare demands. The play begins to
sound right, neither particularly French nor English, but alive.
The qualities of the company become more evident. They are a
language company as the RSC tries to be. Given the problems
of the text, they delight whenever possible in finding the solutions
verbally. And when Shakespeare's rhetoric matches their own
tirade as in Act IV Sc 4—the lamentation of Margaret, Queen
Elizabeth, and the Duchess of York—they give it a quality of
control, yet intensity, I've rarely heard in England. And their
voices are magnificent. Given the freedom to use all their equipment
they seem to me to be ideally suited to this play.

In England most training is still largely Stanislavsky based. In
France one feels the influence of the Commedia Del Arte. Where the
English actor finds no difficulty in accepting the idea of variation
in style he has trouble accomplishing it. Stanislavsky often uses
bridge passages from one emotion to another. Shakespeare rarely.

CRÉATION A LA COMÉDIE-FRANÇAISE

RICHARD III

de WILLIAM SHAKESPEARE

TEXTE FRANÇAIS DE M. JEAN-LOUIS CURTIS

MM.			
		Lovel	Jean-Noël SISSIA
Buckingham	Jacques CHARON	*Richmond*	François BEAULIEU
Richard	Robert HIRSCH	*Ratcliffe*	Nicolas SILBERG
L'Evêque d'Ely	Jacques EYSER	*Lord Hastings*	Hervé SAND
Premier Assassin	Jean-Paul ROUSSILLON	*Rivers*	Jean-François RÉMI
Le Roi Edouard IV		*Tyrrel*	Jean-Luc BOUTTÉ
Le Spectre de Henry VI..	François CHAUMETTE	*Le Lord Maire*	Louis ARBESSIER
Lord Stanley	Michel ETCHEVERRY		
Deuxième Assassin	Michel AUMONT		Mmes
Brackenbury	René CAMOIN	*La Reine Marguerite*	Denise GENCE
Clarence	Michel DUCHAUSSOY	*La Reine Elisabeth*	Catherine SAMIE
Catesby	Simon EINE	*Lady Anne*	Ludmila MIKAËL
Vaughan	MARCO-BÉHAR	*Jane Shore*	Virginie PRADAL
Grey	Marcel TRISTANI	*La Duchesse d'York*	Aline BERTRAND

Décors et costumes de M. FARRAH,
décorateur associé à la Royal Shakespeare Company

Musique de M. Guy WOOLFENDEN.
directeur de la Musique à la Royal Shakespeare Company

Mise en scène de M. Terry HANDS,
metteur en scène associé à la Royal Shakespeare Company

'. . . *with* Terry Hands' *production of* Richard III *the Comédie Française has re-established itself as one of the world's great companies'*—HAROLD HOBSON, The Sunday Times, *June 4th, 1972*

The Comédie Française actors on the other hand find difficulty in accepting the *idea* of variability but have all the training to accomplish it. Hirsch switches from tension to gaiety in a line, and then back again. Laughing clown to pathetic clown by an inflexion. Charon gets all gummed up with speaking well, stops worrying, and starts playing like he plays Feydeau. With their leadership the others respond. The play starts to be revealed rather than explained. Begin to understand why *élan* and *panache* are French words.

March: Problems with the stage-hands. The union clashing with the management. Richard III is made the battle-ground. A work to rule is called. No overtime. Our 11 a.m. to 6 p.m. sessions on the stage become 12 p.m. to 5 p.m. A fortnight before opening three overnight lighting sessions have to be cancelled. The ancient traditions of the theatre creak into action. The committee of the *Sociétaires* meets with Dux. He decides to cancel evening performances on Sunday 19th, Monday 20th and Tuesday 21st to allow time within the stage-staff's normal working hours for the lighting to be done. It's an unheard of decision. The union retaliates by calling a strike from midnight Saturday to midnight Wednesday. Guy Woolfenden and I become very English; mutter '*Tout ira bien*', and check post-horses to Calais. Farrah smiles. Dux decides to call an *Assemblée Générale*. This too is a tradition, but rarely invoked. In times of crisis all the workers in the theatre can be gathered together to talk it out. There is no chairman—all are equal. Three hundred people gather in the auditorium—another half day's rehearsal lost. Foreigners are excluded.

It is an extraordinary sight. The Richard cast in costume scattered amongst blue-overalled stage-hands and electricians. Wardrobe staff, administrators, wig-makers, scene builders, prop men, prompters, stage managers and dressers. The full staff of a great and famous theatre. And to the sentimental observer it suddenly is a great theatre. Muddled, illogical but rooted in traditions of dedication to a common cause. A strange world of charade, perhaps, and illusion maintained with a kind of dogged self-sacrifice and madness. Many speak. The strike is called off. We are called back. Not as director, designer, composer so much as employees of the troupe, hired to help them with what *they* have decided, *their* play.

Determination and pride sweep them through the nerves of the first preview. Audience reaction helps them through the second. They open to the press and public on Wednesday 29th March. Their ovation is timed at just over twenty minutes.

Eric Shorter

Repertory Round-up

The deputy drama critic of the Daily Telegraph *looks back over a year of regional theatregoing.*

Our Reps, like our policemen, are wonderful. Everybody says so. The Americans have all those campus theatres, so well-endowed, so far-flung, so short of first-rate actors; and they also have a few important professional playhouses far away from New York. The Germans have their heavily subsidised civic theatres, as they have their local opera houses; and the French have got those *Maisons de la Culture* which form part of a ponderously generous arrangement by which the arts in France are brought to provincial people.

But no one has anything quite like our repertory movement which has persisted for sixty years and begun of late to prosper with unexpected vivacity just when people had supposed that television was going to wipe it off the map. It hasn't of course prospered alone. It has had its share of subsidy, variously stumped up by the Arts Council and local authorities and relatively little from most local authorities; and if it hadn't been for the Arts Council's policy of making grants only to theatres which showed signs of raising their standards (moving up say from a weekly to a fortnightly change of bill or producing new plays and rare revivals from time to time) the nation-wide network of repertory theatres would today be scarcely worth talking about, assuming it existed.

Since, however, all serious theatre where a policy is proclaimed seems now to need support beyond box-office revenue, it would be wrong to regard the Arts Council's benefactions as wholly respon-

sible for the cheerful picture. The main force in the renewed health
of our reps has come from the people who run them; and the main
distinction about the repertory movement has always been that
no two reps are ever run in the same way. They may find themselves
choosing the same play for production. Their approach, standards,
resources and achievement will remain stubbornly their own. Thus
each theatre has its own personality.

And whether that personality is bright or dull, orthodox, adventurous, imaginative or prosaic depends largely upon the director.
The status of the director in the modern theatre may be causing
Henry Irving to turn in his grave but the power of the director, for
good or ill, in the reps is a good deal more potent in the end; and
although he can, if he misbehaves or loses the confidence of local
people, be ejected and replaced by someone more manageable,
there is the risk of a public loss of confidence and intervention by
those who provide subsidies.

But it happens from time to time. It happened at Nottingham
Playhouse a few years ago when John Neville was replaced by
Stuart Burge. It nearly happened at Stoke-on-Trent when Peter
Cheeseman resisted an effort to dislodge him from his position as
director of a distinguished theatre-in-the-round company; and it
happened in 1971 at Leeds Playhouse when Bill Hays lost his job
as director of that exciting new theatre.

The announcement came only a year after the theatre's opening;
and though its policy had shown every sign of attracting a new
young audience to a playhouse which curiously bore a marked
resemblance to the National Theatre's new proposed auditorium
there was apparently not enough of the traditionalist in young Mr
Hays to satisfy the theatre's management committee. And so he
had to go—even before, as he protested, he had been given the time
to make a real go of this lively theatre. Whether it was just his
choice of plays—a stimulating if not always successful mixture of
classics, musicals, and difficult new works —or (more likely) a clash
of personalities, the unseating of an ambitious young director of an
important new civic theatre so soon after its opening looks like
mismanagement somewhere, or misjudgement. Mr Hays, a likeable
but determined individualist whose taste in drama did not avoid
a certain trendiness, told the annual meeting of the British Drama
League in York in 1971 that he had rejected Stan Barstow's domes-

LEFT: *Sheffield: Ian McKellen in* Swansong
RIGHT: *Guildford: John Stride and Eileen Atkins in* Suzanna Andler

BELOW: *'Cartoon humour': Eleanor Bron and Joe Melia in Michael Frayn's* The Sandboy *at Greenwich*

tic Northern comedy *Stringer's Last Stand* when it was sent to Leeds
Playhouse because it wasn't that open-stage theatre's kind of play,
though it subsequently gave great pleasure to audiences at the
traditional Theatre Royal, York; and one suspects that it might
also have given much pleasure to audiences at Leeds Playhouse
with its well-told story of a Yorkshire working-class Dad whose
family finds out he had a fancy woman.

But if Mr Hays's tastes veered predictably away from anything
that might be called conventional his choice and Roger Chapman's
production of *Dracula* showed an admirable feeling for pastiche;
and a musical comedy with football for its theme, *Tight At The
Back* by Leonard Barras, caught from time to time a racy, ribald
Northern zest which suggested that this company was depending
on its brashness to a monotonous extent. Do open stages perhaps
encourage it? Do they, as the Mermaid has always done, inspire a
kind of rompiness?

The new Sheffield Playhouse, which was opened in November
and re-christened The Crucible, suggested this might be so.
Beautifully appointed and with a seating capacity double that of
the old Playhouse, this gleaming amphitheatre with its long thrust
stage had the audience looking down on it from three sides and the
players entering from beneath the rows of seats as at a circus (or
Chichester). Colin George was still the director (keen, young,
forward-looking, self-confident, same generation as the dismissed
Hays but possibly more tactful); and having shrewdly anticipated
the problems of unveiling new theatres he boldly cut across all
tradition and put on three one-act entertainments: local schoolchildren in a semi-spontaneous cowboys and Indians action-sketch
which had them rolling round the promontory stage, Ian McKellen
in Chekhov's soliloquy for an ageing, fading actor, and the whole
company led by the jovial and rotund Douglas Campbell in a bout
of pseudo-music hall.

There were protests, of course; but Mr George was right. He
wanted an opening night without tensions. He wanted the theatre to
show its paces, and for people to remember that drama meant more
than just three-act classics—that it could involve everyone at
different levels in a single evening. It remained, however, rather dim
entertainment and we had to go back a week later for what we
hoped would be real theatre—Ibsen's *Peer Gynt*. This should have

suited the open stage but the talents of the company were not yet up to the epic's other demands. Yawns were politely suppressed as the funny bits made their effect with crudity and the sublimity went for nothing; though if you sat at the back of the gallery, so to speak, in the remotest row the general impression could be very striking and beautiful as the lights played down on the oblong thrust stage and the rest of the thousand-strong audience remained faintly in view.

The new Birmingham Rep, still keeping its old name, but similarly impressive as a new civic building, opened its doors a few weeks before Sheffield and seemed much better from a front-of-house point of view. Unlike Sheffield, it is a theatre which tempts you somehow not to enter the auditorium until the very last minute; and when you do it feels a bit like Drury Lane without the grandeur. In other words the new Birmingham Rep is very large and wide with a proscenium arch that would accommodate opera, ballet or musical comedy but hardly anything less spectacular.

So it began perhaps wisely with a musical comedy. This was *First Impressions*, a Broadway rendering by Abe Burrows and others of Jane Austen's *Pride and Prejudice*, and it had several advantages. To begin with Finlay James's elaborate settings more or less filled the huge stage. Then there was Patricia Routledge as Mrs Bennett, tongue-in-cheek with Gingoldian bravado; and the dainty period background sometimes wittily offset the solemn absurdities of song and sketch downstage. But neither the show nor the leading members of the company seemed to have much bearing on the occasion. We might have been at any touring 'date' rather than the first night of an opulent new rep which always used to take itself so seriously as one of our leading regional theatres.

What did Peter Dews have next up his sleeve? A sort of sub-Steptoe junkyard comedy *Roll Me Over* for which the stage was crammed with old lorry tyres, in and out of which a dismal assortment of Cockney layabouts wandered and gossiped in search of wit or character. Lots of better writers had been there before. Then, for Christmas, came Ronnie Barker in a boisterous updating of *The Merry Wives of Windsor* called *Good Time Johnny*: predictable nonsense but suited to the season.

Still, it is an old critical mistake to pass early judgements. Given time, no doubt both these handsome new theatres will settle down to do their proper job as it used to be done at the Sheffield Play-house and at the Rep in Station Street, Birmingham. Since the wonder of our reps is less their individual achievements than their capacity for variable and ambitious enterprise, their failures possess more interest for the student of theatre than, say, a short sharp West End flop. At Greenwich Theatre, for example, they battled during the year with Ibsen, Sophocles, Euripides, Feydeau, Shakespeare and Michael Frayn, all under the valiant banner of Ewan Hooper who had made of this theatre such a resoundingly intelligent oasis of drama in the London suburbs. And mostly it seemed to be a losing battle. Ibsen's *The Lady From The Sea*, awkwardly set for this open-ended stage, is a difficult piece at the best of times, and Ann Lynn, drifting wanly about the coastline, haunted by a past indistinctly nautical, looked emotionally sub-merged by a role which has defeated many finer actresses. But one admired the courage. Then Leo Aylen had a shot at re-creating *Antigone* so that its presumably original musical elements should be allowed to have their fling; but I'm afraid the fling was all too full as Freddie Jones's Creon, moody and moping, and Freda Dowie, miserably overparted, struggled ineffectually against the surround-ing host of dithyrambic jollification, most of it unintelligible. Euripides fared marginally better under the strong influence of another Greek scholar Hovhaness I. Pilikian who saw the original musical and comical elements in terms of intimate revue for his revival of *Electra*. As a result the evening proved unexpectedly jovial and perky. Yvonne Mitchell's Clytemnestra echoed Her-mione Gingold and Derek Jacobi's Orestes Henry Kendall; and Miss Dowie this time had more chance to express the heroine's misery. Feydeau's *La Main Passe*, adapted as *Fish Out of Water* by Caryl Brahms and Ned Sherrin, yielded one or two notable farcical performances from David Stroll and Trevor Ray among others in a typically exuberant and mistakenly stylised production by Peter Coe with Fenella Fielding as the errant wife; but when will directors learn that Feydeau should be acted as if tragic?

At Greenwich there was certainly a tendency in 1971 to play tragedy as comedy; not that they went all out for laughs in *Macbeth* as they determined to do with the Greeks, but the laughs came nonetheless. The Macbeths seemed to live in a kind of log cabin from which they did their entertaining. As director Mr Hooper saw the play as a chance to demonstrate several slightly cinematic effects when it came to the witches and the general's visions. There was a deal of Scots mist; and as Macbeth Alan Dobie seemed merely bored. His lady, however, fairly simmered sexually in Hildegard Neil's shapely performance which helped at once to explain her power and Mr Dobie's air of abstraction. But again one was reminded that Shakespearean tragedy is not to be trifled with. Michael Frayn, of course, is; and he brings to his trifling a light, literary touch which is so often absent in modern comedy. *The Sandboy*, as we remembered from this author's *The Two of Us*, was about and addressed to the more prosperous members of the young middle-class professional society to which Mr Frayn himself belongs and among which the Greenwich Theatre finds itself. Thus, Joe Melia was admirably cast as an ambitious architect-planner giving an interview for the box; and Eleanor Bron, all genteel apology for his fame and their affluence, came diffidently forward as his smart wife. To offset their complacency a pair of glum neighbours turned up to count their own misfortunes. And much of the dialogue was funny and sharply observed. But it remained essentially cartoon humour: short winded though stretched for a full length play. Where, on the other hand, were satirical playwrights who could find the length without stretching? Mr Frayn, I felt, should be encouraged.

Peter Terson needs no encouragement. He has a feeling for the theatre (not the West End theatre) and produces two, three or four plays every year, good, bad and indifferent. In 1971 he supplied two to the University Theatre at Newcastle-upon-Tyne, one to the Victoria at Stoke-on-Trent, and one to the National Youth Theatre. Because he is such an unassuming writer, so indifferent to worldly success, he has always had the critics on his side; and they sided with *The Samaritan* at Stoke-on-Trent and with *Good Lads at Heart* (Jeannetta Cochrane) but it had to be admitted that his works for Newcastle-upon-Tyne, *Prisoners of the War* and *Slip Road Wedding*, were not up to scratch. Was he writing too much or too quickly?

You can never say that of Marguerite Duras, though a lot of other things may be said about her theatrical style—or rather untheatrical style—which one felt like saying about *Suzanna Andler* at the Yvonne Arnaud, Guildford, a theatre hardly given to any recognisable policy but often apt to come up with surprises. This

was a surprise. Having seen the original production in Paris
(widely slated) I doubted whether it was worth re-producing in
English, seeing how typically introspective and anecdotal its
story of a wealthy if neglected wife came out on the stage. All she
does is moon and mope about an expensive Riviera apartment,
wondering whether to rent it or not, and what to do about her
marriage and her latest boy-friend. But as luck, or rather the art of
Eileen Atkins, would have it the mooning and the moping exercised a pleasantly hypnotic spell of emotional indecision, though
the low-keyed nature of the writing was not likely to be of much
general appeal.

For sheer contrast how about the bawdy brashness of Lan-
cashire's Bill Naughton? Never an author to render a point with
too much subtlety, his robustly candid comedy for Liverpool
Playhouse called itself *Lighthearted Intercourse* and concerned for
the most part the hazards of sexual fatigue facing a husband whose
wife habitually seduced him before he went to work—to look for
work, rather, since for some reason or other Mr Naughton set his
frolic in the grim 1930s, perhaps as sociological makeweight. The
vein of ribaldry in the dialogue made for laughter; but the joking
seemed basically as tired as the husband seemed of sex. This most
pleasantly renovated bourgeois theatre also offered Ken Dodd as
Malvolio in a production of *Twelfth Night* which was otherwise
considered unremarkable; and Mr Dodd did his stuff with generally
admired devotion to the script. But as usual the more striking and
original work was going on up the hill at the Everyman Theatre
which seems to concentrate on attracting the under-thirties where
the Playhouse appeals to their parents. In a festival of new plays
Charles Wood and John McGrath offered typically racy entertainments: fragmented, unpolished, but humming with vitality and
satirical force.

In *Unruly Elements* McGrath took an amusingly disgruntled
and ironical view of family life in Liverpool today and in *Welfare*
Charles Wood cobbled three of his vaudevilles together to make a
somewhat surrealist comment on contemporary values in music
hall terms, including a re-write, mercifully trimmed, of *Meals On
Wheels*, vaguely remembered from a Royal Court production.
Neither of these shows was a complete success. Their styles, and
Alan Dossor's vigorous productions, wore a makeshift air as if

ABOVE: *Liverpool Playhouse; Ken Dodd in 'an otherwise un-remarkable'* Twelfth Night

LEFT: *Liverpool Everyman: Roger Sloman, Gillian Hanna in* Unruly Elements. RIGHT: *Nottingham Playhouse: Donal McCann and Peter O'Toole in* Waiting for Godot

much of the material had been dredged from the authors' bottom drawers; but the spirit of the satire, the attack of the performances (led by Roger Sloman) and the atmosphere of a theatre so essentially informal overcame a good deal of the inadequacy which elsewhere must have looked more stark.

The atmosphere is always good at Nottingham Playhouse. No one ever knows quite why. It was well designed, of course, but then so are other theatres without half the sense of occasion generated by every new Nottingham production. Nor can this important aspect of its appeal be attributed mainly to the director Stuart Burge since the same feeling of liveliness was noted in John Neville's day. Whatever the cause, however, the effect is beneficial to the audience and therefore to the plays; and it was felt with extra pleasure at the revival of Beckett's *Waiting for Godot* with Peter O'Toole as Vladimir and Donal McCann as Estragon.

This production had originated in Dublin where its Irish tones found full and fresh expression; and I feared that by the time it came to Nottingham the Irishness might be too stage-Oirish. In the event it seemed to have achieved an even greater depth of humour and heartbreak. O'Toole's scarecrow Vladimir came in the Chaplin tradition: baggy trousers, battered bowler, clownish, absent-mindedly surveying the audience as if we were infinity; and Mr McCann, who seemed unaware of our presence, gave Estragon a pitiably comic sincerity, with his pinching boots and poor memory. Frank Middlemass's Lucky, gibbering pathetically, and Niall Toibin's Pozzo, a moralising tyrant, had been brought in to strengthen the original production, and Daniel Figgis, boy-messenger without a message, completed a memorable evening. But who directed? The name of Frederick Monnoyer on the programme rang no bells. Mr O'Toole, I presume?

The rest of the year at Nottingham could hardly hope to reach that standard but the repertoire (and it was worth remembering that this theatre is one of the few reps to have one) was notable for a striking *Richard the Third* by Leonard Rossiter under the equally novel direction of Peter McEnery, an amusingly Welsh if rather too discursive village comedy *Lilywhite Liars* by Alun Richards, and some pseudo-Gothic Christmas japes by Beverley Cross called *The Owl on the Battlements*.

For sheer absence of atmosphere the Forum at Billingham takes

'There is no livelier example of a policy-based company surviving on that policy': Two excursions into the theatrical past staged by the '69 Theatre Company in Manchester and London. ABOVE: Journey's End (*Peter Egan, James Maxwell*); BELOW: Charley's Aunt (*Johanna McCallum, Tom Courtenay, Celia Bannerman*)

a lot of beating. The industrial landscape of surrounding Tees-side can claim its own distinctive desolation. It may be dreary; it is at least mostly natural. The Forum is a theatre unnaturally in the corner of a civic sports centre where art is bound to take second place or third or fourth place to athletics. At this energetic complex I found a revival of *The Clandestine Marriage* setting off on a tour with the Denisons at its head and Brian Shelton, then artistic director of the Forum, as producer. Having last seen him at the Pitlochry Festival where his work had been admired for several years (it was he who first unearthed *The Revenger's Tragedy* and restored it to the national attention) it was hard to tell what he was doing amid this cultural wasteland, except that he had been born there and presumably felt a sense of mission. He did not, however, stay for long. And who can wonder? If ever a theatre was built without the means to run it in regional terms, the Forum seemed to be that theatre. It remained (at last hearing) an oasis for tours; and an example of the widespread civic assumption that by putting up a theatre you have done your cultural duty to the drama. The question of its policy, who runs it and how to make it go can be settled (or overlooked) later—as it was with the ever-ailing Adeline Genee at East Grinstead in Sussex.

Sometimes it seems healthier for companies to come first, and the actual theatres later—like the National, the Royal Shakespeare. Stephen Joseph's theatre-in-the-round group (now rooted at Stoke-on-Trent) or Joan Littlewood's Theatre Workshop (Manchester and the north before E.15) and Prospect Productions (which have always had Cambridge to fall back on). Given a company, there's a policy, however queer. Given a theatre, there's only cleaners. Take the Sixty-Nine Theatre Company of Manchester which bases itself on that city's new-fangled University Theatre. Founded by the people who made so much, in so short a time, of the '59 Theatre Company at the Lyric, Hammersmith, there is no livelier example of a policy-based company surviving on that policy two hundred miles away ten years later—though admittedly it lacks today the classical grandeur of its Hammersmith days. The best thing it did in the year under review was *Journey's End*, though it sent to London *Charley's Aunt* (with Tom Courtenay) for Christmas. Sherriff's craftmanship was not the war play's only wonder. There was its lack of sentimentality; and Alan Pickford's impressive setting placed its perils with subterranean obedience in a world of confused, class-ridden loyalties from which all the acting could take powerful shape. James Maxwell, Peter Egan, Christopher Good, Harry Landis and Bruce Robinson drew out the tensions and the humours of trench life in France with detailed pathos; and Eric Thompson directed with assurance.

Whatever policy was lurking at the Gardner Arts Centre of Sussex University did not become apparent during 1971, though its choice of play and the quality of players must be the envy of more conventional reps. Eric Porter came forward in Jean Vauthier's *The Protagonist,* a familiar vehicle in Paris for Jean-Louis Barrault which hardly suited Mr Porter's talents. Other good players came forward in other unlikely things, as if a well-endowed theatre were suffering from more subsidy than imagination—a lack of the proper leadership. Which brings us back to the basic problem for reps. In a word, who is to run them? Most of them appeared, in 1971, to be in suitable hands. At Leatherhead's Thorndike, in Surrey, Hazel Vincent-Wallace continued to show that measure of her audience which had been evident in this theatre's club days. Likewise Peter Cheeseman at Stoke-on-Trent pursued that theatre's distinctive policy of mixing imaginative documentaries with revivals from the classical repertoire and one or two notable adaptations from, say, Hardy or Arnold Bennett; while Ted Craig at Worthing, Warren Jenkins at Coventry and Jane Howell at Exeter (succeeding Tony Church) were the directors of those reps which—if not consistently wonderful—made their national mark during the year without resorting to try-outs for West End managers.

The One That Got Away

After two years and more than 800 performances of How the Other Half Loves, *its star looks back at the making of a West End success.*

In April 1970 there seemed little point in going to Leicester, where *How The Other Half Loves* was being given a second chance at the local repertory theatre, the first production of the play at Scarborough some months before having satisfied neither author nor management. The invitation had come from Peter Bridge, whom I knew only slightly. On the other hand, I had to find myself a play and a new management. The firm of H. M. Tennent, with whom I had been closely connected for much of my theatrical life, and I, had come to the parting of the ways.

The split, for which I was entirely responsible, came during the run of *Half Way Up The Tree*, a play by Peter Ustinov, the success of which in the West End had not been repeated in other countries where it had been produced. I am never slow to apportion credit to myself, and regarded the whole episode as a personal triumph for my acumen and theatrical knowhow. I had saved Ustinov from himself.

Tennent's must, I was sure, be grateful to their old friend, so that when I needed a quick thousand pounds, I approached full of confidence and goodwill. I had taken it upon myself to raise a few thousand pounds to buy and equip a school for autistic children

'In the forty years I have been sitting around in dressing-rooms I don't believe I have ever sat in a new armchair'

and contacted a number of the rich whom I considered would be fairly easy touches.

Lew Grade, for instance, is a natural giver. I approached him across a crowded room and sniffed his cigar for a time while he told a story. I am not a good listener to other people's anecdotes, and after a time thinking, or perhaps just hoping, that he had reached the point, I asked him for the money.

'Of course,' he replied, 'you shall have it in the morning. Don't interrupt,' and went on with his tale.

On the books of ATV Lew owes me very little. Indeed I must have cost the company a small fortune in my unsuccessful attempts to launch a series on their network. But Lew Grade is a generous man, not given to jobbing back. I am not praising him. I don't think generous men should be praised, they are the lucky ones. Another of my successes on this occasion was John Lennon, who whipped out his cheque book and gave me the bread on the spot. I hardly knew John Lennon.

On the other hand Hugh Beaumont (H. M. Tennent's managing director) was on this occasion one of my failures. When I told him that if he didn't give me the money I would sit in his outer office till he did, he seemed only mildly amused. When, this ploy having failed, two days later I told him that unless he gave the money I would never darken his door again, he called it blackmail, which it was. I am not a reasonable man; on this occasion I stuck to my guns.

What finally decided me to go to Leicester was a race meeting at Stratford-on-Avon, where a horse of mine was entered to run. On the map Leicester seemed fairly close. There was a time when I knew every provincial city in England. I spent ten years of my life on tour, but I had forgotten Leicester. In any case it appeared to have been replanned recently with multi-storey car parks to depress me with their cement understains and crush barriers to keep back non-existent crowds. The object of the exercise is that you should drive straight through such cities these days without stopping, or indeed noticing that they are there at all.

I was surprised to find the theatre in a bus depot, but I suppose even that makes sense in a way. A handy sort of house with raked seats and a flat stage, the convenience of a curtain was dispensed with, so that when the furniture had to be changed halfway through the first act, an entirely separate production was mounted with a ringmaster and uniformed circus hands. The audience enjoyed it hugely. I thought they quite liked the play.

After the performance several patrons accosted Robin Midgley, who had directed the piece, with advice on how to improve it. He struck me then, as he does now, as an eminently patient, reasonable and above all resourceful fellow. About the play I was not so certain. The most serious snag seemed to me that most of the goods were displayed in the first act, the climax of which was an immensely complicated *coup de théâtre* in which two players contrived to attend separate and simultaneous dinner parties.

'Is it, do you suppose,' I asked John Jonas, who drives me around on these occasions and nurses me through the performances I do decide to give, 'is it, do you suppose, too clever by half?' Mr Jonas on this occasion seemed not to share my anxiety. 'A thoroughly good evening,' he insisted on the way home. 'I don't know why you didn't enjoy it more.'

I think it was his enthusiasm as much as anything else that decided me to go ahead. It was after all an even money chance, and this has always seemed generous odds to me. I had certain reservations, and having told Peter Bridge that I was game at least up to a point, tried for the next couple of weeks to get the play altered, but found Alan Ayckbourn, the author, fairly obdurate and inclined to prefer his own ideas to mine.

I started out by demanding that the baby in the play should be replaced by an elkhound, and that I should be encouraged to participate in the celebrated dinner scene dressed in Japanese costume. Both suggestions were resisted tooth and nail, and on reflection correctly. After two years I can't pretend to have made much of Alan Ayckbourn, an eminently cautious fellow, not given to hanging round the cast, remembering the anniversaries of the play or bunching his leading ladies. About his play's quite phenomenal success he evinces little emotion, hugging himself, if he does so at all, in secret.

Having got me to agree to do the play, Peter Bridge's immediate tasks were to find the money and the theatre with which, and in which, to present *How The Other Half Loves*. The money presented no problem. There was an embarrassment of would-be investors. All he had to do was to circularise the list of prospective backers with which all managers provide themselves, and the £18,000 for which he asked to mount the production was subscribed overnight. The Angels on this occasion smelt success. Both the author and myself had been previous winners over the course, and almost uniquely Peter was able to produce two notices written by national critics on the strength of the Leicester production, predicting a London success for the play when it was eventually produced there. You could hardly ask for more, and no one did. Indeed one of the backers, Eddie Kulukundis, of whom we shall hear more later, wanted to provide all the capital required from his own pocket.

Without the Sunday notices written by Ronald Bryden (*The Observer*) and Frank Marcus (*Sunday Telegraph*) it is possible that nothing much more would ever have been heard of the play after Leicester. The local notices for the piece were not particularly encouraging, and interest in a London production had all but ceased.

The problem of obtaining a suitable West End theatre was, as usual, more complicated. In order to appreciate the singular good fortune which attended its arrival at the Lyric, we must inform ourselves not so much about the state of the theatre in London and the provinces, as the state of the theatres themselves.

In a business which is by nature optimistic and essentially fly-by-night, the ground landlords of theatre land have been, ever since I can remember, in a class by themselves for sober mien and general lack of high spirits. Grave and reverend seigneurs to a man, they are the farmers of this never-never land of ours, always complaining of the harvest, but raking in the shekels whenever and wherever possible.

In the years between the wars such men were typified by the late Stuart Cruikshank, who controlled the giant Howard Wyndham circuit in the then flourishing provincial theatre. Here was a card index man after the heart of IBM itself. No employee however insignificant, no star however famous, no gown however dilapidated, no piece of scenery or property however unlikely ever to be used again, escaped his filing system. He once let me scan some of the cards on his desk awaiting redeployment.

'Miss A', I read, 'asks £30, is worth half. Good personality and clothes sense, but poor personal wardrobe. Not a hard worker at matinées. Blond (natural).' Then followed the dates she had fulfilled and the fees paid. The card beneath referred to a ball dress which, although now alas damaged at the hem, was considered by E. J., who had supplied the information, as still suitable for second lead singer in the finale or ballroom scenes.

If there is one thing that theatre owners have in common it is a pathological horror of throwing anything away, for this would entail the purchase of a replacement. In the forty years I have been sitting around in dressing-rooms I don't believe I have ever sat in a new armchair. I have never used a lavatory which hadn't been designed half a century before, or looked into a mirror which wasn't lit by a naked bulb. I have never seen a carpet in a corridor or a picture on a wall.

The higher you climb in most theatres the more sparse the furniture becomes. Understudies are not encouraged to relax. They must sit for the three hours each evening on upright chairs, no two of which ever match each other. To strip an average theatre of its furniture and fittings, most self-respecting junk men would demand a fee.

Does it matter? Well, the answer is it doesn't really matter all that much to the actors. It may be good for us not to be able to relax too much backstage, and we are used to such conditions, but broken window sashes and sagging armchairs are a symptom of bad management. They do little to dispel the belief that theatre owners in this country are a bunch of frustrated property developers who spend a good deal of their time flattening their noses against the grimy window panes and gazing out enviously across the street at the car parks and supermarkets which luckier colleagues have been allowed to build.

A theatre site is rarely a profitable one, particularly if one takes into account how much more could be made by turning out the actors and installing the businessmen and tourists. Yet these same tourists now come to this country in large numbers partly because of the theatres and it is the height of folly that so many of the latter should be in the hands of vast conglomerates who treat them like unwanted children, allowing them each year to grow a little shabbier and more uncared for, evincing no pride in their achievement, grudging them even a coat of paint.

However, when it comes to renting them out for profit, parental interest revives somewhat. Heads we win, tails you lose is the rule, and the empty shell, for such each house virtually becomes with every fresh lease, is let to the producing manager on the harshest possible terms. The average rent demanded is in the region of a thousand pounds a week against 20 per cent of the box office takings, whichever is the larger, and the lease can be terminated by the landlords two weeks after the takings drop below an agreed sum which is known as the 'stop figure'.

Over and above that the tenant is expected to pay for light, heating and staff and nowadays the landlords are chary of providing even a bulb, let alone a spotlight, so all this has to be hired afresh. The landlords, however, insist on retaining the right to sell programmes and operate the bars, an enormously profitable business. One might be forgiven for supposing that they are often more concerned with the brand of whisky on sale in the foyers than the brand of entertainment advertised on the marquee.

Not all London or provincial theatres find themselves in this sorry state. There are producing managers who maintain their establishments in reasonable repair and one house especially, acquired some years ago by Peter Saunders, has been extensively redecorated and redesigned. The Vaudeville Theatre shines forth like a good deed in this naughty world. But these theatres are not as a rule available to managers such as Bridge. Their proprietors prefer to have a finger in the pie if they have not actually baked it themselves, and do not as a rule let their theatres on a strict rental basis.

Bridge was now free to proceed at his peril, the date when he would be able to conclude negotiations for a theatre being some weeks off, and no guarantee that he would get one at all, should business in the West End suddenly spurt. He could find himself, as he did with his recent production of *On the Rocks*, up in the clouds circling the airport without permission to land, and if the tour proved financially disastrous, running out of gas.

Rehearsals began on my birthday at the Irish Club. I had not then, and still haven't, the faintest idea what normally goes on at the Irish Club, apart from the sale of the *Irish Times* in the hall, but I climbed the stairs to the room reserved for the first rehearsal and found Bridge had invited a few Press photographers along for a drink in the hope that they would take pictures of myself cutting my birthday cake. There is surely no duller subject for portraiture, or one an editor is more easily able to reject, than an actor poised over confectionery, but the attempt has to be made.

Robin Fox turned up and I was as always reassured in his company, and managed the ritual bonhomie and drank the champagne, blissfully unaware of the impending catastrophe. A few days later I was to learn that my trusted friend and manager had terminal cancer and the shadow of his approaching death made life suddenly much colder. In the evenings after rehearsing I would drive down to the King Edward Hospital at Midhurst for a picnic in his bedroom, bearing caviare and curious mousses from Fortnums, and drinking champagne by his bedside. It didn't really make matters better, but in times of crisis I find extravagance sometimes helps me.

Late one evening I left him and walked along the corridor to where a nurse sat at a table, writing reports on her patients. 'I'm off now,' I told her unnecessarily. 'I gather the news is rather good about Mr Fox. They haven't found anything sinister.' She didn't answer for a moment. I had caught her, I suppose, off guard. Into her eyes came a look of disbelief, instantly checked by a professional caution. 'Oh yes,' she said, 'Mr Fox is doing very well,' and that as far as I was concerned was that. I never again had any hope at all.

It was at the first rehearsal that I met Eddie Kulukundis and learnt he was to be a partner in the enterprise which Bridge, possibly scenting battle, had christened Agincourt Productions Ltd. My first impression was that of a large, untidy and likeable Greek who was constantly ducking his head in a basin, not to cool it, but to get his hair to lie down.

His recent impact on theatreland was already proving sensational. Word had got round that there was a stranger in town and back at the old saloon they were busy polishing the glasses and getting out the old deck of cards. Here was a tenderfoot aiming to join in the poker game and there was no lack of players anxious for him to draw up a chair and sweeten the pot.

They found out almost immediately that he was a man after their own heart. When I asked him once how much a particular hand had cost him, he assured me he would break even. 'Come now, Eddie, what do you mean by even?' I persisted. 'You think you'll lose five thousand?' 'A bit more than that,' he assured me with a smile.

He is the only son of a wealthy Greek shipowner. 'I suppose you would call us wealthy,' he told me. 'As a boy I lived in Wembley; it's not all that rich a neighbourhood. On the other hand my father always had chauffeurs.'

'Chauffeurs?' I queried.

'One at a time. Mother's dowry when she married—we Greeks have dowries, you know—was twenty thousand, a lot of money in those days.'

Mother was strict with him, I gathered. Until he was 22 he didn't go out with girls. Then, as is often the way, it all happened too quickly. He fell deeply in love and for the first time really started to go places in his father's business. He managed the English branch from the Minories. He made a small fortune, intent on marriage and settling down possibly in Wembley himself, although by this time the rest of the family had moved abroad. Eddie, as the son of the eldest brother, was more or less the boss. 'There's not,' he explained, 'much difference really between a good shipowner and a bad shipowner. In good times everyone makes money because they can't help doing so. In bad times we all lose.' He was not, however, to find the same conditions prevailing in the theatre.

He finds it surprising, for instance, that managers should transfer so high a percentage of their office expenses to the production account. When he rents a playhouse he doesn't, or least didn't, expect to have to pay several hundreds a week over and above the agreed sum for the illuminated signs directing patrons to the theatre. When told he can mount a production of a play already in the repertory of one of the subsidised companies for four thousand, he is dazed to find his production bill has shot up to twenty thousand because the scenery has deteriorated through damp and the dresses have been claimed back and rented out afresh by the costumiers to amateur groups. He is gradually being weaned from the theatre. 'If I could find a nice girl and marry her, I'd give it up tomorrow,' he told me, and I rather hope he does.

Meanwhile he flits from function to function, automatically accosted, perpetually propositioned by those who seek his patronage and his fortune. 'In point of fact,' he told me, 'it's not strictly true that I still have to pick up the checks. Quite often I get a free lunch and there's really nothing to pay at the cocktail parties. All I have to remember to do is not to take my cheque book.'

LEFT: '*An eminently cautious fellow*': *Alan Ayckbourn (playwright)*
RIGHT: '*His tasks were to find the money and the theatre*':
Peter Bridge (producer)

BELOW (l. to r.): *Brian Miller, Heather Sears, Donald Burton, Elizabeth Ashton, Robert Morley and Joan Tetzel in* How the Other Half Loves

When I asked Bridge why we were rehearsing at the Irish Club, he told me proudly that coming up from Berkshire every morning I would find it easier to park. 'On the first night,' I told him, 'I am expected to make a speech excusing our state of unpreparedness on the grounds that we are all keen motorists?' I hate rehearsing in rooms as opposed to on stage. I find the space confining, the stage management sits on top of you, prompt book in hand, my mind wanders, reflecting on the décor, marvelling that people normally carouse in these surroundings, give wedding receptions and children's parties. Public rooms are haunted for me by the ghosts of failed functions.

I seldom enjoy myself at rehearsals. I am back in the classroom I so hated; the director is a beak, sometimes a decent beak, but a beak nevertheless. This is his hour, his month in fact. We normally rehearse for about that long. He is here to see we do the work as he wishes it done. Some actors suck up to the master, follow him around, take his hand on the walk, call him Sir, bring him flowers. I am not one of them. Between him and me there is always hostility of a kind often manufactured by myself. I am stimulated by conflict, like to be the one who hurls the rubber while he is intent on the blackboard.

In all my theatrical career, only Guthrie willingly enslaved me. I longed to please him, accepted his rule absolutely in triumph and disaster, and no one brought the temple down more effectively on occasions than this curious Irish giant whom I met almost at the outset of my career, who directed my first two plays and later myself in *Pygmalion*. I had stepped into the breach at the last moment, learnt Higgins in a weekend, gone on ill-prepared and triumphed at Buxton of all places, or so I thought. He came to the dressing-room afterwards.

'Very dull,' he said, 'most of it.' It seemed like praise, perhaps it was intended to be. He never bored one, was never bored himself, stopped in time, dismissed the class, sent us home for prep, a lovely man. When he died, his bailiff came to his wife. 'The great tree has fallen,' he told her. On the morning of his memorial service at St Paul's, Covent Garden, the tree in the churchyard fell. There was no wind. A great director.

Of course I have liked some of the others, some of them I suppose have liked me, but not many. Peter Brook irritated me by his sup-

preme dedication to the task we both had in hand. He tried everything to get me to do what he wanted: I did everything not to. We
even quarrelled about who should fetch the Coca-Cola. Perhaps
because of him, perhaps despite him, *The Little Hut* was a great
success, but I don't think either of us would ever go through it
again. To enjoy oneself is the supreme duty of an actor. I cannot
bear the rack of effort, if acting doesn't come easily I'd rather it
didn't come at all. I cannot bear dedication when it is paraded in
front of me. I like my director corked, but frothy. The late Jack
Minster was the flattest director I ever knew, and the most amusing.
He sat in the stalls, wrapped in an overcoat and sustained despair.
'Don't look on the floor,' he would tell us, 'there's nothing there but
the play.'

'It gets a laugh,' an actor would expostulate.

'I didn't hear it,' he would reply, 'I was deafened by the ones
who weren't laughing.'

Peter Ashmore directed me in *Edward, My Son*, and *Hippo
Dancing* and *A Likely Tale*. I enjoyed it. Willie Hyde White
summed him up. 'What a civil little chap. I find him invaluable,
always ready to fetch the script when I've left it in the Rolls.' But
Ashmore was cleverer than that, cleverer with me than anyone
else has been. He came into money and wisely didn't press his luck
after that. Directors are alchemists, their hour is brief.

Gielgud I admired enormously, but the trouble was everyone
else did the same. I was perpetually comforting the cast in the
wings during rehearsals of *Halfway Up The Tree*. 'I don't think
John likes what I'm doing,' they would sob. 'Has he said so?' 'No,
I just sense it.' 'I like it,' I would tell them, but the tears didn't
stop. After a time I began to resent it. He did rather take Ustinov's
side at the beginning, but luckily Ustinov wasn't there most of the
time. I like a director to take my side. I demand it. My current
task-master, Robin Midgley, took my side from the first.

I've got so old now that I am no longer a challenge to directors,
just something they wish they could move around and can't. Which
is not to say I don't make concessions; on this occasion I made one
or two. I didn't interfere with the casting, except to insist that
Joan Tetzel played my wife. No one seemed all that keen, not even
Tetzel. She had done *The Little Hut* with me, so was more or less
prepared.

It's strange about Tetzel. I worked with her before the war in radio in New York City when she was only a child. She was the darling of the networks because able to play opposite any leading man in the Rudy Vallee Hour. French, British, Japanese, she took them all on and I never forgot her astringent poise. When I decided to play *The Little Hut* I told Beaumont about her, adding that I hadn't seen her for twenty years and was possibly out of the business. 'She was in my office this morning,' he told me, 'suddenly turned up out of the blue.' 'Grab her,' I insisted, and he did. It was the same with *How The Other Half Loves*. I hadn't met her since *The Little Hut* finished again more than twenty years before. On the day I agreed to sign the contract, I lunched with Robin at Wilton's.

'The girl we need,' I told him, 'is Tetzel. Where has she gone, do you suppose?' That evening I walked into a cocktail party, the first one I'd been to for seven years, and there she was by the door. 'Do you want to do a play?' I asked. 'I might,' she said.

As is usually the case with playwrights who deliver their plays into my hands, Ayckbourn began to grow restless quite early on. He had already seen his play rehearsed twice before and had fairly set notions of what it was all about. At the back of his mind, as indeed is nearly always at the back of authors' minds, was the idea that he had written a more significant play than I supposed. Moreover he insisted that all the characters except perhaps my own were fundamentally unlikeable.

This didn't do for Tetzel. She was not, as far as she was concerned, playing a bitch and had no intention of doing so. The final confrontation was to come later at Leeds, but meanwhile there was a certain amount of muttering on both sides. I have always held that to make a steady income in our business, which should be all actors' ambition, one cannot afford to play unsympathetic parts. However much praise is lavished on you by the critics, the audience gradually comes to associate you with the unlikeable characteristics you have assumed in the cause of art. After a time they simply won't pay to go and see you. With the notable exception of Vincent Price, who keeps his tongue firmly in his cheek, few heavies grow rich. Tetzel and I were quite determined on this point. 'If they don't like us,' we told Ayckbourn, 'they won't come, and where will your little play be then?'

After a week rehearsals moved to the Haymarket, where

Midgley could sit in the stalls and leave us to get on with it. But for some reason he seemed to prefer a chair at the side of the stage. I have never known a director who sat so long on top of a company. Otherwise I had no fault to find with him, or with the script.

Normally I am a glutton for rewriting, but after my initial failure with this piece I thought it best to bide my time, say the lines the author had written and only when I found they didn't work with an audience, get him to alter them or preferably alter them myself. Directing is like cooking in the sense that all the dishes should ideally come to perfection at the same moment. Some actors boil almost immediately, while others take ages to rise.

There comes a time too when all of us demand an audience. 'Mummy, watch me!' we cry, and if Mummy isn't planning to visit the nursery for another week, the squabbles are liable to start. At the end of the month we were just about ready. The curtains had been drawn, the stage set. Arrayed in our costumes, we awaited the arrival of the grown-ups. They could hardly have been more appreciative in Leeds had they in fact been our relatives. We didn't pack the theatre, but business built, and we were complimented in tea-shops. There is nothing the English dislike more than having to talk to people they haven't met. When it happens to an actor, he knows he is on a winner.

These days I drive to Leeds, put up at the Queen's and come down after the performances on Saturday and am in my own bed at four. I do not choose to linger. As one gets older, time grows more precious. Years and years ago we travelled on Sundays in special reserved coaches. Long, slow journeys without restaurant cars, but always with a pack of cards and beer, sometimes sandwiches, sometimes we rushed the buffet on the stations where we halted. A pleasant sort of day, particularly if one was sure of digs on arrival. I knew most of the towns in England then, sad, dead slums like Rochdale and Oldham and gay, comfortable, happy places like Southport and York. Blackpool was best of all, but all seaside towns were fun, Bournemouth, Brighton, Morecambe, even Southend.

I was twenty-one at Blackpool and had melon flown from Manchester for my birthday party. I was always a show-off. I opened *Edward, My Son* in Leeds at a matinée on a Tuesday. It ran for four and a half hours with the hitches, but I knew we had a success. In those days the Grand was really grand, an opera house really, with goodness knows how many floors and a lift and an enormous stage. It was a number one date, full more often than not and when it was full there was a lot of brass. The manager wore white tie and tails and was a VC.

You put your best foot forward when you stepped on that stage. You lived in the Roundhay Park district. There were plenty of good rooms with wonderful Yorkshire teas before the performance and hot suppers afterwards. There were bits of the city which were unexpected, Marshall and Snelgrove for instance, and Austin Reeds. If like me you had a bad memory, there was always the excitement of rediscovery. Round here, you would tell yourself, somewhere round here there is a shop window in which stuffed squirrels were skating.

But Leeds has changed and like Leicester it too has barricades in preparation for some future riot perhaps, or just possibly a pageant. There is a new complex near the theatre and a new hotel and this time I wondered if I should have done better to have stayed there. But hotel bedrooms grow ever smaller and I like to be near the station. The theatre had given Bridge a guarantee, and we stayed a fortnight. Business was not sensational, but remained above average. The Grand breaks a good many hearts these days. There was a note for me at the stage-door, left by Leonard Rossiter, who had been there the week before. 'Help!' was all it said.

One morning saw a glorious row on the stage. A last attempt by the director and the author to get Tetzel to play it tough. She held firm. 'Do you mean to tell me,' asked Robin, 'that you are not going to play the part as we wish it played?' 'Yes. If you want it played that way, you must get someone else.' 'Two someone elses,' I told them, relishing the confrontation. That was the end, more or less.

After a fortnight we moved to Nottingham, where once two theatres stood side by side, like elderly maiden aunts, but one has now passed on, her grave a car park, though goodness knows what is planned as a headstone. The other used at one time to have a notice written on the wall, 'Do not embarrass the management with requests for complimentary passes. If your friends will not pay to see you, you can hardly expect the general public to do so.' Is it still there? I am not sure.

There is a brand new hotel reached by a tunnel or underpass, but extremely comfortable once you are inside. There is a lot of money about in Nottingham, lace and cigarettes. Do people still wear lace? At least they still smoke, and dose themselves. Boots and Players, a great deal of swapping around of Diners Cards. People sitting down for business huddles over the dinner table just when they should be turning out to watch me. Ah well, perhaps another night.

There is a brand new theatre too, run by a friend, Stuart Burge. I pay him a visit and find myself watching a dress rehearsal of a new play by Christopher Fry, who hasn't written a play for a long time. Celia Johnson's daughter looks as if someone has poured water over her. More beautiful than her mother ever was, but not fledged yet. These are early days for her. Not for me alas, although I don't think I'd want to start again, certainly not in the provinces. How I hate one-way streets and having to go round and about and burrow like a mole.

It is in Nottingham that I hear Bridge has been offered the Lyric. By now the production has been evaluated by head office, the reports are in. The head brass of course doesn't come itself, but somewhere in the chain of command is a warrant officer on whose judgement they rely.

Years ago in the days when the ticket agencies made deals and put down their money in advance, there was a faceless, anonymous taster to whom they appealed for a verdict. If he said buy, they bought and the success was a foregone conclusion. Once they had the seats, they pushed the show. In those days too everyone relied on Fred Carter. When you opened out of town he came along and if he liked what he saw, found you a theatre in London. On the try-out of *Edward, My Son* he waited till we got to Manchester. 'You can have,' he told me, 'any theatre you want in London. Which is it to be?' 'His Majesty's,' I told him, and so it was. My God, I felt proud. I didn't have the same pride with this one, but then of course I hadn't written it. I counselled Bridge to try not for the Lyric but the Apollo if he was offered a choice. He was and he didn't, and was right.

We still had three more weeks on the road, Wimbledon and Brighton, but these passed uneventfully. There was not a lot more rehearsing to be done, and no rewrites. Everything would now depend on the first night at the Lyric.

The first night of a play in London is still a formidable obstacle, the Bechers Brook of the National course. In recent years attempts have been made to modify the jump somewhat. The supreme confrontation is no longer sought by management, as used to be the case.

Before the war, when the theatre catered largely for the Stalls public, managers regarded their first night list as all important, and spent hours at work on the Sheet. The idea was to seat the critics in warm nests of appreciation, although taking care they should not be irritated by loud laughter and bursts of applause while they themselves were scribbling notes in the dusk.

Some managers, like the late Gilbert Miller, prided themselves on knowing the social scene and which Marquis was talking to which Marchioness. Gilbert had a profound suspicion of princesses. 'If possible,' he confided in me once, 'I keep them out. They are too casual, like racehorses.' Beaumont is another who is a great expert on such occasions, leaving as little as possible to chance. He has been reported to carry a thermometer to check the exact temperature of the auditorium.

But the days when first nights were great social occasions are over. In point of fact nowadays it is quite difficult to fill the house at all, and after the friends of the cast have been accommodated, the manager may be hard put to it to find a representative audience and not one composed almost exclusively of fellow managers, agents, film producers and television directors who have seen it all before and are not all that keen to see it again. This is one of the reasons why previews are encouraged. The actors get a chance of playing themselves in and the professionally interested need no longer all come on the same evening.

On the whole, *How The Other Half Loves* at the Lyric Theatre on the night of 5 August 1970 played much as it had been playing for the last six weeks and the notices, when they appeared, were with one exception uniformly encouraging. Only Harold Hobson in the *Sunday Times* was unwontedly abrasive. He reported that most of the cast gave performances which looked as if they had been recruited from the rejects of the annual pantomime in a backward village, or could he have written originally a backwoods village? We shall never know. By the time his notice appeared we were home and dried.

Reference Section

The first checklist gives brief details of all commercial theatre productions in central London over a period of twelve months; it does not include lunchtime, Sunday-night or club productions, nor does it take account of vaudeville seasons, ice shows or fringe ventures. Transfers are only noted where they were inter-London, and principal cast changes are in the footnotes. Separate checklists for the subsidised companies and certain seasonal theatres as well as opera and ballet companies will be found on subsequent pages.

CHECKLISTS

T.72—R

London First Night Diary

DIRECTOR	LEADING PLAYERS
Jonathan Miller	Hugh Thomas, Mike Baker, Andrew Hilton
Laurier Lister	Max Adrian
Harold Fielding	Tommy Steele, Young Generation, Susan Maughan
Roger Williams	Roy Dotrice, Frances Cuka, George Pravda
William Chappell	Gladys Cooper, Joan Greenwood, Michael Goodliffe
Bernard Miles	Bernard Miles
Michael Blakemore	Anton Rodgers, Priscilla Morgan, Michael Bates
Jonathan Hales	Paul Angelis, James Hazeldine, Clare Sutcliffe
Warren Jenkins	Paul Massie, Margaretta Scott, Rhoda Lewis
Tom Eyen	Madeleine le Roux, Peggy Ledger, Jeffrey Herman
Alan Strachan	Anna Cropper, Patrick McAlinney, Edward Petherbridge
Max Stafford-Clark	Anna Massey, Lynn Redgrave, Barbara Ferris
Richard Digby Day	Marilyn Taylerson, Hugh Ross, Maureen Pryor
Allan Davis	Michael Crawford, Linda Thorsen,[1] Evelyn Laye
Virginia Mason	Harold Kasket, Al Mancini, Douglas Lambert
James Grout	Norman Rodway, Moira Redmond, Godfrey Quigley
Jonathan Miller	Kenneth Haigh, Dennis Carey, Angela Thorne
Michael Croft	Tom Bell, Ray McAnally, Ronald Hines
Jonathan Hales	Peggy Ashcroft, Maurice Denham, Gordon Jackson
Keith Hack	Trevor Peacock, Barry Dennen, Ann Mitchell
Richard Digby Day	Gary Raymond, Delena Kidd, Ian Talbot
Harold Pinter	Alan Bates,[2] Richard O'Callaghan, Mary Wimbush
Peter Cotes	Gerald Flood, Gladys Henson, Janet Munro
Wendy Toye	Cleo Laine,[3] André Jobin, Thomas Carey[4]
Alan Strachan	Michael Redgrave, Peter Copley, Bernard Hepton
Leslie Phillips	Simon Oates, Sue Lloyd, Kate O'Mara
Doreen Cannon	Suzanne Smith, Julia Breck, Michael Mundell
Ronald Eyre	Alec Guinness,[5] Jeremy Brett,[6] Leueen McGrath[7]

[1] Later replaced by Carolyn Lyster
[2] Later replaced by Richard Briers
[3] Later replaced by Jan Waters
[4] Later replaced by Valentine Pringle
[5] Later replaced by Michael Redgrave
[6] Later replaced by Barry Justice
[7] Later replaced by Jane Baxter

DATE	THEATRE	PLAY	AUTHOR
Aug. 5	Cambridge	*Hamlet*	William Shakespeare
Aug. 17	Royal Court	*West of Suez*	John Osborne
Aug. 23	Jeanetta Cochrane	*Good Lads At Heart*	Peter Terson
Aug. 24	Old Vic	*The Father*	August Strindberg
Aug. 25	Shaw	*The Shoemaker's Holiday*	Thomas Dekker
Aug. 31	Queen's	*Jump!*	Larry Gelbart
Sept. 6	Old Vic	*Last Sweet Days of Isaac*	Gretchen Cryer & Nancy Ford
Sept. 7	Shaw	*Henry IV, Part 2*	William Shakespeare
Sept. 8	Roundhouse	*Skyvers*	Barry Reckord
Sept. 14	Prince of Wales	*Big Bad Mouse*	Philip King & Falkland Cary
Sept. 15	Garrick	*Don't Just Lie There, Say Something!*	Michael Pertwee
Sept. 16	Mermaid	*Othello*	William Shakespeare
Sept. 16	Old Vic	*Pantagleize*	Michel de Ghelderode
Sept. 17	Old Vic	*The 7th Commandment*	Dariofo
Sept. 22	Shaw	*The Samaritan*	Peter Terson
Sept. 28	Duke of York's	*Romance!*	John Spurling/Charles Ross
Sept. 29	Royal Court	*Lear*	Edward Bond
Sept. 30	Fortune	*Suddenly At Home*	Francis Durbridge
Oct. 6	Cambridge (from Royal Court)	*West of Suez*	John Osborne
Oct. 12	Roundhouse	*1789*	Ariane Mnouchkine
Oct. 12	Shaw	*Slip Road Wedding*	Peter Terson
Oct. 13	Duke of York's	*Talking About Yeats*	W. B. Yeats
Oct. 14	Queen's	*Getting On*	Alan Bennett
Oct. 19	Her Majesty's	*Ambassador*	Gohman/Hackady/Ettlinger
Nov. 3	Piccadilly	*Dear Antoine*	Jean Anouilh
Nov. 4	Duke of York's	*The Douglas Cause*	William Douglas Home
Nov. 4	Mermaid	*Geneva*	Bernard Shaw

DIRECTOR	LEADING PLAYERS
Robert Chetwyn	Ian McKellen, Faith Brook, John Woodvine
Anthony Page	Ralph Richardson, Jill Bennett, Sheila Ballantine
Michael Croft/	Gareth Thomas, Anthony Conaboy, Philip Davis
Barrie Rutter	
Geoffrey Ost (for	Wilfred Harrison, Lorraine Peters, Jenny Laird
Octagon Theatre,	
Bolton)	
David Weston	Alan Halliday, John Hodgson, George Irving
Charles Marowitz	Warren Mitchell, Sheila Steafel, Sheila Scott-Wilkinson
Donald Bodley (for	Bob Sherman, Julia McKenzie, Philip Miller
Theatre Royal, York)	
Andrew Murray	Neil Phillips, Ian Redfern
Pam Brighton	Leonard Fenton, William Hoyland, Mike Kitchen
John Downing	Jimmy Edwards, Eric Sykes, Joan Young
Wallace Douglas	Brian Rix, Alfred Marks, Leo Franklyn
Peter Oyston/	Bruce Purchase, Bernard Miles, Josephine Wilson
Julius Gellner	
Frank Dunlop (for the	Georges Bossair, Anne Marev, Vanderic
Belgian National	
Theatre)	
Arturo Corso (for the	André Debaar, Anne Marev, Paul Clairy
Belgian National	
Theatre)	
Ron Daniels	Timothy Dalton, David Cook, Richard Moore
Charles Ross	Bill Simpson, Joyce Blair, Jess Conrad
William Gaskill	Harry Andrews, George Howe, Carmel McSharry
Basil Coleman	Gerald Harper, Jennifer Daniel, Terence Longdon
Anthony Page	Ralph Richardson, Jill Bennett, Sheila Ballantine
Ariane Mnouchkine	Mario Gonzales, Gerard Hardy, Anne Demeyer
Gareth Morgan	Avis Bunnage, Joseph O'Conor, Gwen Nelson
Hilton Edwards	Micheál Mac Liammóir
Patrick Garland	Kenneth More, Gemma Jones, Mona Washbourne
Stone Widney	Howard Keel, Danielle Darrieux, Margaret Courtenay
Robin Phillips	Isabel Jeans, John Clements, Joyce Redman
Clive Perry	Andrew Cruikshank, Sophie Stewart, Duncan Lamont
Philip Grout	Barbara Ferris, Christopher Hancock, George Benson

261

DATE	THEATRE	PLAY	AUTHOR
Nov. 9	Royal Court	*The Changing Room*	David Storey
Nov. 15	Young Vic	*Cato Street*	Robert Shaw
Nov. 17	Roundhouse	*Godspell*	Schwarz/Tebelak
Nov. 30	Arts	*Mother Adam*	Charles Dyer
Dec. 6	Apollo	*Charley's Aunt*	Brandon Thomas
Dec. 8	Apollo	*Owl and The Pussycat* (matineés only)	David Wood
Dec. 9	Westminster	*Give A Dog A Bone*	Peter Howard
Dec. 14	Mermaid	*Dick Turpin*	Loynes/Pember
Dec. 15	Globe	*The Changing Room* (from Royal Court)	David Storey
Dec. 15	Shaw	*The Plotters of Cabbage Patch Corner*	David Wood
Dec. 16	Piccadilly	*Straight Up*	Syd Cheatle
Dec. 16	Phoenix	*Winnie The Pooh* (matineés only)	A. A. Milne/Julian Slade
Dec. 20	Duke of York's	*Toad of Toad Hall* (matineés only)	A. A. Milne/Kenneth Graham
Dec. 20	Duke of York's	*The Man Most Likely To . . .*	Joyce Rayburn
Dec. 21	Palladium	*Cinderella*	Blackburn, Cryer, Park
Dec. 27	Coliseum	*Peter Pan*	J. M. Barrie
Dec. 30	Mermaid	*Love, Love, Love*	Raleigh, Shakespeare, etc.
Jan. 18	Her Majesty's	*Company*	Sondheim/Furth
Jan. 26	Wyndhams (from Roundhouse)	*Godspell*	Schwarz/Tebelak
Jan. 26	Royal Court	*Alpha Beta*	E. A. Whitehead
Jan. 27	Mermaid	*The Price of Justice*	Albert Camus
Feb. 1	Shaw	*Romeo and Juliet*	William Shakespeare
Feb. 7	Roundhouse	*Lilla*	Boeler/Kent/Butler
Feb. 10	Prince of Wales	*The Threepenny Opera*	Brecht/Weill
Feb. 15	Cambridge	*Siege*	David Ambrose
Feb. 16	Mermaid (from Greenwich)	*Never the Twain*	Kipling/Brecht
Feb. 17	Piccadilly	*Reunion in Vienna*	Robert E. Sherwood
Feb. 22	Roundhouse	*Black Macbeth*	William Shakespeare
Feb. 24	Apollo	*The Beheading*	Thomas Muschamp
Mar. 2	Mermaid	*The Caretaker*	Harold Pinter
Mar. 9	Royal Court	*Veterans*	Charles Wood

DIRECTOR	LEADING PLAYERS
Lindsay Anderson	Edward Judd, Barry Keegan, Paul Dawkins
Peter Gill	Vanessa Redgrave, John Arnatt, John Sharp
John-Michael Tebelak	Julie Covington, Marti Webb, David Essex
Charles Dyer	Beatrix Lehmann, Roy Dotrice
Braham Murray	Tom Courtenay, Dilys Hamlett, Wolfe Morris
Barry Booth	Christopher Biggins, Jenny Wren, Michael Elwyn
Henry Cass	Donald Scott, Tony Jackson, Louise Rush
Sally Miles	Gary Raymond, Arthur Mullard, Penny Ryder
Lindsay Anderson	Edward Judd, Barry Keegan, Paul Dawkins
Jonathan Lynn	Paul McDowell, Bridget Turner, Ben Aris
Michael Rudman	Antonia Pemberton, Doug Fisher, Marty Cruikshank
Malcolm Farquhar	Jimmy Thompson, Frank Thornton, Zulema Dene
David Conville	James Cairncross, Richard Goolden, Derek Smith
Leslie Phillips	Leslie Phillips, Gail Granger, Tim Block
Albert J. Knight	Ronnie Corbett, Clodagh Rogers, Terry Scott
Robert Helpmann	Dorothy Tutin, Eric Porter, Belinda Carroll
Barrie Ingham	Barrie Ingham
Harold Prince	Larry Kert, Elaine Stritch, Marti Stevens
John-Michael Tebelak	Julie Covington, Marti Webb, David Essex
Anthony Page	Albert Finney, Rachel Roberts
Bernard Miles	Kate Coleridge, Gary Raymond, Josephine Wilson
Michael Croft	Simon Ward, Sinead Cusack, Maurice Roeves
Joe Donovan	Dilip Bannerjee, Andy Lehner, Shyam Das
Rufus Collins	
Tony Richardson	Vanessa Redgrave, Joe Melia, Hermione Baddeley
Robert Kidd	Alistair Sim, Stanley Holloway, Michael Bryant
John Cox	John Dalby, Jerome Willis, Eliza Ward
Frith Banbury	Margaret Leighton, Nigel Patrick, Beatrix Lehmann
Peter Coe	Oscar James, Mona Hammond, Jeffrey Kissoon
Noel Willman	John Moffatt, Virginia McKenna, Robert Lang
Christopher Morahan	Leonard Rossiter, Jeremy Kemp, John Hurt
Ronald Eyre	John Gielgud, John Mills, Ann Bell

263

DATE	THEATRE	PLAY	AUTHOR
Mar. 13	New	*Julius Caesar*	William Shakespeare
Mar. 16	Apollo (from Royal Court)	*Alpha Beta*	E. A. Whitehead
Mar. 23	Globe	*Notes On A Love Affair*	Frank Marcus
Mar. 27	Stratford East	*Londoners*	Stephen Lewis/Lionel Bart
Mar. 27	Sadler's Wells	*Lord Arthur Savile's Crime*	Oscar Wilde

DIRECTOR	LEADING PLAYERS
Jonathan Miller	Jonathan James-Moore, David Snodin, Andrew Hilton
Anthony Page	Albert Finney, Rachel Roberts
Robin Phillips	Irene Worth, Nigel Davenport, Julia Foster
Joan Littlewood	Bob Grant, Yootha Joyce, Stephen Lewis
John Downing	Elsie Randolph, Jack Hulbert, Bill Kerr

The ten productions with longest runs as at August 1st 1972 were:

The Mousetrap	8167
There's a Girl in My Soup	2539
Canterbury Tales	1800
Magic of the Minstrels	1624
Hair	1591
Pyjama Tops	1171
Sleuth	1008
Oh! Calcutta!	827
How The Other Half Loves	755
The Philanthropist	719

The National Theatre 1971–72

Old Vic and New Theatres
DIRECTOR: Sir Laurence Olivier

CORIOLANUS
by William Shakespeare
PROD: Manfred Wekwerth/
Joachim Tenschert
THE CAPTAIN OF KOPENICK
by Carl Zuckmayer
PROD: Frank Dunlop
MRS WARREN'S PROFESSION
by Bernard Shaw
PROD: Ronald Eyre
THE MERCHANT OF VENICE
by William Shakespeare
PROD: Jonathan Miller
AMPHITRYON 38
by Jean Giraudoux
PROD: Laurence Olivier
THE RULES OF THE GAME
by Luigi Pirandello
PROD: Anthony Page
THE GOOD-NATURED MAN
by Oliver Goldsmith
PROD: John Dexter
CYRANO
by Edmond Rostand
PROD: Patrick Garland

A WOMAN KILLED WITH KINDNESS
by Thomas Heywood
PROD: John Dexter
THE ARCHITECT & THE EMPEROR
by Fernando Arrabal
PROD: Victor Garcia
THE NATIONAL HEALTH
by Peter Nichols
PROD: Michael Blakemore
DANTON'S DEATH
by Georg Buchner
PROD: Jonathan Miller
TYGER
by William Blake/Adrian
Mitchell
PROD: Michael Blakemore/John
Dexter
LONG DAY'S JOURNEY INTO NIGHT
by Eugene O'Neill
PROD: Michael Blakemore
JUMPERS
by Tom Stoppard
PROD: Peter Wood
THE IDIOT
by Simon Gray
PROD: Anthony Quayle

The Company included: Sarah Badel; Tom Baker; Gillian Barge; Frank Barrie; Dai Bradley; Coral Browne; Anna Carteret; Kate Coleridge; Graham Crowden; Constance Cummings; Paul Curran; Jim Dale; Bill Fraser; Edward Hardwicke; William Hobbs; Anthony Hopkins; Michael Hordern; Hazel Hughes; Derek Jacobi; Gerald James; Charles Kay; Jane Lapotaire; Gabrielle Laye; Harry Lomax; Kenneth Mackintosh; Jo Maxwell-Muller; Geraldine McEwan; Desmond McNamara; John Moffatt; Anthony Nicholls; Laurence Olivier; Ronald Pickup; Joan Plowright; Christopher Plummer; Louise Purnell; Dennis Quilley; Louis Ramsay; Malcolm Reid; Diana Rigg; David Ryall; Paul Scofield; Cleo Sylvestre; Jeanne Watts; Jane Wenham.

Royal Shakespeare Company 1971–72

ARTISTIC DIRECTOR: Trevor Nunn

Stratford 1972:
THE ROMANS:
CORIOLANUS
JULIUS CAESAR
ANTONY AND CLEOPATRA
TITUS ANDRONICUS
Directed by Trevor Nunn with John Barton, Buzz Goodbody
and Euan Smith

THE COMEDY OF ERRORS
Directed by Clifford Williams

The Company included: Darien Angadi; John Atkinson; Wendy Bailey;
Colin Blakely; Loftus Burton; Joseph Charles; Judy Cornwell; Hans
De Vries; Mark Dignam; Michael Egan; Edwina Ford; Paul Gaymon;
Patrick Godfrey; Peter Godfrey; Ian Hogg; Geoffrey Hutchings; Gerald
James; Richard Johnson; Malcolm Kaye; Calvin Lockhart; Clement
McCallin; Rosemary McHale; Philip Manikum; Joe Marcell; Robert
Oates; Lennard Pearce; Tim Pigott-Smith; Michael Radcliffe; Corin
Redgrave; Kevin Sheehan; Patrick Stewart; Desmond Stokes; Janet
Suzman; Keith Taylor; Margaret Tyzack; John Wood.

Aldwych 1971–72:

OLD TIMES
by Harold Pinter
PROD: Peter Hall

ENEMIES
by Maxim Gorky
PROD: David Jones

EXILES
by James Joyce
PROD: Harold Pinter

ALL OVER
by Edward Albee
PROD: Peter Hall

MUCH ADO ABOUT NOTHING
by William Shakespeare
PROD: Ronald Eyre

A MIDSUMMER NIGHT'S DREAM
by William Shakespeare
PROD: Peter Brook

THE MAN OF MODE
by George Etherege
PROD: Terry Hands

THE BALCONY
by Jean Genet
PROD: Terry Hands

THE OZ TRIAL
by Illingworth & Robertson
PROD: Buzz Goodbody

The Company included: Peggy Ashcroft; Isla Blair; Colin Blakely;
Brenda Bruce; Patience Collier; Frances de la Tour; Michael Egan;
Julian Glover; Patrick Godfrey; Sheila Hancock; Alan Howard; John

Kane; Lila Kaye; Sara Kestelman; Ben Kingsley; Estelle Kohler; Angela Lansbury; Philip Locke; Clement McCallin; T. P. McKenna; David Markham; Vivien Merchant; Helen Mirren; Sebastian Shaw; Barry Stanton; Patrick Stewart; Dorothy Tutin; David Waller; John Wood; John York.

The Place 1971:

OCCUPATIONS
by Trevor Griffiths
PROD: Buzz Goodbody

MISS JULIE
by August Strindberg
PROD: Robin Phillips

SUBJECT TO FITS
by Robert Montgomery
PROD: A. J. Antoon

The Company included: Isla Blair; Heather Canning; Ralph Cotterill; Julian Glover; Paul Hardwick; John Kane; Lila Kaye; Sara Kestelman; Estelle Kohler; Philip Locke; Clement McCallin; Donal McCann; Helen Mirren; Sebastian Shaw; Patrick Stewart; John York.

World Theatre Season

Aldwych Theatre
ARTISTIC DIRECTOR: Peter Daubeny

1972

SOUTH AFRICA: *Natal Theatre Workshop:*
Welcome Msomi: UMABATHA

SPAIN: *Nuria Espert Company:*
Lorca: YERMA

GREECE: *Greek National Theatre:*
Aeschylus: AGAMEMNON
THE CHOEPHORI
THE EUMENIDES

ITALY: *Eduardo de Filippo Company:*
De Filippo: NAPOLI MILIONARIA

INDIA: *Kathakali Drama Company:*
THE RAMAYANA
THE MAHABHARATA

POLAND: *Cracow Stary Theatre Company:*
Wajda: THE POSSESSED

Chichester Festival Theatre

ARTISTIC DIRECTOR: Sir John Clements

1972

THE BEGGAR'S OPERA
by John Gay
PROD: Robin Phillips

THE DOCTOR'S DILEMMA
by Bernard Shaw
PROD: John Clements

THE TAMING OF THE SHREW
by William Shakespeare
PROD: Jonathan Miller

THE LADY'S NOT FOR BURNING
by Christopher Fry
PROD: Robin Phillips

The Company included: Michael Aldridge; Sarah Atkinson; Kim Braden; Alan Brown; Anna Calder-Marshall; Richard Chamberlain; John Clements; Richard Cornish; Charles Dance; Bee Duffell; Jonathan Elsom; Maggie Fitzgibbon; Leslie French; Josephine Gordon; Anthony Hopkins; Harold Innocent; June Jago; Myvanwy Jenn; Harold Kasket; Millicent Martin; William Mervyn; John Neville; Robin Phillips; Joan Plowright; Brian Poyser; Angela Richards; Laurie Webb.

Opera 1971–72

Royal Opera House, Covent Garden:
CARMEN: Bizet/Atherton
LUCIA DI LAMMERMOOR: Donizetti/Pritchard
TURANDOT: Puccini/Mackerras
DIE MEISTERSINGER VON NURNBERG: Wagner/Krips
EUGENE ONEGIN: Tschaikovsky/Solti/Hall
LA SONNAMBULA: Bellini/Cillario
SALOME: Strauss/Semkow
COSI FAN TUTTE: Mozart/Davis
RIGOLETTO: Verdi/Downes
UN BALLO IN MASCHERA: Verdi/Guadagno
PARSIFAL: Wagner/Goodall
MADAME BUTTERFLY: Puccini/Matheson
OTELLO: Verdi/Ceccato
BORIS GUDUNOV: Mussorgsky–Rimsky Korsakov/Rozhdestvensky
HAMLET: Searle/Downes
IL BARBIERE DI SIVIGLIA: Rossini/Atherton
TRISTAN UND ISOLDE: Wagner/Solti/Hall
PETER GRIMES: Britten/Davis
ORFEO ED EURIDICE: Gluck/Mackerras
DAS RHEINGOLD: Wagner/Downes
DIE WALKÜRE: Wagner/Downes
SIEGFRIED: Wagner/Downes
GÖTTERDÄMMERUNG: Wagner/Downes
FIDELIO: Beethoven/Davis
FALSTAFF: Verdi/Ceccato
DER ROSENKAVALIER: Strauss/Krips
AIDA: Verdi/Matheson
LE NOZZE DI FIGARO: Mozart/Davis/Copley
TOSCA: Puccini/Downes
BILLY BUDD: Britten/Mackerras

Sadler's Wells Company, Coliseum:
KISS ME, KATE: Porter/Dodds/Coe
FIDELIO: Beethoven/Mackerras/Coleman
DIE FLEDERMAUS: Strauss/Matheson
THE TWILIGHT OF THE GODS: Wagner/Goodall/Byam Shaw–Blatchley
CARMEN: Bizet/Mackerras/Copley
MADAM BUTTERFLY: Puccini/Mackerras
THE MAKROPOULOS CASE: Janaćek/Mackerras
THE TALES OF HOFFMAN: Offenbach/Lloyd–Jones/Graham
THE BARBER OF SEVILLE: Rossini/Montgomery
THE VALKYRIE: Wagner/Goodall/Byam Shaw-Blatchley
SEMELE: Handel/Mackerras/Sanjust
THE SERAGLIO: Mozart/Mackerras/Copley

LOHENGRIN: Wagner/Mackerras/Graham
THE MARRIAGE OF FIGARO: Mozart/Mackerras
CAVALLERIA RUSTICANA: Mascagni/Barker/Blatchley
PAGLIACCI: Leoncavallo/Braithwaite/Blatchley
RIGOLETTO: Verdi/Balkwill
THE CORONATION OF POPPEA: Monteverdi/Leppard/Graham
THE FORCE OF DESTINY: Verdi/Barker/Graham
THE DAMNATION OF FAUST: Berlioz/Mackerras

Glyndebourne Festival:
THE QUEEN OF SPADES: Tchaikovsky/Pritchard/Hadjimischev
ARIADNE AUF NAXOS: Strauss/Ceccato/Cox
THE RISING OF THE MOON: Maw/Fredman/Graham
LA CALISTO: Cavalli/Leppard/Hall
COSI FAN TUTTE: Mozart/Pritchard/Montarsolo

Welsh National Company:
THE MAGIC FLUTE: Mozart/Lockhart/Geliot
LULU: Berg/Lockhart/Geliot
AIDA: Verdi/Armstrong/Geliot–Stubbs
FALSTAFF: Verdi/Mannino/Copley–Evans
SIMON BOCCANEGRA: Verdi/Lockhart/Moody
BORIS GODUNOV: Mussorgsky–Rimsky Korsakov/Armstrong/Moody
DIE FLEDERMAUS: Strauss/Hose/Geliot
THE BARBER OF SEVILLE: Rossini/Armstrong/Moody
LA TRAVIATA: Verdi/Lockhart/Copley

Scottish Opera Company:
THE TURN OF THE SCREW: Britten/Brydon/Besch
ROSENKAVALIER: Strauss/Gibson/Besch
SIEGFRIED: Wagner/Gibson/Ebert
ALBERT HERRING: Britten/Brydon/Besch
LA TRAVIATA: Verdi/Loughran/Watt-Smith
THE MAGIC FLUTE: Mozart/Gibson–Seaman/Ebert
RHEINGOLD: Wagner/Gibson/Ebert
THE BARBER OF SEVILLE: Rossini/Bertini/Watt–Smith
WALKÜRE: Wagner/Gilson/Ebert
THE RAKE'S PROGRESS: Stravinsky/Gibson–Brydon/Pountney
DON GIOVANNI: Mozart/Thomson/Ebert
GÖTTERDÄMMERUNG: Wagner/Gibson/Ebert

Ballet 1971-72

Royal Ballet (large company)
New productions:
ANASTASIA (Kenneth MacMillan/Tchaikovsky & Martinu/Barry Kay)
FIELD FIGURES (Glen Tetley/Stockhausen/Nadine Baylis)
AFTERNOON OF A FAUN (Jerome Robbins/Debussy/Jean Rosenthal & Irene Sharaff)
Also in repertory during the year:
APOLLO (Balanchine/Stravinsky), LA BAYADÈRE (Petipa/prod. Nureyev/Minkus), LES BICHES (Nijinska/Poulenc), CHECKMATE (de Valois/Bliss), THE CREATURES OF PROMETHEUS (Ashton/Beethoven), DANCES AT A GATHERING (Robbins/Chopin), DANSES CONCERTANTES (MacMillan/Stravinsky), THE DREAM (Ashton/Mendelssohn), ENIGMA VARIATIONS (Ashton/Elgar), LA FILLE MAL GARDÉE (Ashton/Hérold, arr. Lanchbery), GISELLE (Pepita, prod. Wright/Adam), THE INVITATION (MacMillan/Sieber), JAZZ CALENDAR (Ashton/Bennett), MARGUERITE AND ARMAND (Ashton/Liszt), RAYMONDA ACT 3 (Nureyev after Petipa/Glazunov), THE RITE OF SPRING (MacMillan/Stravinsky), ROMEO AND JULIET (MacMillan/Prokofiev), SCÈNES DE BALLET (Ashton/Stravinsky), SERENADE (Balanchine/Tchaikovsky), SHADOWPLAY (Tudor/Koechlin), SONG OF THE EARTH (MacMillan/Mahler), SWAN LAKE (Petipa, Ivanov & Ashton/Tchaikovsky), SYMPHONIC VARIATIONS (Ashton/Franck), THE TWO PIGEONS (Ashton/Messager).

Royal Ballet (small company)
New productions:
OVERTURE (Joe Layton/Bernstein/John Conklin)
THE GRAND TOUR (Layton/Coward, arr. Hershy Kay/Conklin)
LAS HERMANAS (MacMillan/Martin/Nicholas Georgiadis)
ST THOMAS' WAKE (David Drew/Maxwell Davies/Peter Logan)
ANTE ROOM (Geoffrey Cauley/Bernard Hermann/Cauley)
CAPRICHOS (Herbert Ross/Bartok)
THE MAIDS (Ross/Milhaud/William Pitkin)
THE MIRROR WALKERS PAS DE DEUX (Peter Wright/Tchaikovsky)
Also in repertory during the year:
APOLLO, BEAUTY AND THE BEAST (Cranko/Ravel), CHECKPOINT (MacMillan/Gerhard), CONCERTO PAS DE DEUX (MacMillan/Shostakovich), DANSES CONCERTANTES DIVERSIONS (MacMillan/Bliss), FAÇADE (Ashton/Walton), FIELD FIGURES, LILAC GARDEN (Tudor/Chausson), MONOTONES 2 (Ashton/Satie), LES PATINEURS (Ashton/Meyerbeer arr. Lambert), PINEAPPLE POLL (Cranko/Sullivan arr. Mackerras), THE RAKE'S PROGRESS (de Valois/Gordon), LES RENDEZVOUS (Ashton/Auber arr. Lambert), SOLITAIRE (MacMillan/Arnold).

273

Ballet Rambert:
New productions:
SWERVES AND CURVES (Mary Prestidge/Seixas/Peter Cazalet)*
SPANDANGO (Ann Whitley/Moskovski/Cazalet)*
HOE-DOWN (Susan Cooper/Anthony Hymas & Burl Ives/Cazalet)*
THE STRONG MAN (Amanda Knott/Blood, Sweat and Tears/Cazalet)*
MISFITS (Peter Curtis/Lasry/Cazalet)*
    * for 'Bertram Batell' programmes
THAT IS THE SHOW (Norman Morrice/Berio/Baylis)
METAFLOW (Joseph Scoglio/Rudnik, Malovec & Smiley/Cazalet)
WINGS (Christopher Bruce/Downes)
RAG-DANCES (Tetley/Hymas/Baylis)
SOLO (Morrice/Downes/Baylis)
Also in repertory during the year:
THE ACT (Linda Hodes/Page & Johnson), L'APRÈS-MIDI D'UN FAUNE
(Nijinsky/Debussy), BERTRAM BATELL'S SIDESHOW, BLIND-SIGHT
(Morrice/Downes), DANCE AND DANCERS, DARK ELEGIES (Tudor/
Mahler), DESERTS (Sokolow/Varèse), EMBRACE TIGER AND RETURN TO
MOUNTAIN (Tetley/Subotnick), THE EMPTY SUIT (Morrice/Salzedo),
FOUR ACCORDING (Chesworth/Bacewicz), GEORGE FRIDERIC (Bruce/
Handel), LIVING SPACE (Bruce/Cockburn), OPUS '65 (Sokolow/Macero),
PAWN TO KING FIVE (Chesworth/Pink Floyd), PIERROT LUNAIRE
(Tetley/Schoenberg), RICERCARE (Tetley/Seter), 'TIS GOODLY SPORT
(J. Taylor/16th-century court music), 1–2–3 (Morrice/Orgad),

Festival Ballet:
New productions:
GISELLE (Petipa, prod. Mary Skeaping/Adam/David Walker)
LE BEAU DANUBE (Leonide Massine/Johann Strauss/Polunin)
PETROUCHKA (Michel Fokine, prod. Nicholas Beriozoff/Stravinsky/
Benois)
BOURNONVILLE DIVERTISSEMENT (August Bournonville, prod. Mona
Vangsaa/Paulli, Helsted & Gade)
Also in repertory during the year:
BOURRÉE FANTASQUE (Balanchine/Chabrier), COPPELIA (Jack Carter/
Delibes), CORSAIR PAS DE DEUX (Klavin/Minkus), DON QUIXOTE
(Gorsky, prod. Borkowski/Minkus), DVOŘÁK VARIATIONS (Hynd/
Dvořák), ETUDES (Lander/Riisager), GRADUATION BALL (Lichine/
Strauss arr. Dorati), NIGHT SHADOW (Balanchine/Rieti after Bellini),
THE NUTCRACKER (J. Carter/Tchaikovsky), SCHEHERAZADE (Fokine,
prod. Beriozoff/Rimsky–Korsakoff), THE SLEEPING BEAUTY (Petipa,
prod. Stevenson/Tchaikovsky), LES SYLPHIDES (Fokine/Chopin).

Scottish Theatre Ballet:
New productions:
PEEPSHOW (Walter Gore/Françaix/Gore)

FOUR PORTRAITS (Peter Darrell/Prokofiev/Peter Docherty)
GISELLE (Petipa, prod. Darrell/Adam/Cazalet)
ARRIVING BELLEVUE SUNDAY . . . (Ashley Killar/Janaĉek/Margaret
Mary Preece)
LA FÊTE ETRANGE (Andrée Howard, prod. Helen Starr/Fauré/Sophie
Fedorovitch)
Also in repertory during the year:
BEAUTY AND THE BEAST (Cranko/Ravel), BEAUTY AND THE BEAST
(Darrell/Musgrave), JEUX (Darrell/Debussy), SLEEPERS (Hopps),
SOLITAIRE DUET (MacMillan/Arnold), SONATE À TROIS (Béjart/Bartók),
STREET GAMES (Gore/Ibert), LA VENTANA (Bournonville, prod. Brenaa/
Lumbye), THE WEB (Meyer/Webern).

Northern Dance Theatre:
New productions:
INTRODUCTION PIECE (Laverne Meyer/Poulenc/Vijay Batra)
GAMES FOR FIVE PLAYERS (John Chesworth/Takemitsu/Baylis)
DANCE PICTURES (Gore/Rudolf Maros)
TOWARDS NIGHT (John Haynes/Schumann/Haynes)
NUTCRACKER PAS DE DEUX (Ivanov, prod. Simon Mottram/
Tchaikovsky)
QUARTET (Jonathan Thorpe/Beethoven/Michael Holt)
Also in repertory during the year:
BRAHMS SONATA (Meyer/Brahms), DEATH AND THE MAIDEN (Howard/
Schubert), PAS DE CINQ (Meyer/Suppé), PETER AND THE WOLF (Staff/
Prokofiev), THE PRISONERS (Darrell/Bartók), SILENT EPISODE (Meyer/
Webern), TANCREDI AND CLORINDA (Thorpe/Monteverdi), THE WEB
(Meyer/Webern).

London Contemporary Dance Theatre:
New productions:
NOWHERE SLOWLY (Richard Alston/Stockhausen)
MACROSECONDS (Flora Cushman)
CONSOLATION OF THE RISING MOON (Robert Cohan/John Williams/
Peter Farmer)
THE TROUBADOURS (Barry Moreland/Maxwell Davies/Moreland)
THE ROAD OF THE PHOEBE SNOW (Talley Beatty/Ellington & Strayhorn)
STAGES (Cohen/Arne Nordheim & Bob Downes/Farmer)
Also in repertory during the year:
CANTABILE (Lapzeson/Finnissy), CELL (Cohan/Lloyd), CONVERSATION
PIECE (North/Parsons), DUET (P. Taylor/Haydn), ECLIPSE (Cohan/
Lester), EL PENITENTE (Graham/Horst), HERMIT SONGS (Ailey/Barber),
HUNTER OF ANGELS (Cohan/Maderna), PLAYGROUND OF THE ZODIAC
(Louther/Quincey), RAGA SHANKARA (Cushman/Alford & Sathe),
RAINMAKERS (de Groot/Rommerts), SKY (Cohan/Lester), X (Cohan/
Kagel), 3 EPITAPHS (P. Taylor/early American folk music).

Visiting companies:
Alfred Jarry Mime Company (Prague); *Alwin Nikolais Dance Theatre*
(New York); *Ballet du XXe Siècle* (Brussels); *Ballets Modernes de
Paris; Ballet Théâtre Contemporain* (Amiens); *Black Theatre of
Prague; Burmese National Dance Company; Chitrasena Dance
Company* (Ceylon); *City Center Joffrey Ballet* (New York); *Cullberg
Ballet* (Stockholm); *Darpana Dance Company* (India); *Dora Stratou
Dance Company* (Athens); *Dukla Dance Company* (Czechoslovakia);
Fialka Mime Company (Prague); *Fiesta Gitana* (Spain); *Korean Folk
Arts Company; Lado Jugoslav Ensemble; The Little Angels* (Korea);
The Mevlevis (*Whirling Dervishes*); *Paco Pena's Flamenco Pura*
(Spain); *Rajko Hungarian Gypsy Company; Red Army Ensemble;
Royal Classical Javanese Dancers of the Sultan of Jogjakarta; Royal
Danish Ballet; Wakashu Kabuki Company* (New York).

Theatre Honours and Awards 1971-72

Birthday Honours 1971:
KNIGHTHOOD: Terence Rattigan
C.B.E.: George Baker, Harold Hobson
O.B.E.: Michael Croft, Wendy Hiller
HON.K.B.E.: Georg Solti

New Year Honours 1972:
KNIGHTHOOD: Cecil Beaton
D.B.E.: Cicely Courtneidge
C.B.E.: Martin Cooper, Michael Hordern, David Ward
C.M.G.: Joan Hammond
O.B.E.: Charles Chilton, Martin Esslin, Alec McCowen, Stanford Robinson
M.B.E.: Edmonds Gateley

Plays & Players *1971 London Drama Critics' Awards: New Play:* OLD TIMES; *New Musical:* CATCH MY SOUL; *Male Performance:* Ralph Richardson; *Female Performance:* Peggy Ashcroft; *Breakthrough Actor:* Anthony Hopkins; *Breakthrough Actress:* Heather Canning; *Director:* Lindsay Anderson; *Designer:* Farrah.

Evening Standard *1971 Drama Awards:*
Actor: Alan Bates; *Actress:* Peggy Ashcroft; *Play:* BUTLEY (Simon Gray); *Comedy:* GETTING ON (Alan Bennett); *Most Promising Playwright:* E. A. Whitehead (THE FOURSOME).

Broadway 1971 'Tony' Awards:
Best Play: STICKS AND BONES; *Best Musical:* 2 GENTLEMEN OF VERONA; *Actor (play):* Cliff Gorman; *Actor (musical):* Phil Silvers; *Actress (play):* Sada Thompson; *Actress (musical):* Alexis Smith.

George Devine Awards: Shane Connaughton, Wilson John Haire, Robert Thornton.

Clarence Derwent Awards: Michael Bates, Rosemary McHale.

John Whiting Award: Mustapha Matura.

Theatrical Obituary

Sir Bronson Albery, *Theatre Manager* (90)

Pier Angeli, *Actress*

Stephen Arlen, *Managing Director, Sadler's Wells* (58)

Catherine Armstrong, *Actress*

Robert Atkins, *Actor/Manager* (85)

Mary Austin, *Actress* (98)

Hilda Bayley, *Actress* (81)

Esmé Beringer, *Actress* (96)

John Brint, *Stage Doorkeeper, Birmingham* (72)

Edgar K. Bruce, *Actor* (78)

Maurice Chevalier, *Singer* (83)

Viola Compton, *Actress* (85)

Dame Gladys Cooper, *Actress* (82)

Alec Coppel, *Playwright* (63)

Elisabethe Corathiel, *Author* (77)

May Craig, *Actress*

David Curtis, *Designer* (48)

Bella Darvi, *Actress*

Edith Day, *Actress/Singer* (75)

Terence De Marney, *Actor/Manager* (62)

Doris Dorée, *Soprano* (66)

Pete Duel, *Actor* (31)

Hamilton Dyce, *Actor*

Eleanor Elder, *Actress* (85)

Lionel Falck, *Manager, Strand Theatre*

Jon Farrell, *Actor* (61)

Eric Fawcett, *Actor/Producer*

Alexander Field, *Actor* (79)

Alfred Gelin, *Playwright* (76)

Gene Gerrard, *Actor* (81)

Denne Gilkes, *Stratford Voice Coach*

Tom Gill, *Actor* (54)

Becky Goldstein, *Actress* (94)

Eric Gorman, *Actor/Secretary, Abbey Theatre* (89)

Sir Tyrone Guthrie, *Director* (70)

Cyril Harper, *Stage Doorkeeper, Wimbledon* (62)

Libby Helmar, *Torch Singer* (65)

Sir A. P. Herbert, *Composer/Lyricist* (81)

Phoebe Hodgson, *Actress*

N. C. Hunter, *Playwright* (62)

Rita James, *Actress* (73)

Dennis King, *Actor* (73)

Mathilde Kschessinska, *Ballerina* (99)

Harold Lander, *Dancer/Choreographer* (66)

Jessie Royce Landis, *Actress* (67)

Alois Lang, *Oberammergau Actor* (80)

Ulysses Lappas, *Tenor* (81)

Joe E. Lewis, *Comedian* (69)

Albert Lieven, *Actor* (65)

Molly McArthur, *Designer* (71)

Esther McCracken, *Playwright* (69)

Hugh McDermott, *Actor* (64)

Moray McLaren, *Playwright* (70)

Austin Melford, *Actor* (86)

Herbert Menges, *Conductor* (69)

Josephine Middleton, *Actress* (88)

Maria Minetti, *Actress*

Janet Morrison, *Actress*

Mignon Nevada, *Soprano* (83)

Bronislava Nijinska, *Dancer* (81)

Max Oldaker, *Actor* (64)

Edith Outram, *Actress* (87)

Cecil Parker, *Actor* (73)

George Porter, *Critic* (66)

Tom Pyper, *General Manager* (56)

Peggy Rae, *Actress* (77)

Peter Randall, *Director* (55)

David Raven, *Actor* (58)

Clarence Raybould, *Conductor* (85)

Kynaston Reeves, *Actor* (78)

Dick Richards, *Critic*

Arthur Rigby, *Actor* (70)

Dominic Roche, *Actor/Director* (69)

Milton Rosmer, *Actor* (89)

Alec Ross, *Actor*
Ian Sadler, *Actor* (69)
Michel St. Denis, *Director* (73)
Ivy St. Helier, *Actress/Singer*
Ted Shawn, *Dancer* (80)
Frank Staff, *Choreographer* (52)
Jerome Stephens, *Stage Manager* (76)
Igor Stravinsky, *Composer* (88)
Jean Stuart, *Actress*
Sylvester Stuart, *Actor/Manager* (81)
Ellaline Terris, Lady Hicks, *Actress* (100)
William Thorburn, *Tenor* (61)
Veronica Turleigh, *Actress* (68)
Val Valentine, *Scriptwriter* (74)
Madame Verishka, *Ballet teacher*

Jean Vilar, *Actor/Director* (58)
Hugh Wakefield, *Actor* (83)
C. Denier Warren, *Actor* (82)
Malcolm Watson, *Actor* (76)
John Webley, *Singer* (24)
Sir David Webster, *Administrator, Covent Garden* (67)
Helene Weigel, *Actress* (70)
Cyril Wheeler, *Actor* (59)
Inia Te Wiata, *Actor/Singer* (55)
Theodore Wilhelm, *Actor* (62)
Rita Williams, *Singer* (51)
Jessie Winter, *Actress*
Edward J. Wood, *Actor* (80)
Robert Woollard, *Actor/Producer* (83)
Maxwell Wray, *Director/Actor* (73)

Index

Compiled by Gordon Robinson

Page numbers in italics refer to illustrations